Basic Anatomy and Physiology

Basic Anatomy and Physiology

N. KUMAR
B.Sc., M.Sc., Ph.D., PGDCA, PGDPM
Bangalore University, Karnataka

A.I.T.B.S.
AITBS PUBLISHERS, INDIA
MEDICAL PUBLISHERS
J-5/6, Krishan Nagar, Delhi-110051 (INDIA)
Phone: 011-40167052, 49067602; Fax: 011-22009074
E-mail: aitbsindia@gmail.com & aitbsindia@hotmail.com

First Edition : 2009
Revised Edition : 2011
Second Edition : 2025

ISBN: 978-81-7473-442-6

Published by:
Virender Kumar Arya for
AITBS Publishers, India
MEDICAL PUBLISHERS
J-5/6, Krishan Nagar, Delhi-110051 (INDIA)
Phone: 011-40167052, 49067602; Fax: 011-22009074
E-mail: aitbsindia@gmail.com & aitbsindia@hotmail.com

Printed by AITBS, Delhi

PREFACE

As we know that the human body is explained system by system. The reader must, however, remember that "Anatomy and Physiology" is an integrated subject. The human body is rather like a highly technical and sophisticated machine. It operates as a single-entity, but is made up of a number of systems that works interdependently. *Anatomy* is the study of the structure of the body and physical relationships involved between body systems and on the other hand, *Physiology* is the study of how the systems of the body work, and the ways in which their integrated co-operation maintains life and health of the individual. The book "Basic Anatomy and Physiology" is designed to help you master the terminology, basic concepts, and principles important to an understanding of the human body. It help us in building a foundation of essential knowledge. Such a foundation will support further courses dealing with specific topics in human anatomy and physiology. It providing a framework for interpreting and applying related information obtained outside the classroom.

A large work is difficult because it is large, even though all its parts might singly be performed with facility; where there are many things to be done, each must be allowed its share of time and labour, in the proportion only which it bears to the whole; nor can it be expected, that the stones which form the dome of a temple, should be squared and polished like the diamond of a ring.

I extend my sincere and whole-heartly thanks to *Virender Kumar Arya,* the publisher of A.I.T.B.S. Publishers, India for his motivating guidance and cheerful co-operation of his staff members during preparation of this book.

Author

CONTENTS

1 CHAPTER

INTRODUCTION TO ANATOMICAL TERMS

INTRODUCTION

Anatomy is the science of the structure of the body. In relation to the size of the parts studied, anatomy is usually divided into: (i) *macroscopic* or *gross anatomy,* and (ii) *microscopic anatomy* or histology (now used synonymously). In addition, *embryology* is the study of the embryo and the fetus, that is, the study of prenatal development, whereas the study of congenital malformations is known as *teratology.*

In general, works dealing with human anatomy are arranged either (i) systemically, that is, according to the various systems of the body (skeletal, muscular, digestive, etc.) or (ii) regionally, that is, according to the natural, main subdivisions of the body (head and neck, upper limb, thorax, etc.).

ANATOMICAL TERMINOLOGY

All descriptions in human anatomy are expressed in relation to the anatomical position, a convention whereby the body is erect, with the head, eyes, and toes directed forward and the upper limbs by the side and held so that the palms of the hands face forward.

There is no implication that the anatomical position is one of rest. It is often necessary, however, to describe the position of the viscera also in the recumbent posture, because this is a posture in which patients are frequently examined clinically.

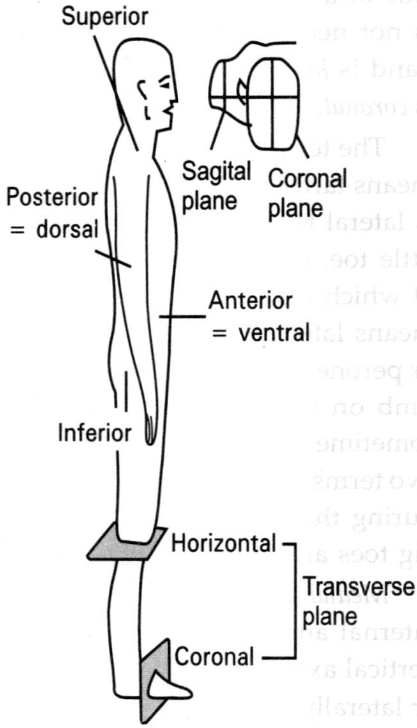

Fig. 1.1 *Anatomical position of a human body.*

The *median plane* is an imaginary vertical plane of section that passes longitudinally through the body and divides it into right and left halves. The median plane intersects the surface of the front and back of the body at what are called the anterior and posterior median lines. It is a common error, however, to refer to the "midline" when the median plane is meant.

Any *vertical plane* through the body that is parallel with the median plane is called a sagittal plane. The sagittal planes are named after the sagittal suture of the skull, to which they are parallel. The term "parasagittal" is redundant: anything parallel with a sagittal plane is still sagittal.

Any vertical plane that intersects the median plane at a right angle and separates the body into anterior and posterior parts is termed a coronal, or frontal, plane.

The term *horizontal plane* refers to a plane at a right angle to both the median and coronal planes: it separates the body into superior and inferior parts. This is often termed an axial plane, particularly in radiology.

The term *transverse* means at a right angle to the longitudinal axis of a structure. Thus, a transverse section through an artery is not necessarily horizontal. A transverse section through the hand is *horizontal,* whereas a transverse section through the foot is *coronal.*

The term *medial* means nearer to the median plane, and lateral means farther from it. Thus, in the anatomical position, the thumb is lateral to the little finger, whereas the big toe is medial to the little toe. Intermediate means lying between two structures, one of which is medial and the other lateral. In the upper limb radial means lateral and ulnar means medial: in the lower limb fibular or peroneal means lateral and tibial means medial. The border of a limb on which either the thumb or the big toe is situated is sometimes called preaxial, and the opposite border, postaxial. These two terms are based on the arrangement of the limbs in the embryo during the sixth postovulatory week, when the thumbs and the big toes are both on the rostral border of the limbs.

Medial and *lateral rotation* (which should never be referred to as internal and external) means rotation (e.g., of the hip) around a vertical axis so that the anterior aspect of the part moves medially or laterally, respectively.

Anterior or *ventral* means nearer the front of the body. Posterior or dorsal means nearer the back. In the upper limb, the term palmar (formerly volar) means anterior. In the foot, plantar means *inferior,* and the term dorsal is commonly used for *superior* in the foot.

Superior means nearer the top or upper end of the body. Inferior means nearer the lower end. Cranial or cephalic is sometimes used in stead of superior, and caudal instead of inferior. Rostral means nearer the "front end," that is, the region of the nose and mouth. this is superior in the most of the body althoug it represents the anterior aspect of the head.

The suffix "-ad" is sometimes added to a positional term to indicate the idea of motion. Thus, cephalad means proceeding toward the head. Such terms are useful occasionally in describing growth processes, but their application is best limited.

In the limbs, *proximal* and *distal* are used to indicate, respectively, nearer to and farther from the root or attached end of the limb. (Proximal and distal have a special meaning in the case of the teeth.)

Internal and *external* mean, respectively, nearer to and farther from the center of an organ or a cavity. Superficial and deep mean, respectively, nearer to and farther from the surface of the body.

The term *middle* is used for a structure lying between two others that are anterior and posterior, or superior and inferior, or internal and external.

In addition to the technical terms of *position* and *direction*, certain common expressions may be cautiously used in anatomical descriptions: front, back, in front of, behind, forward, backward, upper, lower, above, below, upward, downward, ascending, and descending.

BODY CAVITIES

The cavities, or spaces, of the body contain the internal organs, or viscera. The two main cavities are called the ventral and dorsal cavities. The ventral is the larger cavity and is subdivided into two parts: thoracic and abdominal or pelvic cavities by the diaphragm, a dome-shaped respiratory muscle.

(i) *Thoracic cavity:* The upper ventral, thoracic, or chest cavity contains the heart, lungs, trachea, esophagus, large blood vessels, and nerves. The thoracic cavity is bound laterally by the ribs (covered by costal pleura) and the diaphragm caudally (covered by diaphragmatic pleura).

(ii) *Abdominal and pelvic cavity:* The lower part of the ventral (abdomino-pelvic) cavity can be further divided into two portions: abdominal portion and pelvic portion. The abdominal cavity contains most of the gastrointestinal tract as well as the kidneys and adrenal glands. The abdominal cavity is bound cranially by the diaphragm, laterally by the body wall, and caudally by the pelvic cavity. The pelvic cavity contains most of the urogenital system as well as the rectum.

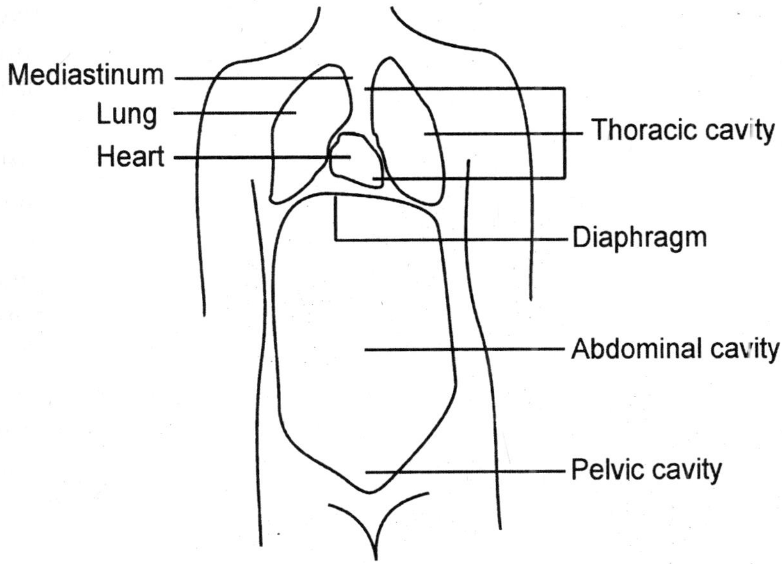

Fig.1.2 *Major abdominal cavities of a human body.*

The pelvic cavity is bounded cranially by the abdominal cavity, dorsally by the sacrum, and laterally by the pelvis.

(iii) *Dorsal cavity*: The smaller of the two main cavities is called the dorsal cavity. As its name implies, it contains organs lying more posterior in the body. The dorsal cavity, again, can be divided into two portions: the upper portion, or the cranial cavity, houses the brain, and the lower portion, or vertebral canal houses the spinal cord.

STUDY QUESTIONS

1. Which type of plane would include the entire length of the vertebral column?
2. A sagittal plane, especially the median plane, could include the entire length of the vertebral column. The column is too curved to be seen in its entirety in a coronal section.
3. Horizontal and coronal planes could pass through both shoulder joints.
4. Planes transverse to the little finger or neck would be horizontal. A plane transverse to the big toe would be coronal.

2

CHAPTER

ORGANISATION OF BODY CELLS, TISSUES, ORGANS SYSTEMS, MEMBRANE AND GLANDS

WHAT IS A CELL ?

Cells are the microscopic fundamental units of all living things. Every living thing has *cells*: *bacteria, protozoans, fungi, plants,* and *animals* are the main groups (kingdoms) of living things. Some organisms are made up of just one cell means *unicelluler* (e.g., bacteria and protozoans), but animals, including human beings, are *multicellular*.

An adult human body is composed of about 100,000,000,000,000 cells. Each cell has basic requirements to sustain it, and the body's organ systems are largely built around providing the many trillions of cells with those basic needs (such as oxygen, food, and waste removal). There are about 200 different kinds of specialized cells in the human body.

When many identical cells are organized together it is called a *tissue* (such as muscle tissue, nervous tissue, etc.). Various tissues organized together for a common purpose are called *organs* (e.g., the stomach is an organ, and so is the skin, the brain, and the uterus).

Early biologists saw cells as simple membranous sacs containing fluid and a few floating particles. Today's biologists know that cells are infinitely more complex than this. Therefore, a strong knowledge of the various cellular organelles and their functions is important to any physiologist. If a person's cells are healthy, then that person is healthy. All physiological processes, growth and development, and disease can be described at the cellular level.

SPECIALIZED CELLS OF THE HUMAN BODY

Although there are specialized cells — both in *structure and function* — within the body, all cells have similarities in their structural organization and metabolic needs (such as maintaining energy levels via conversion of carbohydrate to ATP and using genes to create and maintain proteins). Here are some of the different types of specialized cells within the human body.

Nerve cells: Also called *neurons,* these cells are in the nervous system and function to process and transmit information. They are the core components of the brain, spinal cord and peripheral nerves. They use chemical and electrical synapses to relay signals throughout the body.

Epithelial cells: Functions of epithelial cells include secretion, absorption, protection, transcellular transport, sensation detection, and selective permeability. Epithelium lines both the outside (skin) and the inside cavities and lumen of bodies.

Exocrine cells: These cells secrete products through ducts, such as mucus, sweat, or digestive enzymes.

Endocrine cells: These cells are similar to exocrine cells, but secrete their products directly into the bloodstream instead of through a duct. Endocrine cells are found throughout the body but are concentrated in hormone-secreting glands such as the pituitary.

Blood cells: The most common types of blood cells are :

Red blood cells (erythrocytes): The main function of red blood cells is to collect oxygen in the lungs and deliver it through the blood to the body tissues. Gas exchange is carried out by simple diffusion.

Various types of white blood cells (leukocytes): They are produced in the bone marrow and help the body to fight infectious disease and foreign objects in the immune system. White cells are found in the circulatory system, lymphatic system, spleen, and other body tissues.

CELL SIZE

Cells are the smallest living units within our body, but play a big role in making our body function properly. Many cells never have a large increase in size after they are first formed from a parental cell. Typical stem cells reproduce, double in size, then reproduce again. Most cytosolic contents such as the endomembrane system and the cytoplasm easily scale to larger sizes in larger cells. If a cell becomes too large, the normal cellular amount of DNA may not be adequate to keep the cell supplied with RNA. Large cells often replicate their chromosomes to an abnormally high amount or become multinucleated. Large cells that are primarily for nutrient storage can have a smooth surface membrane, but metabolically active large cells often have some sort of folding of the cell surface membrane in order to increase the surface area available for transport functions.

CELLULAR ORGANIZATION

Several different molecules interact to form organelles with our body. Each type of organelle has a specific function. Organelles perform the vital functions that keep our cells alive.

PLASMA MEMBRANE OR CELL MEMBRANES

The boundary of the cell, sometimes called the *plasma membrane,* separates internal metabolic events from the external environment and controls the movement of materials into and out of the cell. This membrane is very selective about what it allows to pass through; this characteristic is referred to as "selective permeability." For example, it allows oxygen and nutrients to enter the cell while keeping toxins and waste products out.

The plasma membrane is a double *phospholipid membrane.* From which two primary building blocks include protein (about 60%

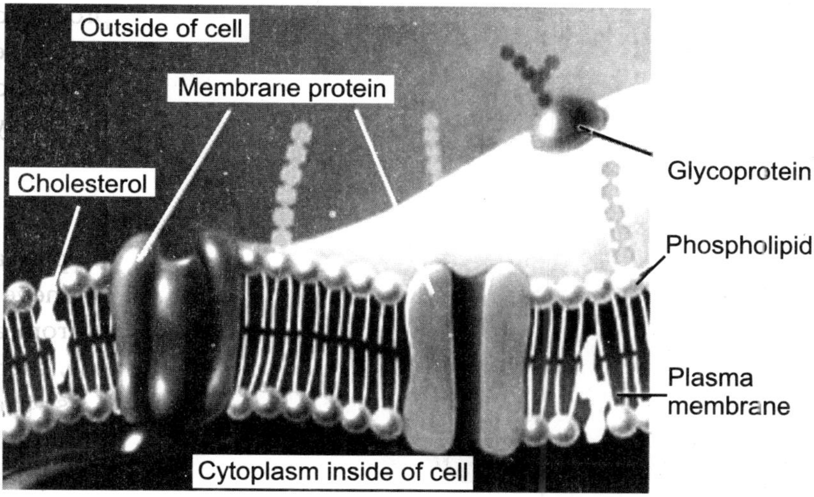

Fig. 2.1 *Structure of plasma membrane.*

of the membrane) and lipid, or fat (about 40% of the membrane). The primary lipid is called *phospholipid*, and molecules of phospholipid form a '*phospholipid bilayer*' (two layers of phospholipid molecules). This bilayer forms because the two 'ends' of phospholipid molecules have very different characteristics: one end is polar (or *hydrophilic*) and one (the hydrocarbon tails below) is non-polar (or *hydrophobic*).

PARTS OF THE CELL

1. CYTOPLASM

The gel-like material within the cell membrane is referred to as the *cytoplasm*. It is a fluid matrix, the cytosol, which consists of 80% to 90% water, salts, organic molecules and many enzymes that catalyse reactions, along with dissolved substances such as proteins and nutrients. The cytoplasm plays an important role in a cell, serving as a "molecular soup" in which organelles are suspended and held together by a fatty membrane.

2. CYTOSKELETON

Thread-like proteins that make up the cytoskeleton continually reconstruct to adapt to the cells constantly changing needs. It helps cells maintain their shape and allows cells and their contents to move. The cytoskeleton allows certain cells such as neutrophils and macrophages to make amoeboid movements. The network is composed of three elements: microtubules, actin filaments, and intermediate fibres.

Fig. 2.2 *Structure of cytoskeleton.*

3. ORGANELLES

Organelles are bodies embedded in the cytoplasm that serve to physically separate the various metabolic activities that occur within cells. The organelles are each like separate little factories, each organelle is responsible for producing a certain product that is used elsewhere in the cell or body.

Nucleus

The nucleus is the largest of the cells organelles. Cells can have more than one nucleus or lack a nucleus all together. Skeletal muscle cells contain more than one nucleus whereas red blood cells do not contain a nucleus at all. The nucleus is bounded by the nuclear envelope, a phospholipid bilayer similar to the plasma membrane. The space between these two layers is the nucleolemma cisterna. The nucleus also serves as the site for the separation of the chromosomes during cell division.

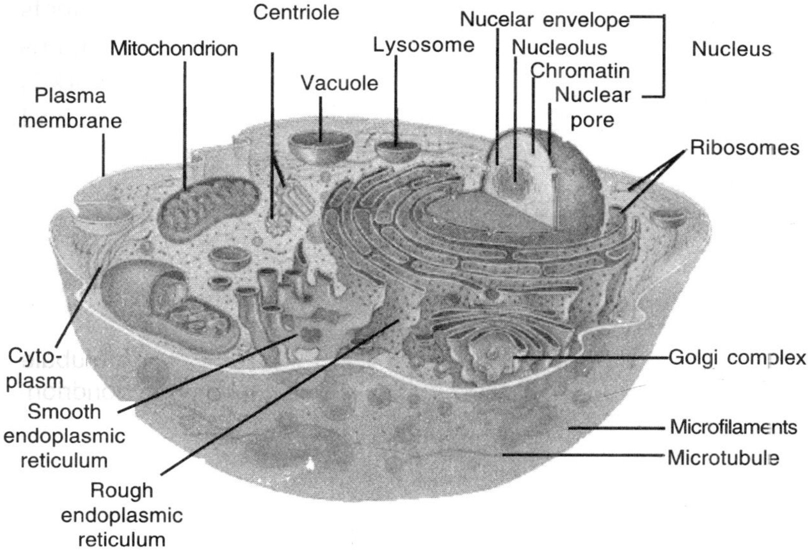

Fig. 2.3 *Structure of organelles.*

Chromosomes

A rough sketch of a chromosome. Inside each cell nucleus are chromosomes. Chromosomes are made up of chromatin, which is made up of protein and deoxyribonucleic acid strands. Deoxyribonucleic acid is DNA, the genetic material that is in the shape of a twisted ladder, also called the double helix. Humans have 23 pairs of chromosomes. Down syndrome and Cri du Chat syndrome result from having an abnormal number of chromosomes.

Centrioles

Centrioles are rod-like structures composed of 9 bundles which contain three microtubules each. Two perpendicularly placed centrioles surrounded by proteins make up the centrosome. Centrioles are very important in cellular division, where they arrange the mitotic spindles that pull the chromosome apart. Centrioles and basal bodies act as microtubule organizing centres. A pair of centrioles (enclosed in a centrosome) located outside the nuclear envelope gives rise to the microtubules that make up the spindle apparatus used during cell division. Basal bodies are at the base of each flagellum and cilium and appear to organize their development.

Ribosomes

Ribosomes play an active role in the complex process of protein synthesis, where they serve as the structures that facilitate the joining of amino acids. Each ribosome is composed of a large and small subunit which are made up of ribosomal proteins and ribosomal RNAs. They can either be found in groups called polyribosomes within the cytoplasm or found alone. Occasionally they are attached to the endoplasmic reticulum.

Mitochondria

Mitochondria are the organelles that function as the cell "powerhouse", generating ATP, the universal form of energy used by all cells. It converts food nutrients such as glucose, to a fuel (ATP) that the cells of the body can use. Mitochondria are tiny sac-like structures found near the nucleus. Little shelves called cristae are formed from folds in the inner membrane. Cells that are metabolically active such as muscle, liver and kidney cells have high energy requirements and therefore have more mitochondria. Mitochondria are unique in that they have their own mitochondrial DNA (separate from the DNA that is in the nucleus). It is believed that eukaryotes evolved from one cell living inside

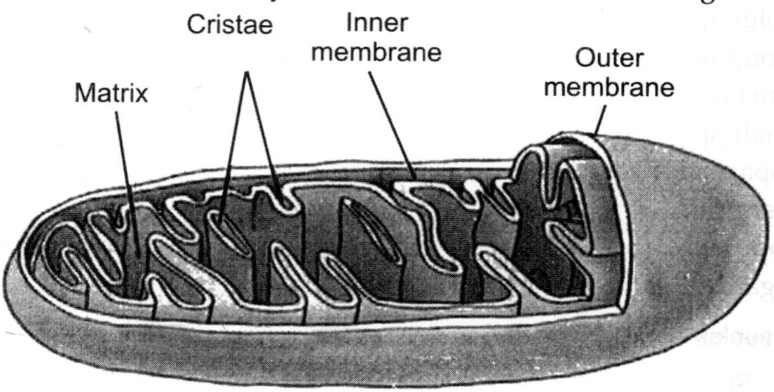

Fig. 2.4 *Mitochondria.*

another cell, and mitochondria share many traits with free-living bacteria (similar chromosome, similar ribosomes, etc.).

Endoplasmic Reticulum

Endoplasmic means "within the plasm" and reticulum means "network". A complex three-dimensional internal membrane system of flattened sheets, sacs and tubes, that play an important role in making proteins and shuttling cellular products; also involved in metabolisms of fats, and the production of various materials. In cross-section, they appear as a series of maze-like channels, often closely associated with the nucleus. When ribosomes are present, the rough ER attaches polysaccharide groups to the polypeptides as they are assembled by the ribosomes. Smooth ER, without ribosomes, is responsible for various activities, including the synthesis of lipids and hormones, especially in cells that produce these substances for export from the cell.

Rough endoplasmic reticulum has characteristic bumpy appearance due to the multitude of ribosomes coating it. It is the site where proteins not destined for the cytoplasm are synthesized.

Smooth endoplasmic reticulum provides a variety of functions, including lipid synthesis and degradation, and calcium ion storage. In liver cells, the smooth ER is involved in the breakdown of toxins, drugs, and toxic byproducts from cellular reactions.

Golgi Apparatus

"Packages", cellular products in sacs are called vesicles so that the products can cross the cell membrane and exit the cell. The Golgi apparatus is the central delivery system for the cell. It is a group of flattened sacs arranged much like a stack of bowls. They function to modify and package proteins and lipids into vesicles, small spherically shaped sacs that bud from the ends of a Golgi apparatus. Vesicles often migrate to and merge with the plasma membrane, releasing their contents outside the cell. The Golgi apparatus also transports lipids and creates lysosomes and organelles involved in digestion.

Vacuoles

Spaces in the cytoplasm sometimes serve to carry materials to the cell membrane for discharge to the outside of the cell. Vacuoles are formed during endocytosis when portions of the cell membrane are pinched off.

Lysosomes

Lysosomes are sac-like compartments that contain a number of powerful degradative enzymes. They are built in the Golgi apparatus. They breakdown harmful cell products and waste materials, cellular debris, and foreign invaders such as bacteria, and then force them out of the cell. Tay-Sachs disease and Pompe's disease are just two of the malfunctions of lysosomes or their digestive proteins.

Peroxisomes

Organelles in which oxygen is used to oxidize substances, breaking down lipids and detoxifying certain chemicals. Peroxisomes self-replicate by enlarging and then dividing. They are common in liver and kidney cells that breakdown potentially harmful substances. Peroxisomes can convert hydrogen peroxide, a toxin made of H_2O_2 to H_2O.

CELL DIVISION

MITOSIS

(i) Characteristic way in which somatic (non-sex) cells divide:

  (a) A parent cell will copy all its internal components, divide them equally, and then split in half to form 2 daughter cells

  (b) The daughter cells formed are identical to each other

(ii) In single-celled, eukaryotic organisms (*Example:* The protist kingdom) this is the way that they form new individuals.

(iii) In multi-cellular organisms, mitosis is used for growth and repair of damaged tissue. *Example:*

  (a) When an egg is fertilized, it undergoes mitosis to form a large mass of cells that will eventually be known as the embryo.

  (b) When you cut your hand, dead cells are replaced by new ones that come from the division of undamaged cells.

(iv) Mitosis is tightly controlled by the cell cycle to ensure that mitosis happens only when it is needed.

(v) When the cell cycle repeats uncontrollably, the cells continue to divide and produce new daughter cells that are not needed–this can lead to the formation of a tumour and quite possibly to cancer.

(a) Cancer begins with one cell.

(b) If that one cell loses the ability to regulate its cell cycle, the two new daughter cells will not have that ability either.

(c) When the two daughter cells divide, their daughter cells likewise will no longer have the ability to regulate cell cycle, and so on...

(d) After only a few rounds, millions of cells will have lost this ability and a tumour will be formed.

(vi) A normal cell completes the cycle within 24 hours.

(vii) Certain cell types eventually lose their ability to complete the cell cycle and can no longer produce new cells – usually these cells are designed to live the life span of the organism. However, if these cells become injured or die, there is no way for the organism to replace them. *Example:* Nerve cells.

THE CELL CYCLE

Interphase

(i) DNA in the cell is coiled up in the form of special linear structures called chromosomes (these contain both DNA and its associated proteins).

(ii) During the replication process, the DNA changes from one double helix (unreplicated) to two double helices (replicated).

(iii) This change occurs within the nucleus where the DNA is normally housed.

(iv) The two helices in the replicated chromosome are joined to one another in the special region of the chromosome called the centromere – at this point, the two double helices are called sister chromatids (technically though, this is still one chromosome because the two helices are attached to one another.

(v) After replication, the parent cell contains twice the normal amount of DNA.

During interphase the chromosomes are not visible since they are spread out to make DNA replication go smoothly – if they remained coiled during this process, it would not be easy to access the nucleotides to make a copy. At this time, the DNA is very vulnerable because the strands are very thin – if they stayed in this state, they would be subject to tangling and breaking during separation – as you will see, they will recoil and condense during mitosis.

Main steps during mitosis

1. *Interphase*: DNA is replicated along with organelles and other cellular components and the cell prepares for division.

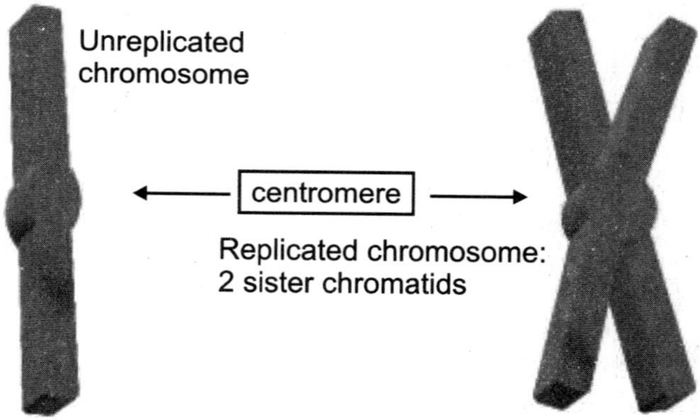

Fig. 2.5 *Interphase.*

2. *Prophase* (*preparation phase*): The DNA recoils, and the chromosomes condense; the nuclear membrane disappears, and the mitotic spindles begin to form.
3. *Metaphase* (*organizational phase*): The chromosomes line up the middle of the cell with the help of spindle fibers attached to the centromere of each replicated chromosome.
4. *Anaphase* (separation phase): the chromosomes split in the middle and the sister chromatids are pulled by the spindle fibers to opposite poles of the cell.

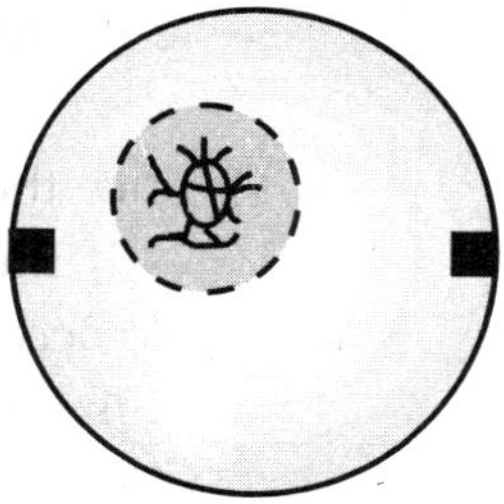

Fig. 2.6 *Prophase.*

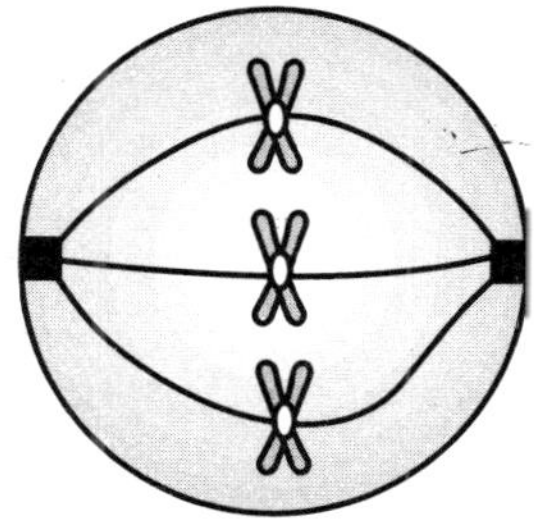

Fig. 2.7 *Metaphase.*

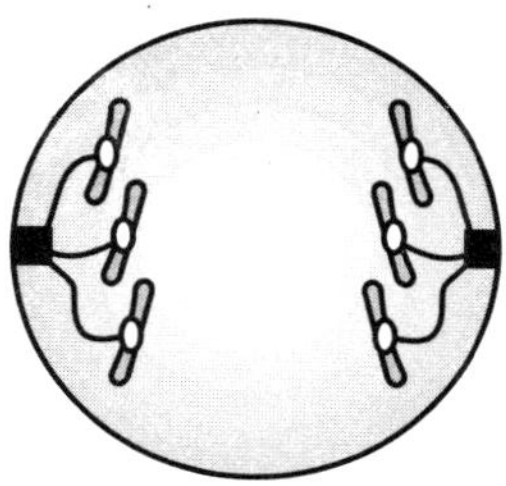

Fig. 2.8 *Anaphase.*

5. *Telophase*: The chromosomes, along with the cytoplasm and its organelles and membranes are divided into two portions. The actual splitting of the daughter cells into two separate cells is called *cytokinesis* and occurs differently in both plant and animal cells as is illustrated below.

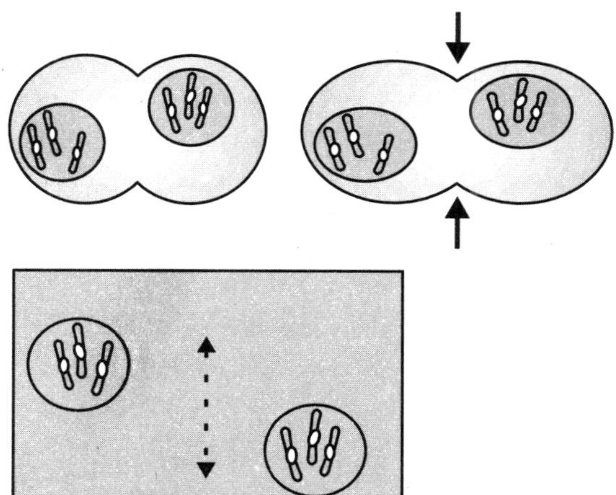

Fig. 2.9 *Telophase.*

Animal cells

The cell pinches in on both sides to form a cleavage furrow. This will gradually move toward the centre to split the parent cell into two daughter cells.

Plant cells

The cell forms a cell plate, which starts in the center and moves towards the outer edges to split the parent cell into two daughter cells.

MEIOSIS

Used in sexual reproduction for the formation of gametes (egg and sperm cells).

Creates genetic diversity

The gametes that are produced as an end result of meiosis are haploid cells, they contain half the genetic material of the parent cell. This will ensure that when gametes combine during fertilization that the new zygote will contain the normal amount of chromosomes instead of double the genetic material.

In the human female, meiosis only occurs within specific cells within the ovary. In the human male, meiosis only occurs within specific cells in the testes. All other cells in the body (somatic cells) undergo mitosis and do not perform meiosis. Both oogenesis (egg production in the female) and spermatogenesis (sperm production in the male) rely on hormones to indicate when to undergo meiosis. After we explain meiosis, we will go back and discuss the differences between these two processes.

MEIOSIS I

Just like in mitosis, during interphase, the DNA is replicated before the cell undergoes the division process.

1. *Prophase I*: The chromosomes coil up and condense and the nuclear membrane disappears. The cell prepares for separation. During this process, the chromosomes of each homologous pair lie so close to one another that the arms can get tangled up. The lining up of homologous chromosomes in pairs is known as synapsis. This can lead to

exchange of genetic material between the homologous pairs known as crossing-over. This will serve to create genetic diversity.

2. *Metaphase I:* The homologous pairs line up in the centre of the cell. During this time, the chromosomes obey the law of independent assortment – this says that each homologous pair arranges itself independently of the others.
3. *Anaphase I*: The homologous pairs are separated and pulled opposite poles of the cell by the spindle fibres.
4. *Telophase I*: The parent cell separates into two daughter cells with the division of the cytoplasm, organelles, and membranes. The new daughter cells now have the number of chromosomes of the parent cell but the chromosomes are still replicated. The two daughter cells are no longer identical to the parent cell or each other.

MEIOSIS II

This is essentially the same as mitosis – we have to split the replicated chromosomes so they are no longer in a replicated state. Remember that this is taking place now in both of the two new daughter cells we have just created.

5. *Prophase II:* This stage resembles that of mitotic prophase – the chromosomes recoil and condense and any nuclear membrane that has formed will now disappear.
6. *Metaphase II*: The chromosomes line up in the middle attached to the spindle fibers and prepare for separation – again, remember this is happening in two different cells simultaneously.
7. *Anaphase II:* The sister chromatids are pulled apart to opposite ends of the cells by the spindle fibres.
8. *Telophase II:* The cells split into 2 daughter cells, and cytokinesis occurs. The end result is four haploid daughter cells that are not identical to one another.

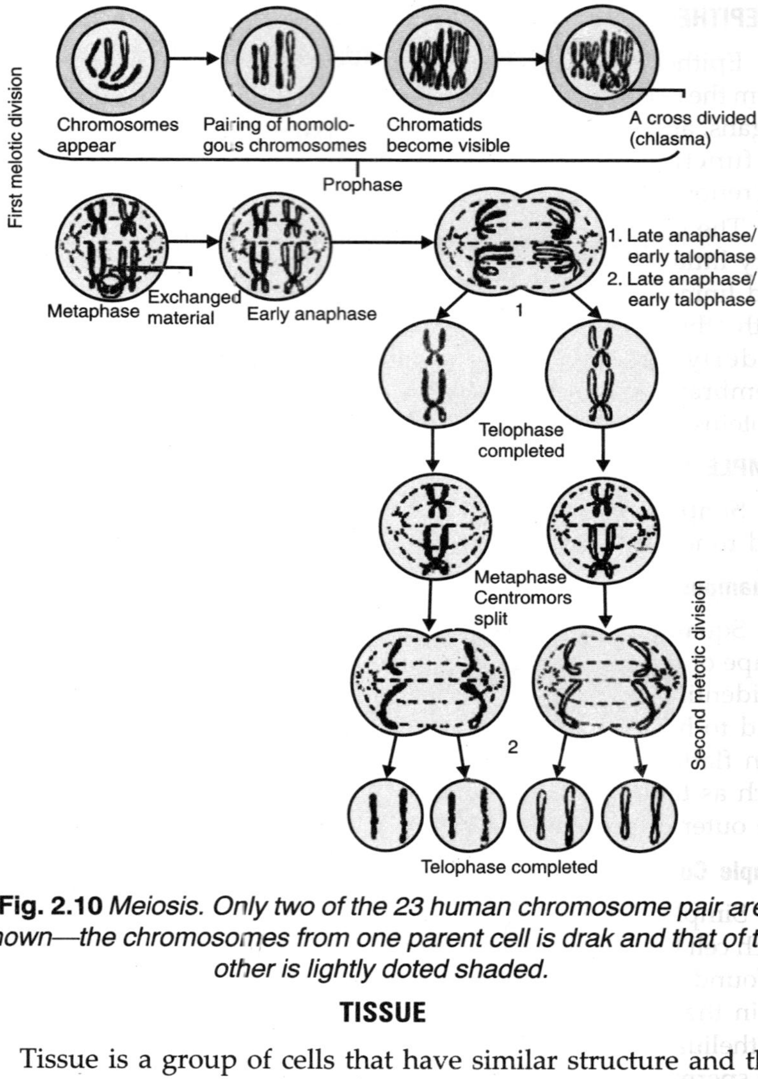

Fig. 2.10 *Meiosis. Only two of the 23 human chromosome pair are shown—the chromosomes from one parent cell is drak and that of the other is lightly doted shaded.*

TISSUE

Tissue is a group of cells that have similar structure and that function together as a unit. A non-living material, called the intercellular matrix, fills the spaces between the cells. This may be abundant in some tissues and minimal in others. The intercellular matrix may contain special substances such as salts and fibers that are unique to a specific tissue and gives that tissue distinctive characteristics. There are four main tissue types in the body: epithelial, connective, muscle, and nervous.

1. EPITHELIAL TISSUES

Epithelial tissues are widespread throughout the body. They form the covering of all body surfaces, line body cavities and hollow organs, and are the major tissue in glands. They perform a variety of functions that include protection, secretion, absorption, excretion, filtration, diffusion, and sensory reception.

The cells in epithelial tissue are tightly packed together with very little intercellular matrix. Because the tissues form coverings and linings, the cells have one free surface that is not in contact with other cells. Opposite the free surface, the cells are attached to underlying connective tissue by a non-cellular basement membrane. This membrane is a mixture of carbohydrates and proteins secreted by the epithelial and connective tissue cells.

SIMPLE EPITHELIUM

Simple epithelium can be subdivided according to the shape and function of its cells.

Squamous (Pavement) Epithelium

Squamous cells have the appearance of thin, flat plates. The shape of the nucleus usually corresponds to the cell form and help to identify the type of epithelium. Squamous cells, for example, tend to have horizontal flattened, elliptical nuclei because of the thin flattened form of the cell. They form the lining of cavities such as the mouth, blood vessels, heart and lungs and make up the outer layers of the skin.

Simple Cuboidal Epithelium

Simple cuboidal cells are roughly square or cuboidal in shape. Each cell has a spherical nucleus in the centre. Cuboidal epithelium is found in glands and in the lining of the kidney tubules as well as in the ducts of the glands. They also constitute the germinal epithelium which produces the egg cells in the female ovary and the sperm cells in the male testes.

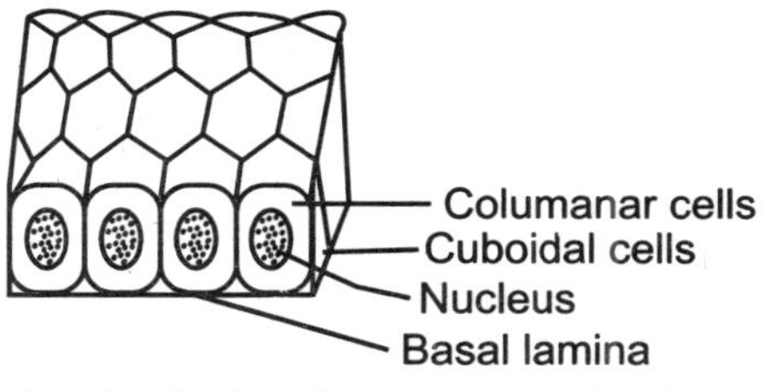

Fig. 2.11 *Simple cuboidal epithelium.*

Simple Columnar Epithelium

Columnar epithelial cells occur in one or more layers. The cells are elongated and column-shaped. The nuclei are elongated and are usually located near the base of the cells.

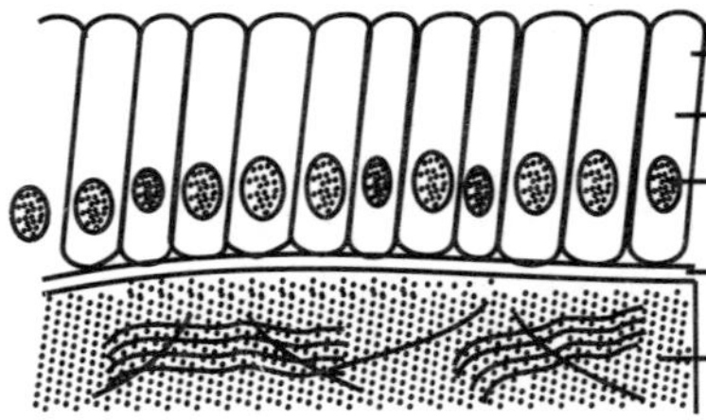

Fig. 2.12. *Simple columnar epithelium*

Columnar epithelium forms the lining of the stomach and intestines. Some columnar cells are specialised for sensory reception such as in the nose, ears and the taste buds of the tongue. Goblet cells (unicellular glands) are found between the columnar epithelial cells of the duodenum. They secrete mucus or slime, a lubricating substance which keeps the surface smooth.

Ciliated Columnar Epithelium

These are simple columnar epithelial cells, but in addition, they possess fine hair-like outgrowths, cilia on their free surfaces. These cilia are capable of rapid, rhythmic, wave-like beatings in a certain direction. This movement of the cilia in a certain direction causes the mucus, which is secreted by the goblet cells, to move (flow or stream) in that direction. Ciliated epithelium is usually found in the air passages like the nose. It is also found in the uterus and fallopian tubes of females. The movement of the cilia propel the ovum to the uterus.

Glandular Epithelium

Columnar epithelium with goblet cells is called glandular epithelium. Some parts of the glandular epithelium consist of such a large number of goblet cells that there are only a few normal epithelial cells left. Columnar and cuboidal epithelial cells often become specialised as gland cells which are capable of synthesising and secreting certain substances such as enzymes, hormones, milk, mucus, sweat, wax and saliva. Unicellular glands consist of single, isolated glandular cells such as the goblet cells. Sometimes a portion of the epithelial tissue becomes invaginated and a multicellular gland is formed. Multicellular glands are composed of clusters of cells. Most glands are multicellular including the salivary glands.

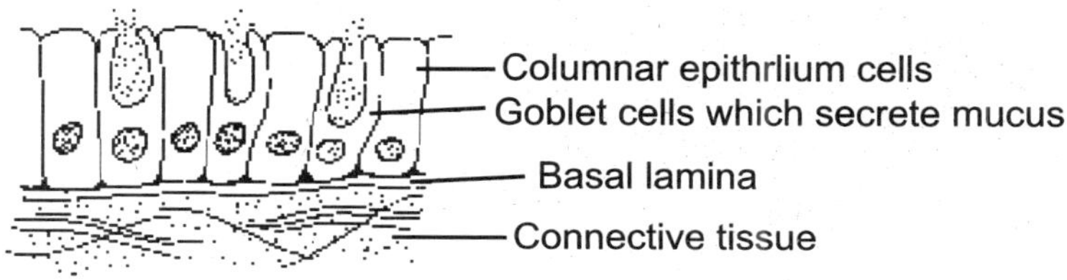

Fig. 2.13 *Glandular epithelium.*

Stratified Epithelium

Where body linings have to withstand wear and tear, the epithelia are composed of several layers of cells and are then called compound or stratified epithelium. The top cells are flat and scaly and it may or may not be keratinised (i.e., containing a tough, resistant protein called keratin). The mammalian skin is an example of dry, keratinised, stratified epithelium. The lining of the mouth cavity is an example of an unkeratinised, stratified epithelium.

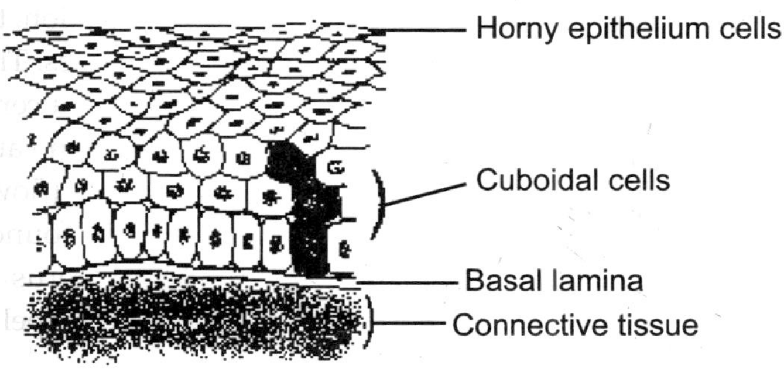

Fig. 2.14 *Stratified epithelium*

Psuedostratified epithelial tissues appear to have more than one layer of cells, but, actually, all the cells of such a tissue reach the underlying tissue just as the cells of a simple epithelial tissue do. Stratified epithelial tissues have two or more layers of cells. In stratified epithelial tissues, the outermost layer of cells determines the name of the tissue: *Stratified squamous, stratified cuboidal,* and *stratified columnar epithelia* are the three types of stratified epithelial tissues.

2. CONNECTIVE TISSUES

Connective tissues bind structures together, form a framework and support for organs and the body as a whole, store fat, transport substances, protect against disease, and help repair tissue damage. They occur throughout the body. Connective tissues are characterized by an abundance of intercellular matrix with relatively few cells. Connective tissue cells are able to reproduce but not as rapidly as epithelial cells. Most connective tissues have a good blood supply but some do not. Numerous cell types are found in connective tissue. Three of the most common are the *fibroblast, macrophage,* and *mast cells.*

Fibroblast: A connective-tissue cell of mesenchymal origin that secretes proteins and especially molecular collagen from which the extracellular fibrillar matrix of connective tissue forms.

Macrophage: A phagocytic tissue cell of the reticuloendothelial system that may be fixed or freely motile, is derived from a monocyte, and functions in the protection of the body against infection and noxious substances —called also histiocyte.

Mast cell : A large cell that occurs especially in connective tissue and has basophilic granules containing substances (as histamine and heparin) which mediate allergic reactions.

Types of Connective Tissue

The types of connective tissue include:

Loose or Areolar Connective Tissue

Loose connective tissue is found just about everywhere in the body, as it provides support for structures passing through it, such as blood and lymph vessels and nerves. As well, it also serves to bind together other tissues, including organs and their components.

Basically, if there's a free space in the body, loose connective tissue fills it. Loose connective tissue can also be called *areolar connective tissue* (from the Latin, *areolatus* meaning, "with small spaces"). The main cells which make up loose connective tissue are fibroblasts. These cells secrete the components which make up the fibres and ground substance that form the non-cellular component of the loose connective tissue.

Adipose Tissue

Adipose tissue is composed of large cells which contain a single large droplet of adipose (fat), surrounded by a thin ring containing the cellular cytoplasm and nucleus. Since the adipose has been removed with the processing of this slice, only a space remains. This gives the cells a "signet ring" appearance, with the ring of cytoplasm making up the band and the nucleus being the "jewellery" on the ring (try that on for size!). Surrounding the adipose cells is a fine network of collagen fibres, which give the cells support.

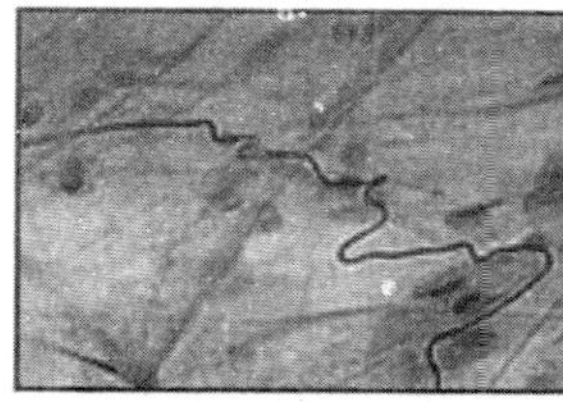

Fig. 2.15 *Loose connective tissue.*

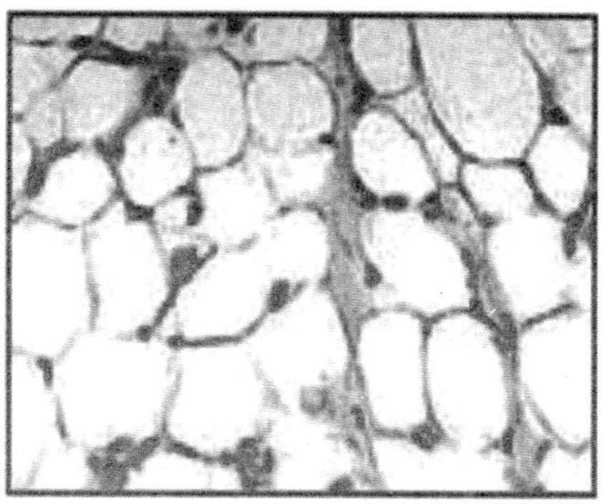

Fig. 2.16 *Adipose tissue*

Fibrous Connective Tissue

Dense connective tissue is divided into two sub-categories:

(i) Dense irregular connective tissue.

(ii) Dense regular connective tissue.

Dense connective tissue contains relatively few cells with much greater numbers of collagen fibres. Dense irregular connective tissue has bundles of collagen fibres that appear to be fairly randomly orientated (as in the dermis).

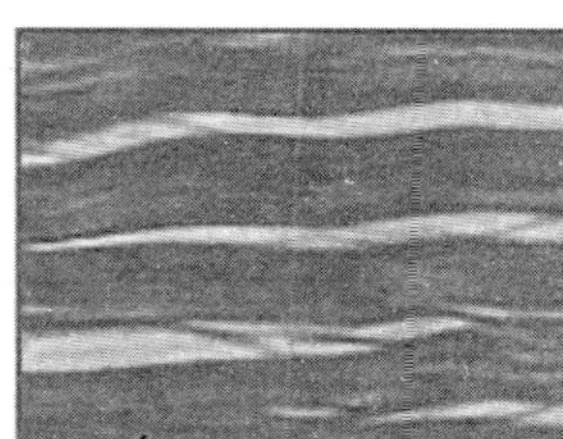

Fig. 2.17 *Fibrous connective tissue.*

Dense regular connective tissue has closely-packed densely-arranged fibre bundles with clear orientation (such as in tendons) and relatively few cells.

Tendons

Tendons are the most common type of dense regular connective tissue. Tendons connect skeletal muscles to bone. Owing to the dominance of the collagen fibers, the tendons have a white colour (stains acidophilic in regular staining). The collagen bundles in tendons are arranged in bundles (primary bundles). Several primary bundles, each surrounded by loose connective tissue, are grouped into larger bundles (secondary bundles). The loose connective tissue surrounding the primary and secondary bundles contains blood vessels and nerves. The whole tendon is surrounded by a denser connective tissue.

Ligaments

Ligaments are a special type of dense regular connective tissue that connects bones to bones. They have a similar structural arrangement to tendons, but differ in their yellow colour, which is due to the abundance of elastic fibres in the tissue. The elastic fibers are stained a dark brown-red with orcein. Elastic fibers provide the ligament with remarkable elasticity (in contrast to tendons).

Mucous tissue

This is found in the umbilical cord (*Wharton's jelly*). It is a loose connective tissue composed of fibroblasts with several long cytoplasmic processes. The intercellular space is filled with a jelly-like amorphous ground substance, rich in hyaluronic acid and fibers.

Elastic Fibres Tissue

Elastic fibers, as the name suggests, are highly elastic and stretch in response to tension. In particular they are formed from the protein elastin. The amino acid composition of elastin, similar to collagen, is rich in glycine and proline, but in addition has two unusual amino acids, desmosine and isodesmosine. Elastic fibers also have a high content of valine. Elastic fibers are very prominent in elastic tissues such as the elastic ligaments. When present in high concentration, the elastin imparts a yellow colour to the tissue. The elastic laminae of arterial blood vessel walls are composed of a non-fibrillar form of elastin. Elastin can be stained in histological preparations using orcein.

Cartilage

Cartilage is a type of dense connective tissue. It is composed of specialized cells called *chondrocytes* that produce a large amount of extracellular matrix composed of collagen fibers, abundant ground substance rich in proteoglycan, and elastin fibers.

Cartilage is found in many places in the body including the articular surface of the bones, the rib cage, the ear, the nose, the bronchial tubes and the intervertebral discs. Its mechanical properties are intermediate between bone and dense connective tissue like tendon.

Unlike other connective tissues, cartilage does not contain blood vessels. The chondrocytes are fed by diffusion, helped by the pumping action generated by compression of the articular cartilage or flexion of the elastic cartilage. Thus, compared to other connective tissues, cartilage grows and repairs more slowly.

Types of Cartilage

Cartilage is classified in three types, elastic cartilage, hyaline cartilage and fibrous cartilage, that differ in the relative amounts of these three main components.

Hyaline cartilage

Hyaline cartilage is a rather hard, translucent material rich in collagen and proteoglycan. It covers the end of bones to form the smooth articular surface of joints. It is also found in the nose, the larynx and between the ribs and the sternum. Bones grow via a hyaline cartilage intermediate, a process called Endochondral ossification.

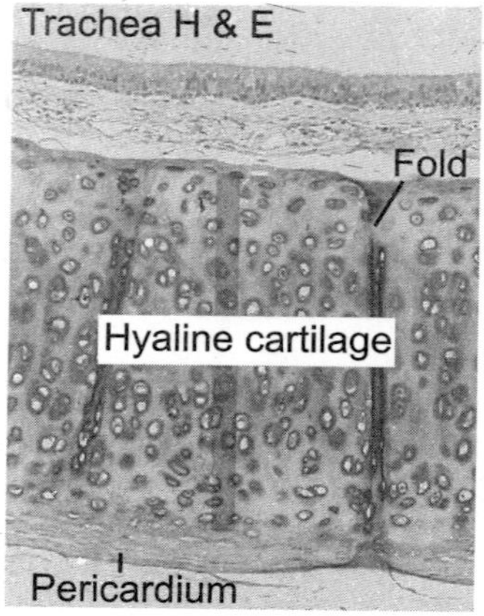

Fig. 2.18 *Hyaline cartilage.*

Elastic cartilage

Elastic cartilage contains large amounts of elastic fibers (elastin) scattered throughout the matrix. It is stiff yet elastic, and is important to prevent tubular structures from collapsing. Elastic cartilage is found in the pinna of the ear, in tubular structures such as the auditory (Eustachian) tubes and in the epiglottis.

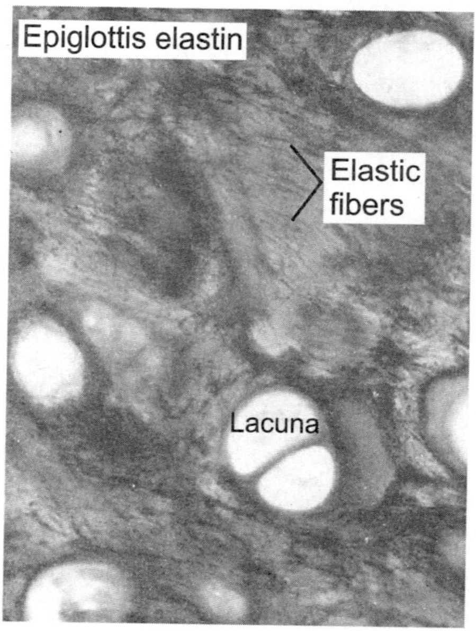

Fig. 2.19 *Elastic cartilage*

Fibrous cartilage

Fibrous cartilage is the most common form of cartilage by weight. It is characterized by a dense network of Type I collagen. It is a white, very tough material that provide high tensile strength and support. It contains more collagen and less proteoglycan than hyaline cartilage. Thus, its properties are closer to those of tendon than hyaline cartilage. It is present in areas most subject to frequent stress like intervertebral discs, the symphysis pubis and the attachments of certain tendons and ligaments.

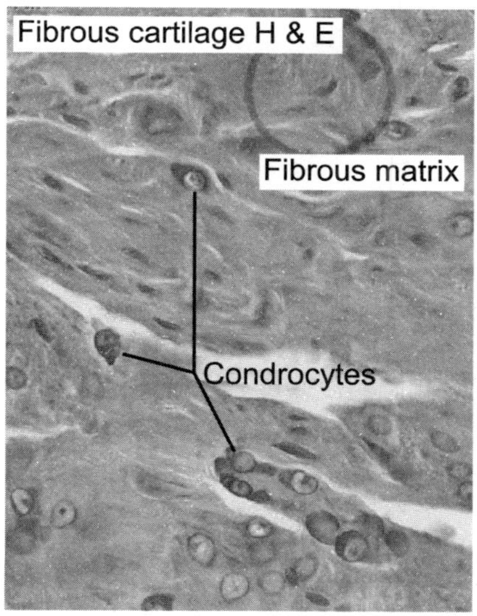

Fig. 2.20 *Fibrous cartilage*

Osseous Tissue (Bone)

The *Haversian system* is the basis for the structural organization of mammalian compact bones and is composed of concentric *lamellae*, the *Haversian canal*, *lacunae* and *canaliculi*. The *lamellae* form the bone matrix surrounding the Haversian canal which carries blood vessels and nerves to and from the bone.

The *lacunae* are the spaces in the bone where the osteocytes are located. These lacunae are interconnected with each other and the Haversian canal (so they get adequate nutrients, as these do not diffuse well through bone) by a system of small tubes in the bone called *canaliculi* ("canals", as the name implies).

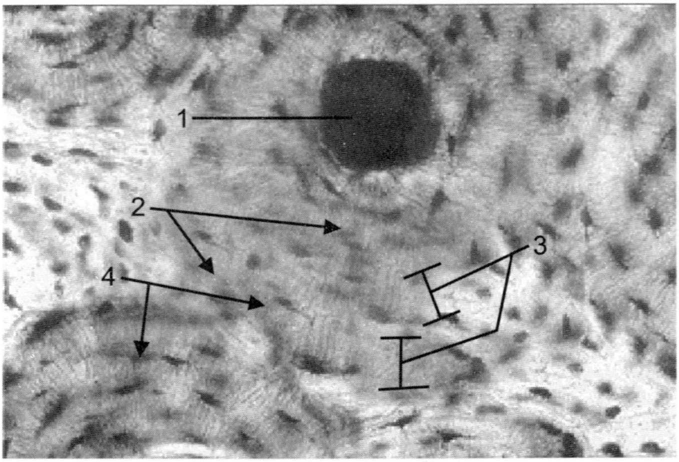

1. Haversian Canal; 2. Canaliculi; 3. Lamellae; 4. Lacunae

Fig. 2.21 *Osseous tissue.*

Blood

Blood is a connective tissue consisting of cells suspended in an intercellular fluid (the blood plasma). Blood functions to transport oxygen, carbon dioxide, nutrients, wastes, hormones, etc. to and from the body's cells. Blood cells consist of *erythrocytes* (red blood cells), *leukocytes* (white blood cells) and *thrombocytes* (platelets).

Erythrocytes have a reddish colour (and, thus so does your blood) due to their high content of the iron – protein complex called *hemoglobin*. Hemoglobin is the molecule that allows erythrocytes to bind oxygen. The other cells seen here are leukocytes, which are part of the immune system. Platelets are small cytoplasmic fragments of a larger cell, known as a *megakaryocyte,* and are important for clotting of the blood.

3. MUSCLE TISSUE

Muscle tissue is composed of cells that have the special ability to shorten or contract in order to produce movement of the body parts. The tissue is highly cellular and is well supplied with blood vessels. The cells are long and slender, so they are sometimes called muscle fibers, and these are usually arranged in bundles or layers that are surrounded by connective tissue. Actin and myosin are contractile proteins in muscle tissue.

Muscle tissue can be categorised into smooth muscle tissue, cardiac muscle tissue and skeletal muscle.

Smooth Muscle

Smooth muscle features long, narrow "spindle" shaped cells with a single central, somewhat elongated, nucleus. These cells are arranged parallel to one another *in situ* and do not show any striations microscopically. This type of muscle is called "involuntary" because it acts to contract and relax without conscious thought (i.e., you can't will your intestines to contract, they just do – this is what causes that embarrassing grumbling half-way through lecture when you're hungry!).

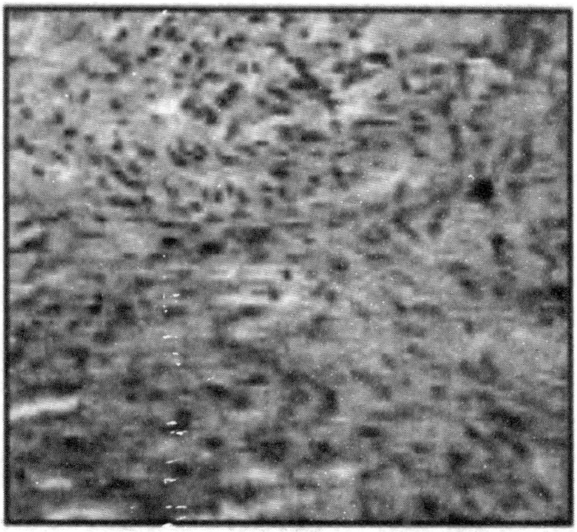

Fig. 2.22 *Smooth muscle.*

Functionally, smooth muscle cells contract as a single unit, with the impulse to contract being passed to small groups of cells by a single innervating nerve, coordinating with other nerves. Smooth muscle is found in the walls of the digestive tract, uterus, bladder, blood vessels and other internal organs.

Cardiac Muscle

Cardiac muscle is similar to skeletal muscle in that it is striated and multinucleate, and similar to smooth muscle in that the nuclei are centrally located and many cells are required to span the length of the muscle. It differs from both skeletal muscle and smooth muscle in that its cells branch and are joined to one another via intercalated discs. Intercalated discs allow communication between the cells such that there is a sequential contraction of the cells from the bottom of the ventricle to the top, facilitating maximal ejection of blood from the ventricle during contraction. This occurs with out nervous innervation to each cell or group of cells.

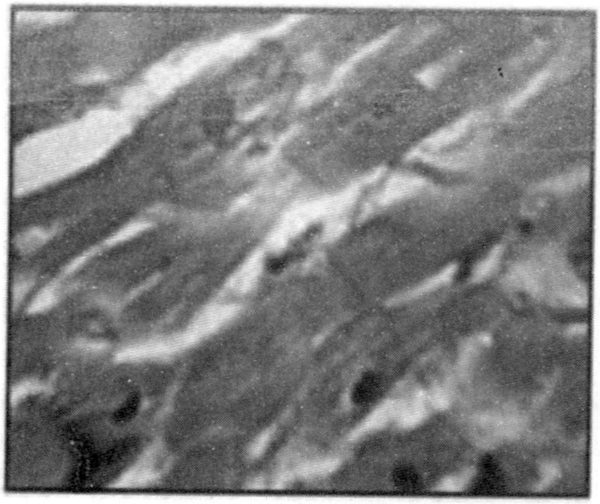

Fig. 2.23 *Cardiac muscle.*

Cardiac muscle also differs from the other two muscle types in that contraction can occur even without an initial nervous input. The cells that produce the stimulation for contraction without nervous input are called the pacemaker cells.

Skeletal Muscle

Skeletal muscle, as its name implies, is the muscle attached to the skeleton. It is also called *striated muscle*. The contraction of skeletal muscle is under *voluntary* control. Skeletal muscle is made up of thousands of cylindrical muscle fibers often running all the way from origin to insertion. The fibers are bound together by connective tissue through which run blood vessels and nerves. Each muscle fibers contains:

Fig. 2.24 *Skeletal muscle.*

- An array of myofibrils that are stacked lengthwise and run the entire length of the fiber.
- Mitochondria.
- An extensive smooth endoplasmic reticulum (SER).
- Many nuclei.

The multiple nuclei arise from the fact that each muscle fiber develops from the fusion of many cells (called *myoblasts*). The number of fibers is probably fixed early in life. This is regulated by myostatin, a cytokine that is synthesized in muscle cells. Myostatin suppresses skeletal muscle development. Cattle and mice with inactivating mutations in their myostatin genes develop much larger muscles. Some athletes and other remarkably strong people have been found to carry one mutant myostatin gene. These discoveries have already led to the growth of an illicit market in drugs supposedly able to suppress myostatin.

4. NERVOUS TISSUE

Nervous tissue is found in the brain, spinal cord, and nerves. It is responsible for coordinating and controlling many body activities. It stimulates muscle contraction, creates an awareness of the environment, and plays a major role in emotions, memory, and reasoning. To do all these things, cells in nervous tissue need

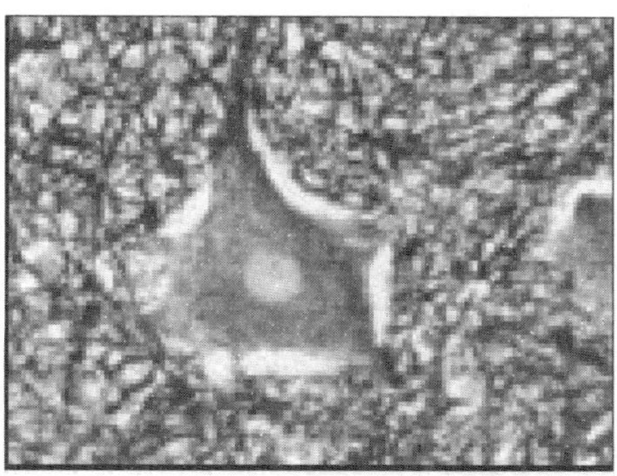

Fig. 2.25 *Nervous tissue (Neuron).*

to be able to communicate with each other by way of electrical nerve impulses. The cells in nervous tissue that generate and conduct impulses are called neurons or nerve cells. These cells have three principal parts: the dendrites, the cell body, and one axon.

The main part of the cell, the part that carries on the general functions, is the cell body. Dendrites are extensions, or processes, of the cytoplasm that carry impulses to the cell body. An extension or process called an axon carries impulses away from the cell body.

Nervous tissue also includes cells that do not transmit impulses, but instead support the activities of the neurons. These are the glial cells (neuroglial cells), together termed the neuroglia. Supporting, or glia, cells bind neurons together and insulate the neurons. Some are phagocytic and protect against bacterial invasion, while others provide nutrients by binding blood vessels to the neurons.

ORGAN

In biology, an organ is a group of tissues that perform a specific function or group of functions. Usually there is a main tissue and sporadic tissues. The main tissue is the one that is unique for the specific organ. For example, main tissue in the heart is the myocardium, while sporadic tissues are the nervous, blood, connective etc.

ORGAN SYSTEM

A group of related organs is an organ system. Organs within a system may be related in any number of ways, but relationships of function are most commonly used. For example, the urinary system comprises organs that work together to produce, store, and carry urine.

The functions of organ systems often share significant overlap. For instance, the nervous and endocrine system both operate via a shared organ, the hypothalamus. For this reason, the two systems are combined and studied as the neuro endocrine system. The same is true for the musculo-skeletal system, which involves the relationship between the muscular and the skeletal system.

List of Major Human Organ Systems

These are typically considered to be eleven major organ systems of the human body:

(i) *Integumentary system*: Body covering.

(ii) *Skeletal system*: Support and movement, lymphocyte production.

(iii) *Muscular system*: Support and movement, production of heat.

(iv) *Nervous system*: Integration and coordination through electrochemical signals.

(v) *Digestive system*: Absorption of nutrients and excretion of waste.

(vi) *Cardiovascular system*: Internal transport.

(vii) *Lymphatic system*: Regulate fluids and immunity.

(viii) *Respiratory system*: Elimination of CO_2 and absorption of O_2.

(ix) *Urinary system*: Excretion of nitrogenous waste, and maintain homeostasis of electrolytes.

(x) *Reproductive system*: Production of offspring.

(xi) *Endocrine system*: Integration and coordination through hormones.

GLAND

A gland is an organ in an animal's body that synthesizes a substance for release such as hormones or breast milk, often into the bloodstream (endocrine gland) or into cavities inside the body or its outer surface (exocrine gland). Every gland is formed by an ingrowth from an epithelial surface. This ingrowth may from the beginning possess a tubular structure, but in other instances glands may start as a solid column of cells which subsequently becomes tubulated.

As growth proceeds, the column of cells may divide or give off offshoots, in which case a compound gland is formed. In many glands the number of branches is limited, in others (salivary, pancreas) a very large structure is finally formed by repeated growth and sub-division. As a rule, the branches do not unite with one another, but in one instance, the liver, this does occur when a reticulated compound gland is produced. In compound glands the more typical or secretory epithelium is found forming the terminal portion of each branch, and the uniting portions form ducts and are lined with a less modified type of epithelial cell.

TYPES

Glands can be divided into two groups:

Endocrine glands

Endocrine glands are glands that secrete their product directly onto a surface rather than through a duct.

Exocrine glands

Exocrine glands secrete their products via a duct, the glands in this group can be divided into three groups:

Apocrine glands

A portion of the secreting cell's body is lost during secretion. Apocrine gland is often used to refer to the apocrine sweat glands, however, it is thought that apocrine sweat glands may not be true apocrine glands as they may not use the apocrine method of secretion.

Holocrine glands

The entire cell disintegrates to secrete its substances (e.g., sebaceous glands).

Merocrine glands

Cells secrete their substances by exocytosis (e.g., mucous and serous glands). Also called '*eccrine*.' The type of secretory product of an exocrine gland may also be one of *three* categories:

(a) *Serous glands*: Secrete a watery, often protein-rich product.
(b) *Mucous glands*: Secrete a viscous product, rich in carbohydrates (e.g., glycoproteins).
(c) *Sebaceous glands*: Secrete a lipid product.

Glands are also classified according to their shape:

(i) *Tubular gland*: If the gland retains its shape as a tube throughout it is termed a tubular gland.
(ii) *Alveolar or saccular glands*. In the second main variety of gland the secretory portion is enlarged and the lumen variously increased in size. These are termed alveolar or saccular glands.

STUDY QUESTIONS

1. Define cell. Explain in detail the structure and functions of various organelles in a cell.

2. Describe the process of meiosis. Explain the functions of different stages of meiosis.
3. Write short notes on the following:
   (a) Tissues
   (b) Organ
   (c) Gland
   (d) Carilage
   (e) Bone.

■■■

3

CHAPTER

THE SKELETAL SYSTEM

INTRODUCTION

The human skeletal system is divided into two main groups: the *axial skeleton* and the *appendicular skeleton*. The axial skeleton includes bones associated with the body's main axis, the spine. This includes the spine, the skull, and the rib cage. The appendicular skeleton is attached to the axial skeleton and consists of the bones associated with the body's appendages—the arms and legs. This includes the bones of the pectoral girdle (shoulder area), the pelvic girdle (hip area), and the arms and legs.

AXIAL SKELETON

The axial skeleton consists of the skull, vertebral column, and rib cage.

SKULL

Its 22 bones feature eight in the cranium (a rigid shell guarding the brain) and fourteen facial bones, including a movable mandible (lower jaw) and a maxilla (upper jaw), with sockets for teeth.

The Cranium

The cranium consists of eight flat bones which are rigidly attached to each other with dentate sutures (joints with teeth-like protrusions). They envelop and protect the brain. The frontal bone forms the forehead and portions of the eye sockets (or orbits). The *occipital bone,* at the base of the skull contains a large opening, called the *foramen magnum,* through which the spinal cord passes. On each side of the opening is the *occipital condyle* — two round protuberances — by means of which the skull articulates with the first neck (or cervical) vertebra (the atlas). The organs of hearing are situated in the *temporal bone,* one on each side. The openings leading into these organs can also be seen on each side.

The Facial Bones

The facial skeleton consists of fourteen irregular bones, which are all (with the exception of the lower jaw bone) firmly attached to the cranium by means of sutures. They include the *nasal bones,* the two jaw bones and the cheek bones. The *lower jaw* articulates with the temporal bone part of the cheek bone, just in front of the ear. This allows for the necessary movement of the lower jaw when food is bitten off and chewed. Both upper and lower jaws have alveolar pockets into which teeth fit.

The teeth are embedded in sockets in the ridges of the upper and lower jaw bones. Three regions can be distinguished in a tooth:

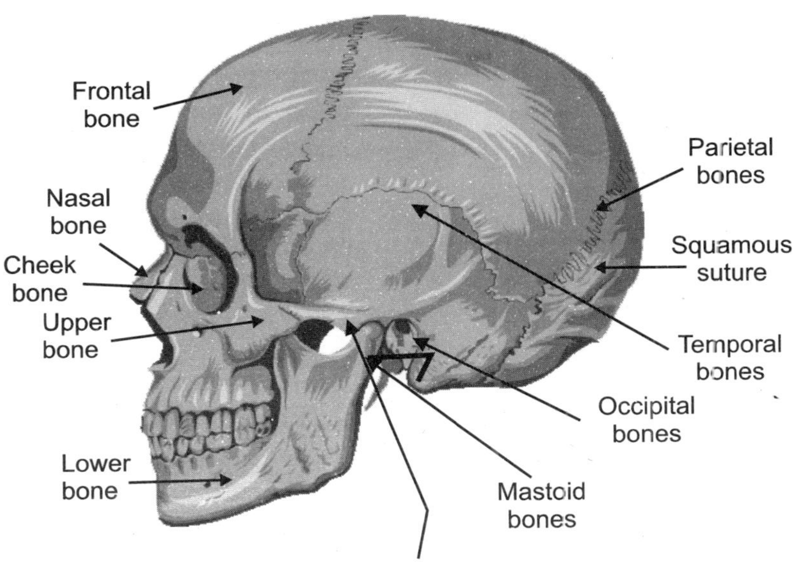

Fig. 3.1 *Facial bones.*

(a) The *root* which are embedded in the alveolar pocket of the jaw. The root is firmly attached to the jaw by a surrounding layer of cement and strong connective tissue.

(b) The *neck* is the area where the root(s) and crown meet.

(c) The *crown* projects above the gum. It is covered with a hard, white layer of enamel. The largest part of the tooth consists of dentine which is a harder substance than ordinary bone. The dentine surrounds the cavity which extends from the root to the crown. Blood capillaries and nerves enter the cavity at a small opening in the tip of the root.

There are four types of teeth:

(i) *Incisors* are chisel-like teeth with sharp cutting edges found at the front of the jaws. They are used for biting off pieces of food.

(ii) *Canines* (eye teeth) are sharp, pointed, cone-shaped teeth which are slightly longer than the other teeth. They flank the incisors and are used for biting, tearing and ripping.

(iii) *Premolars* are situated behind the canines. They have flat surfaces with two pointed protuberances (cusps), which are used for chewing and grinding the food.

(iv) *Molars* are larger and better developed than the premolars. They are found at the back of the mouth, behind the premolars. They have broad, flat surfaces with three pointed protuberances (cusps) and are also used for chewing and grinding the food. They usually have 2 to 3 roots.

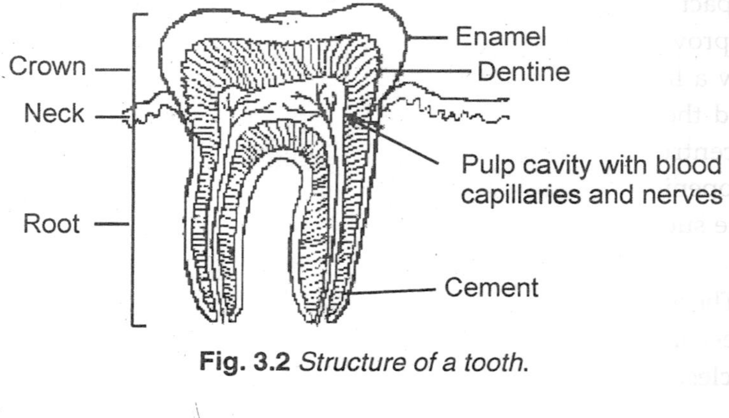

Fig. 3.2 *Structure of a tooth.*

Initially a human has a temporary set, or a milk set of 20 teeth with a tooth formula 2.1.2 over 2.1.2. After shedding the temporary set humans get a permanent set of 32 teeth with a tooth formula 2.1.2.3 over 2.1.2.3.

THE VERTEBRAL COLUMN

The vertebral column forms the central part of the skeleton. It supports the skull and protects the spinal cord. It also serves as attachment for the ribs, the pectoral and pelvic girdles. The vertebral column consists of separate bones, the vertebrae. The different vertebrae are arranged above each other. Because the separate vertebrae are attached to each other by means of fibrous cartilaginous discs they form a flexible column. Each vertebra has articular surfaces above and below, which allow articulation movement between them.

The vertebral column of 33 vertebrae is divided into five regions according to their position and structure. The five regions consist of: seven *cervical* (neck) *vertebrae*, twelve *thoracic* (chest) *vertebrae*, five *lumbar vertebrae*, five fused *sacral vertebrae*, and four *fused vertebrae*.

Structure of a Typical Vertebra

A typical vertebra consists of the centrum, a neural arch, a neural spine, two transverse processes and four articular processes with articulating surfaces. The centrum is the front part (anterior) and consists of a solid piece of spongy bone encircled by a layer of compact bone. The upper and lower surfaces are flat and rough and provide attachment for the cartilaginous discs. These surfaces allow a limited degree of movement. The posterior (back) part is called the *neural arch*. An opening, (foramen) is formed between the centrum and the neural arch. The spinal cord goes through this opening. The neural canal is formed by the vertebral foramina in the successive vertebrae and it encloses and protects the spinal cord.

The *neural spine* is directed backwards. The *two transverse processes* project laterally and serve for the attachment of ligaments and muscles. The neural arch has *four smaller articular processes* with

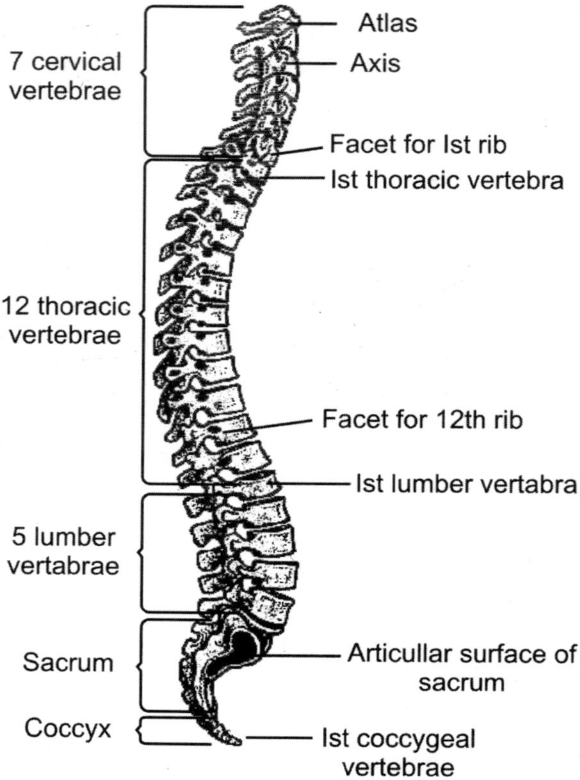

Fig. 3.3 *A typical vertebrae.*

articular surfaces, two on the upper and two on the lower aspect of the vertebra. These articulating surfaces are covered by hyaline cartilage. The *spinal nerves* leave the vertebral column through the openings between each succeeding pair of vertebrae.

The Cervical Vertebrae

The neck region consists of seven cervical vertebrae. These are the smallest vertebrae in the vertebral column. The first two cervical vertebrae are known as the atlas and axis. They are specially adapted to support the skull and to enable it to move. They differ from the structure of the typical vertebra in certain respects.

The Atlas

The atlas is the first neck vertebra and supports the skull. It is ring-shaped and has no centrum. A neural spine is absent. The atlas consists of posterior and anterior neural arches and two short transverse processes. The spinal foramen (neural canal) is very large. The two occipital condyles of the skull fit into the articulating facets on the upper surface of the atlas, on either side of the neural canal. On its lower surface (inferior) surface the atlas has two articular surfaces for articulation with the axis.

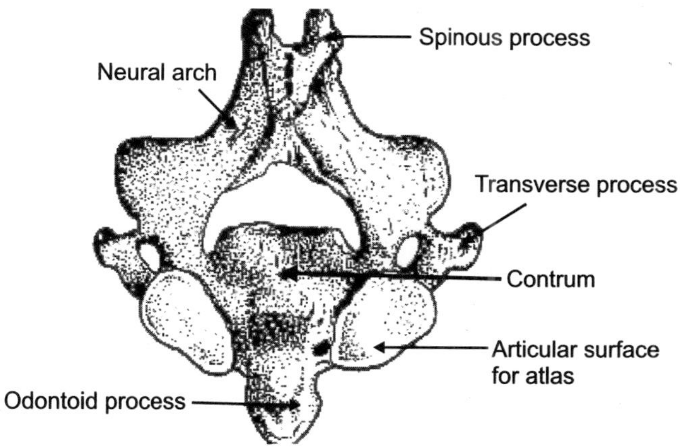

Fig. 3.4 *The atlas.*

The Axis

The axis has a large, strong neural spine. The centrum is small and has become modified to bear the odontoid process (a tooth-like projection) on its upper surface. The odontoid process fits

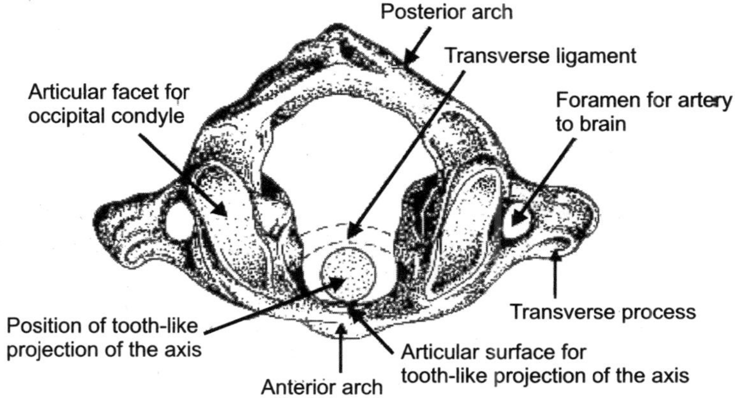

Fig. 3.5 *The axis.*

against the facet in the anterior arch of the atlas. This forms a pivot joint or axis, around which the atlas (together with the skull) can rotate, so allowing the head to turn from side to side.

The Thoracic Vertebrae

There are 12 thoracic vertebrae. The centrum is large and sturdy and the neural spines are long and directed downwards. The long neural spines form an anchorage for the muscles and ligaments that support the head and neck. The head (or capitulum) of each of the first 10 pairs of ribs fits into and articulates with the semi-circular facet which is situated between two successive centra, i.e., between the inferior surface of one and the superior surface of the next centrum. These facets occur on both sides of the centrum. The tubercle of the rib articulates with the facet at the tip of the transverse process.

The Lumbar Vertebrae

These 5 vertebrae are the largest and strongest in the vertebral column. The transverse processes are very long for the attachment of the powerful back muscle that maintain the posture and flex the spine in movement.

The Sacrum

The sacrum is roughly triangular in shape and consists of five fused vertebrae. It lies between the hip bones, with which it articulates. Horizontal ridges indicate the divisions between the fused vertebrae. At the ends of these ridges are openings which allow nerves and blood vessels to pass through.

The Coccyx

The coccyx consists of four fused tail vertebrae which are small and have a relatively simple structure. They do not resemble the structure of a typical vertebra. The muscles of the buttocks are attached to the coccyx.

The Ribs

Twelve pairs of ribs articulate with the 12 vertebrae of the thoracic region. The ribs are flat, narrow bones with a distinctive bow-shaped curve. Each rib consists of a head or capitulum, a small tubercle (which is a short distance back from the head) and the *shaft*. The head of the rib articulates with the semi-circular articulating facets formed by the centra of two successive thoracic vertebrae. The tubercle fits into and articulates with the articulating facets on the transverse process. The first seven ribs on each side are joined to the breastbone by bars of *hyaline cartilage* (called costal cartilage in this region). The first seven pairs of ribs are referred to as *true ribs*. The cartilages of the 8th, 9th and 10th ribs are joined to the *costal cartilage* of the rib immediately above (i.e., to the costal cartilage of the 7th rib). These three pairs of ribs are known as *vertebrochondral ribs*. The last two pairs of ribs have free ends which are not attached to the sternum at all. They are *floating ribs*. The vertebrochondral ribs and the floating ribs are collectively known as *false ribs*. The ribs (together with their muscles) play an important role in the breathing mechanism of a mammal.

The Sternum (Breastbone)

The sternum is a long, flat, dagger-shaped bone. It is about 15 - 18 cm long and is found in the center of the chest region. The broad upper end supports the collar bones. The first seven pairs of ribs are attached to the *articulating facets* on the sides of the sternum. The 12 thoracic vertebrae, the 12 pair of ribs and the sternum forms the thorax which protects the delicate and vital organs of the thorax, viz. the heart and lungs.

APPENDICULAR SKELETON

The appendicular skeleton contains the bones of the appendages (limbs, wings, or flippers/fins), and the *pectoral* and *pelvic girdles*.

The *arms* and *legs* are part of the appendicular skeleton. The upper bones of the limbs are single: *humerus* (arm) and *femur* (leg). Below a joint (elbow or knee), both limbs have a pair of bones (*radius* and *ulna* in the arms; *tibia* and *fibula* in legs) that connect to another joint (*wrist* or *ankle*). The *carpals* makeup the wrist joint; the *tarsals* are in the ankle joint. Each hand or foot ends in 5 digits (fingers or toes) composed of *metacarpals* (hands) or metatarsals (feet).

Limbs are connected to the rest of the skeleton by collections of bones known as *girdles*. The pectoral girdle consists of the *clavicle* (collar bone) and *scapula* (shoulder blade). The humerus is joined to the pectoral girdle at a joint and is held in place by *muscles* and *ligaments*. A dislocated shoulder occurs when the end of the humerus slips out of the socket of the scapula, stretching ligaments and muscles. The *pelvic girdle* consists of two hipbones that form a hollow cavity, the *pelvis*. The vertebral column attaches to the top of the pelvis; the femur of each leg attaches to the bottom. The pelvic girdle in land animals transfers the weight of the body to the legs and feet. Pelvic girdles in fish, which have their weight supported by water, are primitive; land animals have more developed pelvic girdles. Pelvic girdles in bipeds are recognizable different from those or quadrupeds.

THE PECTORAL GIRDLE (UPPER LIMB)

The pectoral girdle is the set of bones which connect the upper limb to the axial skeleton on each side. It consists of the clavicle and scapula in humans and, in those species with three bones in the pectoral girdle, the coracoid. Some mammalian species, e.g., dog and horse have evolved to have only the scapula.

In humans, the only joints between shoulder girdle and axial skeleton are the sternoclavicular joints on each side. No joint exists between each scapula and the thoracic cage, instead the muscular connection between the two permits relatively great mobility of the shoulder girdle in relation to the pelvic girdle. In those species having only the scapula, no joint exists between the forelimb and the thorax, the only attachment being muscular.

(i) The Clavicle

In human anatomy, the clavicle or collar bone is classified as a long bone that makes up part of the shoulder girdle (pectoral girdle). It receives its name from the Latin clavicula ("little key") because the bone rotates along its axis like a key when the shoulder is abducted. (This movement is palpable with the opposite hand.) In some people, particularly females who may have less fat in this region, the location of the bone is clearly visible as it creates a bulge in the skin.

The clavicle is a doubly-curved long bone (the only horizontal long bone in the human body) that connects the arm (upper limb) to the body (trunk), located directly above the first rib. Medially, it articulates with the manubrium of the sternum (breast-bone) at the sternoclavicular joint. At its lateral end it articulates with the acromion of the scapula (shoulder blade) at the acromioclavicular joint. It has a rounded medial end and a flattened lateral end.

From the roughly pyramidal sternal end, each clavicle curves laterally and posteriorly for roughly half its length. It then forms a smooth posterior curve to articulate with a process of the scapula (acromion). The flat, acromial end of the clavicle is broader than the sternal end. The acromial end has a rough inferior surface that bears prominent lines and tubercles. These surface features are attachment sites for muscles and ligaments of the shoulder.

(ii) The Scapula

In anatomy, the scapula, or shoulder blade, is the bone that connects the humerus (arm bone) with the clavicle (collar bone). The scapula forms the posterior part of the shoulder girdle. In humans, it is a flat bone, roughly triangular in shape. It has two surfaces, three borders, and three angles.

The anterior (front) side of the scapula shows the fossa subscapularis (subscapular fossa) to which the subscapularis muscle attaches. In animals, this side is referred to as medial or costal (since it faces the ribs and the middle part of the animal) and also shows the facies serrata, for the insertion of the ventral serratus muscle.

The posterior side (lateral in animals) of the scapula is divided by a bony projection, the spina scapulae (opposite to the fossa subscapularis) into the supraspinous fossa and the infraspinous fossa. This projection is called the spine of the scapula. It begins flat at the base of the shoulder bone, ascends in distal direction to its peak at about the middle of the scapula, this peak is called tuber scapulae. After this peak the spina scapulae steeply decays in height. For humans and carnivores and bovinae the spina runs into a forward pointing hook called *acromion,* which continues past the main part of the bone.

Another hook-like projection comes off the lateral angle of the scapula, and is called the coracoid process. The end of this hook is the site of attachment of many muscles, such as the coracobrachialis muscle. Near the base of the coracoid process, so also on the lateral angle, there is a depression called the glenoid cavity.

THE HUMERUS

The humerus is a long bone in the arm or fore-legs (animals) that runs from the shoulder to the elbow. On a skeleton, it fits between the scapula and the ulna. It consists of the following three sections:

- Upper extremity of humerus
- Body of humerus
- Lower extremity of humerus.

A bursa lies between the scapula and the chest wall, and allows the scapula to move over the chest wall. Movements of the shoulder are actually often combined movements of the glenohumeral joint as well as movement of the scapula on the chest wall.

The distal end of the humerus (at the elbow) creates a hinge joint with the ulna, allowing only flexion and extension. This happens on the trochlea of the humerus. Two pits at this end of the humerus (the coronoid fossa and the olecranon fossa) allow the ulna room to move, but prevent it from over-flexing/extending.

There is also a pivot joint between the capitulum (sometimes called the capitellum) of the humerus, and the head of the radius. This allows the hand to pronate and supinate (turn to face downwards or upwards).

(a) The Ulna

The ulna (elbow bone) is a long bone, prismatic in form, placed at the medial side of the forearm, parallel with the radius. The ulna articulates with:

- The humerus, at the right side elbow as a hinge joint.
- The radius, near the elbow as a pivot joint, this allows the radius to cross over the ulna in pronation.
- The distal radius, where it fits into the ulna notch.

- The radius along its length via the interosseous membrane that forms a syndesmoses joint.

(b) The Radius

The radius is the bone of the forearm that extends from the outside of the limb to the phlangx (lateral) of the elbow to the thumb side of the wrist. The radius is situated on the lateral side of the ulna, which exceeds it in length and size. It is a long bone, prismatic in form and slightly curved longitudinally. The radius articulates with the capitulum of the humerus.

(c) The Wrist and Hand

In human anatomy, the wrist is the flexible and narrower connection between the forearm and the palm. The wrist is essentially a double row of small short bones, called carpals, intertwined to form a malleable hinge. The wrist-joint (articulatio radio carpea) is a condyloid articulation allowing three degrees of freedom.

The hands are the two intricate, prehensile, multi-fingered body parts normally located at the end of each arm medically: "terminating each anterior limb/appendage" of a human or other primate. They are the chief organs for physically manipulating the environment, using anywhere from the roughest motor skills (wielding a club) to the finest (threading a needle), and since the fingertips contain some of the densest areas of nerve endings on the human body, they are also the richest source of tactile feedback, so that sense of touch is intimately associated with human hands. Like other paired organs (eyes, ears and legs), each hand is dominantly controlled by the opposing brain hemisphere, and thus handedness, or preferred hand choice for single-handed activities such as writing with a pen, reflects a significant individual trait.

THE LOWER LIMB

(i) The Pelvis

The pelvis is the bony structure located at the base of the spine (properly known as the caudal end). It is part of the appendicular skeleton. Each os coxae (hipbone) consists of three bones: the illium, ischium, and the pubis.

The illium is the largest and upper most part, the ischium is the posterior-inferior (back-lower) part, and the pubis is the anterior (front) part of the hipbone. The two hipbones are joined anteriorly at the symphysis pubis and posteriorly to the sacrum. The pelvis incorporates the socket portion of the hip joint for each leg (in bipeds) or hind leg (in quadrupeds). It forms the lower limb (or hind-limb) girdle of the skeleton.

(ii) The Femur

The femur is the thigh bone. In humans, it is the longest, most voluminous, and strongest bone. It forms part of the hip and part of the knee.

The word femur is Latin for thigh. Theoretically in strict usage, femur bone is more proper than femur, as in classical Latin femur means "thigh", and os femoris means the bone within it. In medical Latin its genitive is always femoris, but in classical Latin its genitive is often feminis, and should not be confused with case forms of femina, which means "woman".

(iii) The Tibia

The tibia is a long bone with an expanded upper end which articulates with the femur. Its upper surface has two smooth areas. The central portion is raised with attachment areas for the strong cruciate ligaments and the meniscal cartilages. The shaft of the bone is triangular, and its medial side, flat and smooth lies immediately under the skin, easily felt as the shin bone. The lower surface with the prominent medial malleous articulates with the upper surface of the talus.

(iv) The Fibula

The fibula is a thin, twisted bone with many surfaces for the attachment of muscles. The prominent head articulates with the tibia. A large nerve passes close to the neck at the upper end and is easily damaged by pressure. The expanded lower portion, the lateral malleolus, is joined to the tibia by a strong interosscous ligament. The lateral ligament attaches the fibula to the bones of the foot and is often sprained.

(v) The Foot

The foot has seven tarsal bones: the talus, ossicle is, navicular, cuboid and three cunciform bones. These are small bones which glide over each other for short distances. The five metatarsals have the phalanges attached to them. The great toe has two phalanges whilst the others have three. They form a flexible platform with longitudinal and transverse arches which adjust to weight and movement.

BONE TISSUE

Although bones vary greatly in size and shape, they have certain structural similarities. Bones have cells embedded in a mineralized (calcium) matrix and collagen fibers. Compact bone forms the shafts of long bones; it also occurs on the outer side of the bone. Spongy bone forms the inner layer.

Compact bone has a series of Haversian canals around which concentric layers of bone cells (osteocytes) and minerals occur. New bone is formed by the osteocytes. The Haversian canals form a network of blood vessels and nerves that nourish and monitor the osteocytes.

Spongy bone occurs at the ends of long bones and is less dense than compact bone. The spongy bone of the femur, humerus, and sternum contains red marrow, in which stem cells reproduce and form the cellular components of the blood and immune system. Yellow marrow, at the center of these bones, is used to store fats. The outer layer of the bones is known as the periosteum. The inner layer of the periosteum forms new bone or modifies existing bone to meet new conditions. It is rich in nerve endings and blood and lymphatic vessels. When fractures occur, the pain is carried to the brain by nerves running through the periosteum.

BONE GROWTH

Endochondral ossification is the process of converting the cartilage in embryonic skeletons into bone. Cartilage is deposited early in development into shapes resembling the bones-to-be. Cells inside this cartilage grow and begin depositing minerals.

The spongy bone forms, and osteoblasts attach and lay down the mineral portions of spongy bone. Osteoclasts remove material from the center of the bone, forming the central cavity of the long bones. The perichondrium, a connective tissue, forms around the cartilage and begins forming compact bone while the above changes are occurring. Blood vessels form and grow into the perichondrium, transporting stem cells into the interior. Two bands of cartilage remain as the bone develops, one at each end of the bone. During childhood, this cartilage allows for growth and changes in the shape of bones. Eventually the elongation of the bones stops and the cartilage is all converted into bone.

Bones continue to change as adults, to adapt to the stresses generated by physical activity. Exercise can increase the diameter and strength of bone; inactivity can decrease them. Age is a factor: osteoporosis is a disease that primarily affects older, postmenopausal women. Increasing calcium intake, reducing protein intake, exercise and low doses of estrogen are effective treatments for osteoporosis.

BONE MARROW

Bone marrow (or *medulla ossea*) is the soft tissue found in the hollow interior of bones. In adults, marrow in large bones produces new blood cells. There are two types of bone marrow *red marrow* (also known as myeloid tissue) and *yellow marrow*. Red blood cells, platelets and most white blood cells arise in red marrow; some white blood cells develop in yellow marrow. The colour of yellow marrow is due to the much higher number of fat cells. Both types of bone marrow contain numerous blood vessels and capillaries.

At birth, all bone marrow is red. With age, more and more of it is converted to the yellow type. Adults have on average about 2.6 kg (5.7 lb) of bone marrow, with about half of it being red. Red marrow is found mainly in the flat bones such as hip bone, breast bone, skull, ribs, vertebrae and shoulder blades, and in the cancellous ("spongy") material at the proximal ends of the long bones femur and humerus. Yellow marrow is found in the hollow interior of the middle portion of long bones. In cases of severe blood loss, the body can convert yellow marrow back to red marrow in order to increase blood cell production.

JOINTS

A joint is a point of contact between bones, cartilage and bones, or teeth and bones. All joints are classified in a straightforward scheme which names joints according to either their structure (anatomy) or their function (movement).

Relationship between Joints and Movements

(i) There are many different types of joints and movements at joints.

(ii) The structure (anatomy) of a joint determines its function (movements allowed).

(iii) The closer the fit between bones at a joint, the stronger the joint.

(iv) Strong joints exhibit restricted movements. However, in joints with more distance between the articulating bones, a greater range of movements can result.

1. STRUCTURAL CLASSIFICATION

The structural classification scheme is based on two criteria:

(a) Whether or not a space or cavity exists between the bones.

(b) The type of connective tissue that holds the bones together.

Fibrous

Joints have no space between the articulating bones and the bones are held together by fibrous connective tissue.

Cartilaginous

Joints have no space between the articulating bones and the bones are held together tightly by cartilage.

Synovial

Synovial joints permit the greatest degree of flexibility and have the ends of bones covered with a connective tissue filled with synovial fluid; for example, hip.

The outer surface of the synovial joints contains ligaments that strengthen joints and hold bones in position. The inner surface (the synovial membrane) has cells producing synovial fluid that lubricates the joint and prevents the two cartilage caps on the bones from rubbing together. Some joints also have tendons (connective tissue linking muscles to bones). Bursae are small sacs filled with synovial fluid that reduce friction in the joint. The knee joint contains 13 bursae.

2. FUNCTIONAL CLASSIFICATION

The functional classification of joints is based solely on the amount of movement permitted at a particular joint. There are three types of joints classified by the amount of movement they allow: immovable, partly movable, and freely movable.

Immovable joints are *synarthroses*. In this type of joint, the bones are in very close contact and are separated only by a thin layer of fibrous connective tissue. An example of a synarthrosis is the suture in the skull between skull bones.

Partly movable joints are called *amphiarthroses*. This type of joint is characterized by bones that are connected by hyaline cartilage (fibro cartilage). The ribs that connect to the sternum are an example of an amphiarthrosis joint.

Most of the joints in the adult human body are freely *movable joints*. This type of joint is called a *diarthrosis* joint. There are six types of diarthroses joints. These are:

(i) *Ball-and-socket*: The ball-shaped end of one bone fits into a cup shaped socket on the other bone allowing the widest range of motion including rotation. Examples include the shoulder and hip.

(ii) *Condyloid*: Oval shaped condyle fits into elliptical cavity of another allowing angular motion but not rotation. This occurs between the metacarpals (bones in the palm of the hand) and phalanges (fingers) and between the metatarsals (foot bones excluding heel) and phalanges (toes).

(iii) *Saddle*: This type of joint occurs when the touching surfaces of two bones have both concave and convex regions with the shapes of the two bones complementing one other and allowing a wide range of movement. The only saddle joint in the body is in the thumb.

(iv) *Pivot*: Rounded or conical surfaces of one bone fit into a ring of one or tendon allowing rotation. An example is the joint between the axis and atlas in the neck.

(v) *Hinge*: A convex projection on one bone fits into a concave depression in another permitting only flexion and extension as in the elbow and knee joints.

(vi) *Gliding*: Flat or slightly flat surfaces move against each other allowing sliding or twisting without any circular movement. This happens in the carpals in the wrist and the tarsals in the ankle.

STUDY QUESTIONS

Write short notes on the following:

(a) Axial Sekelton

(b) Skulll

(c) Pectoral Girdal

(d) Pelvis

(e) Bones

(f) Joints.

4

CHAPTER

THE MUSCULAR SYSTEM

INTRODUCTION

The muscular system is the body's network of tissues that controls movement both of the body and within it (such as the heart's pumping action and the movement of food through the gut). Movement is generated through the contraction and relaxation of specific muscles.

The muscular system is composed of specialized cells called *muscle fibers*. Their predominant function is contractibility. Muscles, where attached to bones or internal organs and blood vessels, are responsible for movement. Nearly all movement in the body is the result of muscle contraction. There are three types of muscles: skeletal, smooth, and cardiac.

The *longest* muscle in the human body is the *sartorius*. It runs from the waist down across the front of thigh to the knee. Its purpose is to flex the hip and knee. The *largest* muscle in the body is the *gluteus* maximus (buttocks muscles). It moves the thighbone away from the body and straightens out the hip joint.

FUNCTIONS OF MUSCULAR TISSUE

Muscular tissue functions in:

(i) Movement and locomotion, through its direct connection with the skeletal system.

(ii) More subtle movements associated with maintaining posture/ vertical position.

(iii) Help to generate heat due to catabolic reactions that are associated with muscular activity (such that animals shiver or increase overall movement when body temperature drops).

(iv) Can be modified into other structures, such as electric organs in some fish.

MUSCLE STRUCTURE

The organs of the muscular system are the *muscles*. The muscle is composed of subunits called *fascicles*. Fascicles are bundles of individual *muscle fibers*. These fibres are held together by fibrous connective tissue. Each of the muscles is made of muscle tissue. *Capillaries* penetrate this tissue to keep the muscles supplied with oxygen and nutrients that are needed to fuel contraction. Muscle tissue is made up of bundles of muscle cells, which are long, strong threadlike fibers called *myofibrils*. Sarcomeres are the basic contractile subunit of myofibrils.

The general structure of a muscle fiber include *myofibrils* (chains of repeating subunits) composed of two kinds of filaments:

(i) *Thin filaments* (composed of *myosin*); and

(ii) *Thick filaments* (composed of *actin, tropomyosin* and *troponin*) that interact by binding to produce a *sliding movement* between the filaments, and that creates tension in the muscle fiber leading to *muscle contraction*.

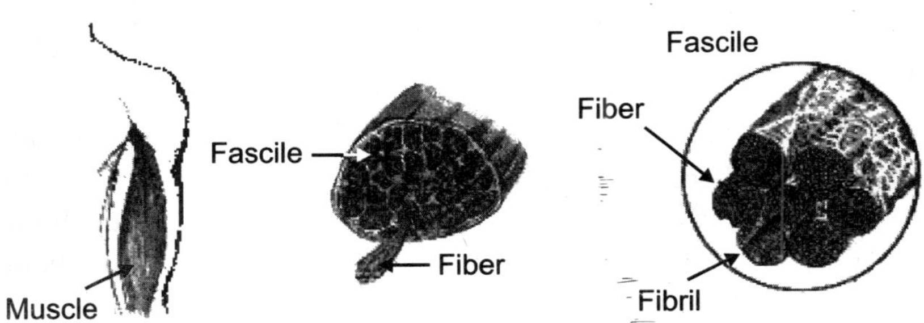

Fig. 4.1 *A muscle structure.*

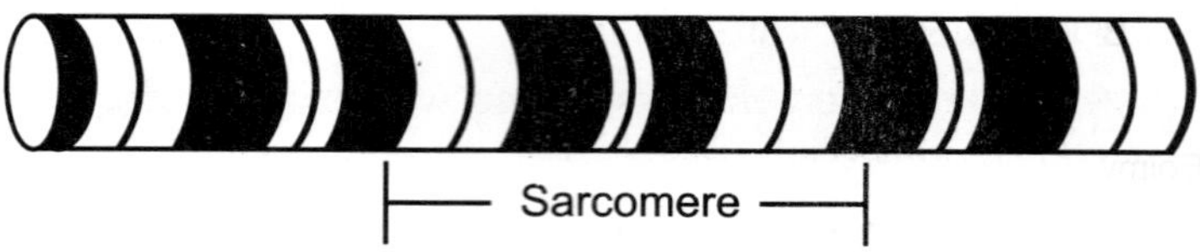

Fig. 4.2 *Structure of a muscle fiber.*

In a relaxed muscle the thick and thin threads within a muscle fibre overlap a little. When a *muscle contracts,* the thick filaments slide further in between the thin filaments like interlacing fingers. This action shortens the entire fibre.

TYPES OF MUSCLE TISSUE

The muscles of the body are divided into *three* main classes:

(I) SKELETAL MUSCLE (VOLUNTARY MUSCLE)

Skeletal muscle is the muscle that is attached to the bones of the skeleton. It is *voluntary* muscle, because a person controls its use, such as in the flexing of an arm or the raising of a foot. There are about 650 skeletal muscles in the whole human body.

Bundles of cylindrical fibers (cells) run in parallel (fascicle); in various arrangements such as spindles, bands, or sheets; typically between two bones and across a joint

Connective tissue subdivided into three parts which together form part of the deep fascia, also merge to form tendons and aponeurosis.

Endomysium: Thin connective tissue layer with capillaries surrounding fiber, includes satellite cells (stem cells) involved in muscle repair

Perimysium: Connective tissue layer of collagenous and reticular fibers with vessels surrounding fascicle

Epimysium: Dense connective tissue layer surrounding groups of fascicles and entire muscle

Motor unit: Functional unit of muscle, consists of a motor neuron and all muscle fibers it innervates. Degree of muscle contraction depends on number of active motor units or recruitment.

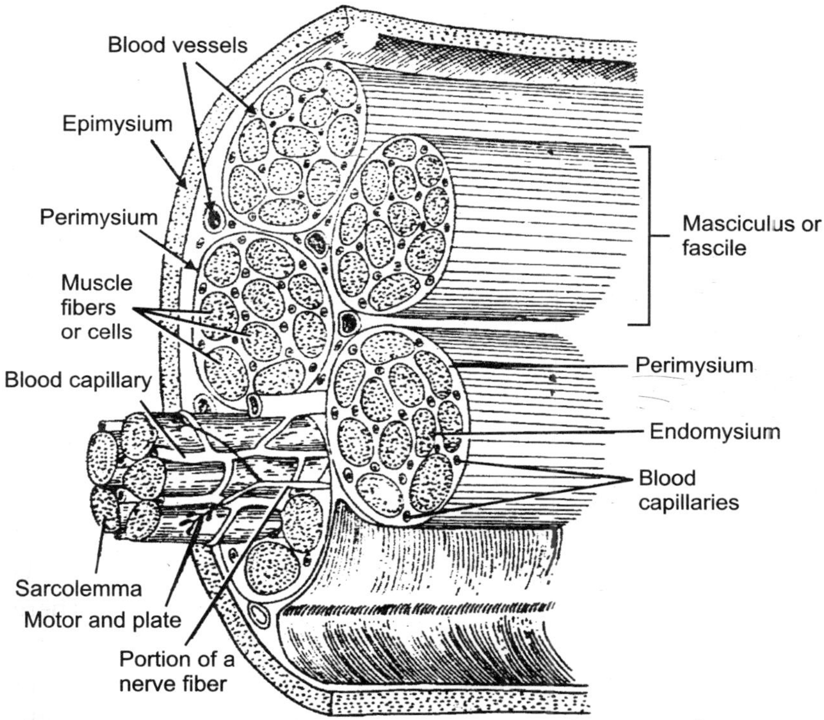

Fig. 4.3 *Sectional view of skeletal muscle.*

Long multinucleate cylinders with peripheral nuclei; striated, actin and myosin arranged in myofibrils.

(II) SMOOTH MUSCLE (INVOLUNTARY MUSCLE)

Smooth muscle makes up the walls of many organs of the body. They are called *involuntary muscles* because a person generally cannot consciously control them. They are regulated by the autonomic nervous system (part of the nervous system that affects internal organs). Smooth muscle is found in such places as the stomach, intestine, and the tubes which move blood around the body (blood vessels).

It occurs in small groups (e.g., arrector pili) or sheets of overlapping cells tightly bound together (e.g., digestive tube, uterus, bladder, respiratory tract, vessels), can regenerate.

Sparse reticular and collagenous connective tissue network, no tendons, sparse capillary network. Two types of innervation:

(a) *Multiunit innervation*: Motor units with each muscle cell innervated by one or more motor neurons, produces rapid coordinated contraction. For example, ductus deferens, ciliary body and iris, arrector pili, large arteries

(b) *Visceral innervation*: One motor neuron innervates several cells, muscle cells connected by gap junctions, produces a wave of contraction (peristalsis). Contraction can also be caused by hormones, stretching, and some chemicals. In absence of stimulation smooth muscle shows rhythmic cycles of contraction.

Spindle-shaped cells with one central nucleus; unstriated, no myofibrils, scattered myosin filaments, actin filaments attached to dense bodies in network of intermediate fibers (desmin), adjacent cells connected by dense bodies. Contraction produces a cellular twisting motion. Action is slower but longer lasting, aerobic, resist fatigue.

(III) CARDIAC MUSCLE

A special type of muscle, the cardiac muscle, is found only in the heart. It is involuntary like the smooth muscle. Branching network of cells forming layers that wind in overlapping spirals to form heart. Cells connected by intercalated discs contain desmosomes and gap junctions.

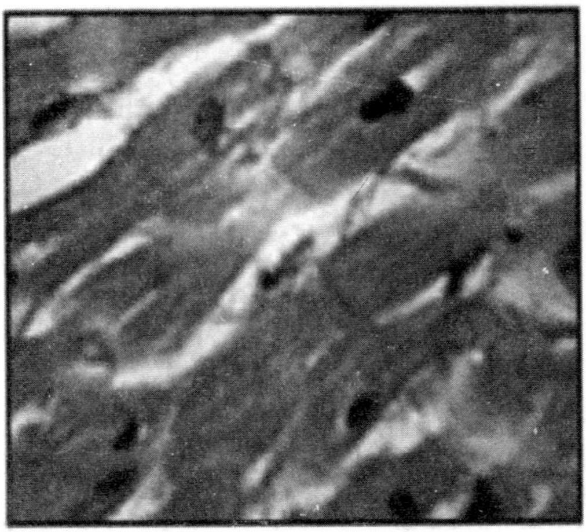

Fig. 4.4 *Cardiac muscle.*

Loose connective tissue with extensive capillary beds. A connective tissue layer separates atria from ventricles.

Inherent rhythmic contraction, pacemaker cells, gap junction connections form functional syncytium of the two atria and of the two ventricles, heart rate moderated by ANS.

Branching cells with one or more central nuclei, striated, actin and myosin in myofibrils, aerobic metabolism of lipids and carbohydrates, resist fatigue.

SKELETAL MUSCLE HISTOLOGY

MUSCLE FIBER STRUCTURE

Long, cylindrical, multinucleated cell containing usual intracellular organelles but in a unique arrangement

(i) *Sarcolemma* — Plasma membrane of muscle cell.
Attached to collagen fibers of tendons.

(ii) *Sarcoplasm* — Cytoplasm of muscle cell including mitochondria and glycogen granules.

(iii) *Sarcoplasmic reticulum*— Modified ER of muscle cell.

  (a) Longitudinal system of membranous tubules and cisternae surrounding myofibrils.

  (b) Functions in calcium storage (Ca^{+2} release channels) and muscle metabolism.

(iv) *T-tubule system* — Infoldings of sarcolemma at A-I junction.

  (a) Produces extension of extracellular space into fiber, encircle myofibrils and filled with ECF.

  (b) Provides for rapid conduction of nerve impulses into and throughout the fiber.

(v) *Myofibrils* — Long, cylindrical contractile fibril composed of filaments (striations).

  (a) Attached at ends of sarcolemma and runs the length of the cell.

  (b) *Sarcomere* — Repeating functional unit of myofibril, 10,000 sarcomeres/myofibril.

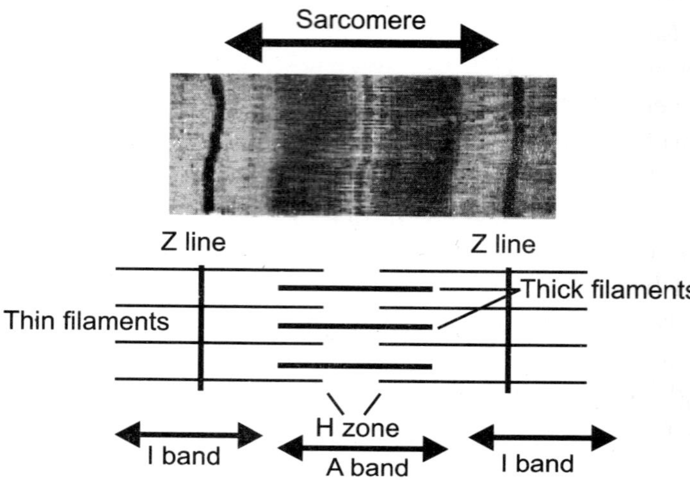

Fig. 4.5 *Structure of fiber muscle.*

MYOFILAMENT STRUCTURE

(i) *Myosin* - Contractile muscle protein.
  (a) Helical rod (light meromyosin), points toward M-line.
  (b) Hinge capable of swiveling.
  (c) Globular head (heavy meromyosin) can form crossbridges with actin filaments, projects outward.

(ii) *Actin* - Contractile muscle protein.
  (a) *F–Actin* in the form of two twisted strands.
    - Composed of G-actin monomers.
    - Each monomer has a myosin binding site.
    - Central strand of nebulin holds monomers in place.
  (b) *Tropomyosin* strands encircle the F-actin strands covering myosin binding sites.
  (c) *Troponin* molecules are scattered at regular intervals along the tropomyosin.
    - Contains three subunits, binding to tropomyosin, G-actin, and calcium.

MYOFIBRIL STRUCTURE

(i) *Z-line* – Forms boundaries of sarcomere.
  (a) Perforated disc holds thin filaments in place.
  (b) Desmin intermediate filaments connect adjacent myofibrils.

(ii) *I-band* — Composed of thin actin filaments only.

(iii) *A-band* — Composed of thick myosin filaments including overlapping actin.

(a) Elastic filament — Composed of titin, anchors thick filaments to Z-lines, acts like spring and is responsible for extensibility and elasticity.

(iv) *H-zone* — In center of A-band, contains only thick filaments

(v) *M-line* — In center of H-zone, cross-connections between adjacent thick filaments.

In adults, increased strength and muscle mass comes about through an increase in the thickness of the individual fibers and increase in the amount of connective tissue.

WHOLE MUSCLE MECHANICS

MUSCLE TWITCH

(i) Contraction of one muscle fiber in response to a single stimulus.

(ii) Twitches in different muscles can vary in duration.

(iii) *Myogram* — Record of muscle fiber contraction.

(iv) *Latent period* — Time between stimulus and when contraction begins, Ca^{+2} release (2 msec).

(v) *Contraction period* — Shortening, produces maximum tension (10-100 msec).

(vi) *Relaxation period* — Lengthening, active transport of Ca^{+2} (10-100 msec).

ALL OR NONE PRINCIPLE

A muscle fiber at a given resting length, when stimulated to contract, always produces the same amount of tension. Variation in the amount of tension produced in a whole muscle is determined by:

(a) Frequency of stimulation — internal and external tension.

(b) Number of muscle fibers stimulated or recruitment.

STIMULATION FREQUENCY

Normal activities require more tension than is produced by single fiber twitch, they involve sustained muscle contractions within the whole muscle.

(i) *Wave summation*: If 2nd stimulus is applied before relaxation is complete, the second contraction is greater.

(ii) *Tetanus*: At higher frequency of stimulation muscle relaxation between contractions is reduced.

(iii) *Incomplete tetanus*: Producing peak tension during rapidly alternating cycles of contraction and partial relaxation.

(iv) *Complete tetanus*: Sustained maximal contraction at peak tension, typical of normal muscle contraction.

(v) *Treppe*: Relaxation is complete before next stimulus occurs, each contraction is a little stronger than previous. Physiological efficiency improves because of temperature rise and gradual increase in Ca^{+2} in sarcoplasm. Basis for warm-up.

EFFECTS OF INTERNAL TENSION AND EXTERNAL TENSION DURING MUSCLE CONTRACTION

(i) *Internal (active) tension*: Force generated in individual muscle fibers by myofibrils.

(ii) *External (passive) tension*: Force generated in the connective tissue and tendons of the whole muscle.

(iii) *Muscle fibers* are surrounded by connective tissue layers which are continuous with the tendons that attach to bones. Connective tissues are flexible and elastic, called *series elastic elements.*

(iv) *Process*: Internal tension is applied to the series elastic elements, which stretch, stiffen and then transfer tension to the resistance. During summation external tension gradually climbs to level of internal tension.

MUSCLE FIBER RECRUITMENT

The amount of tension produced in a whole muscle is also determined by the number of muscle fibers stimulated, called recruitment. Muscle is composed of many muscle fibers each belonging to a motor unit.

Motor unit: All muscle fibers that are innervated by a single motor neuron.

(i) When stimulated muscle fibers contract maximally for conditions (All or None Principle).
(ii) Amount of whole muscle tension is determined by number of muscle fibers contracting, this is controlled by number and size of motor units functioning at one time.
(iii) Small fast-reacting fine-control muscles have few muscle fibers per motor unit, large slower muscles have many fibers per motor unit.
(iv) Gradation of muscle contraction is achieved by multiple motor unit summation, begins with small motor units and then adds larger motor units.
(v) Muscle fibers of a motor unit are typically distributed throughout the fascicles of a muscle producing uniform contraction whether weak or strong.
(vi) Smoothness of contraction is a function of motor units in the muscle firing asynchronously to prevent fatigue of fibers or jerky action.
(vii) Tone is the involuntary activation of a small number of motor units that give firmness to relaxed muscle.

CHARACTERISTICS OF CONTRACTION

(i) *Isotonic contraction*: When a muscle contracts the external tension gradually increases to peak level, slightly exceeding the resistance and causing a change in muscle length. Causes changes in shape of muscle
   (a) *Concentric contraction*: Tension increases as muscle shortens.
   (b) *Eccentric contraction*: Tension is maintained as muscle lengthens.
(ii) *Isometric contraction*: When a muscle contracts the peak tension produced is less than resistance and no significant muscle shortening occurs. Contraction and stretching (gravity) are equal and opposing forces that create tension but no muscle shortening. Produces no movement but stabilizes joints and maintains posture, uses energy.
(iii) *Speed of muscle contraction*: The heavier the resistance, the longer, the muscle takes to reach peak tension and start to shorten,

and the less the muscle will shorten. For any given resistance there is an optimal combination of tension and speed for each muscle.

(iv) *Fatigue*: Nerve impulses arrive but muscle contractions become weaker because of ACh depletion or buildup of metabolic wastes and depletion of ATP.

MUSCLE ENERGETICS

RESTING MUSCLE

(i) ATP is produced by aerobic metabolism of fatty acids faster than needed.

(ii) Excess is used to produce creatine phosphate.

CONTRACTING MUSCLE

(i) Normal stores of ATP last a few seconds (each thick filament uses about 2500 ATP molecules/sec).

(ii) Then muscle switches to aerobic metabolism of pyruvic acid from glucose, stored glycogen, and fatty acids.

PEAK MUSCLE ACTIVITY

(i) There is insufficient O_2 available and muscle switches to anaerobic metabolism of pyruvic acid from glucose and stored creatine phosphate.

(ii) Creatine phosphate can transfer a high energy P to ADP to form ATP, extending activity for 15 sec.

TYPES OF CELLULAR RESPIRATION

(i) *Aerobic respiration:*

(a) For moderate activity longer than 30 sec (marathon is 100% aerobic).

(b) Fatty acids, glucose or glycogen is broken down into pyruvic acid that is used by mitochondria to form ATPs

(c) Slower than glycolysis but yields more ATP (36 net/glucose molecule).

(d) Monosaccharides preferred but can also break down fatty acids and amino acids.

(e) Aerobic requires oxygen and is limited by oxygen availability, oxygen in blood is bound to Hb and in muscle is bound to muscle myoglobin.

(ii) *Anaerobic respiration:*

(a) Upto 3 min supply at maximal muscle activity (aerobic respiration continues to produce about 30% of ATP consumed).

(b) Glucose or glycogen is broken down into pyruvic acid in a series of reactions called glycolysis in the muscle cytoplasm (2 ATP net/glucose molecule). Pyruvic acid is formed too rapidly for mitochondria to use and is converted into lactic acid which diffuses out of the muscle. Anaerobic requires no oxygen.

(iii) *Cori cycle:*

(a) During maximal activity lactic acid accumulates in blood and muscle (oxygen debt).

(b) When oxygen is available lactic acid is converted back into pyruvic acid in the liver and then into glucose and is returned to skeletal muscle to be stored as glycogen.

(c) In skeletal muscle there are different muscle fiber types specialized for different forms of respiration.

SKELETAL MUSCLE FIBER TYPES

(i) *Type I, Red slow-twitch fibers:* Contract slowly and fatigue slowly.

(a) Small diameter cells.

(b) Aerobic with many mitochondria, low glycolytic enzymes.

(c) Very vascular (O_2), high myoglobin levels (binds O_2).

(d) Metabolism of lipids and carbohydrates, some amino acids

(e) Endurance activities, marathon, swimming, jogging.

(ii) *Type IIx, White fast-twitch:* Contract fast and fatigue quickly

(a) Large diameter cells, most common.

(b) Anaerobic with few mitochondria, high glycolytic enzymes

(c) Less vascularized, low myoglobin levels.

(d) Store glycogen, metabolism of carbohydrates.

(e) Dashes and sprints, weight lifting, throwing ball.

(iii) *Type IIa, Intermediate fibers*: Contract fast and fatigue relatively slowly.

(a) Intermediate diameter cells.

(b) Anaerobic with intermediate number of mitochondria, high glycolytic enzymes.

(c) Intermediate vascularization, low myoglobin.

(d) Store glycogen, metabolism mainly carbohydrates.

(e) Increase favors endurance activities.

Percentage of red and white fibers in a muscle is genetically determined, training can convert white fast-twitch (IIx) into intermediate fibers (IIa) and cause muscle hypertrophy (fiber enlargement, but not increase in fiber number).

SMOOTH MUSCLE CONTRACTION

(i) No T-tubules, gap junctions are present.

(ii) Sarcoplasmic retiiculum is a loose network. Calcium enters sarcoplasm from SR and ECF and binds with calmodulin protein, no troponin.

(iii) Actin and myosin myofilaments overlap forming scattered bundles. Calmodulin-Ca activates myosin kinase, which transfers a phosphate from ATP to myosin and crossbridges form. Contraction produces a cellular twisting motion.

(iv) *Relaxation:* Myosin phosphatase removes phophate from myosin.

MUSCLE CONTRACTION

EXCITATION-CONTRACTION COUPLING MECHANISM

Nerve impulse at *neuromuscular junction* induces muscle contraction.

Process

(i) Nerve impulse reaches the synaptic terminal causing the nerve's synaptic knobs to release acetylcholine, ACh crosses the synaptic cleft and binds to the motor endplate receptors causing a depolarization that travels over the sarcolemma and down into the T-tubule system

(ii) Impulse travels to SR cisternae and causes Ca^{+2} release channels to open briefly, Ca^{+2} flows out into sarcoplasm

(iii) Increase of Ca^{+2} above 10^{2} M exposes binding sites on actin filaments (1 msec)

(iv) Sliding filament mechanism

(v) Impulse ends and Ca^{+2} release channels close

(vi) Ca^{+2} active transport pumps return Ca^{+2} to SR or into ECF. Requires ATP expenditure

(vii) When Ca^{+2} level falls below 10^{-6} M, myosin binding sites on G-actin are covered and crossbridges cannot form

SLIDING FILAMENT MECHANISM

Sliding is produced by making and breaking *crossbridges* between actin and myosin. In resting muscle the thick and thin filaments partially overlap. Contraction is due to an increase in the amount of overlap between the filaments; i.e., the actin filaments slide over the myosin filaments. This is known as the *sliding filament theory of muscle contraction*. The sliding is brought about when cross linkages form between the beads of the myosin and their binding sites on the actin molecules.

Process:

(i) *Relaxed muscle*: ATP attaches to myosin heads, which act as ATPase splitting ATP into ADP + P. Myosin heads are activated or cocked.

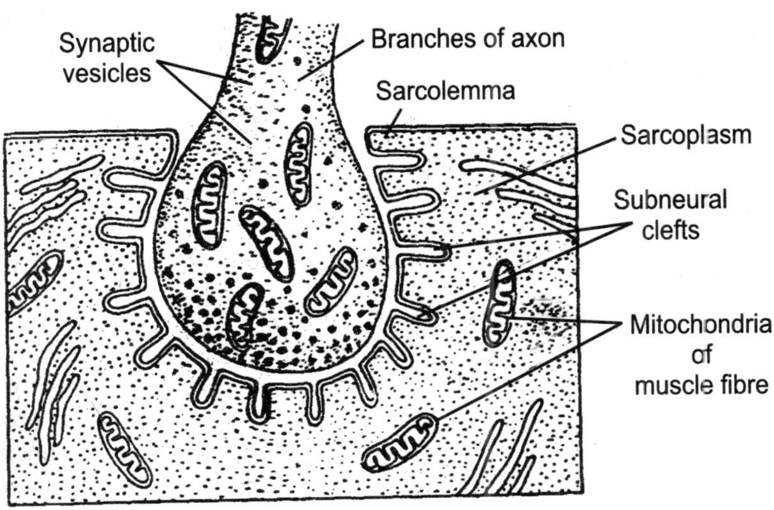

Fig. 4.6 *Showing neuro-muscular junction.*

(ii) When SR releases Ca^{+2}, it combines with a troponin subunit and weakens the troponin-actin bond, troponin moves pulling tropomyosin away and exposes myosin binding site on G-actin monomers.

(iii) Activated (cocked) myosin heads spontaneously bind to exposed myosin binding site on G-actin forming crossbridges.

(iv) *Power stroke*: Myosin heads swivel (conformational change), which pulls actin filaments toward H-zone, then myosin releases the ADP + P.

(v) New ATP binds to myosin heads causing heads to detach from actin filaments and heads swivel back to their original position (conformation change) as ATPase splits ATP.

LENGTH-TENSION RELATIONSHIPS

(i) Amount of tension generated during contraction depends on the number of crossbridges (on all sarcomeres of myofibril) that can form and is based on the degree of overlap of actin and myosin in resting muscle.

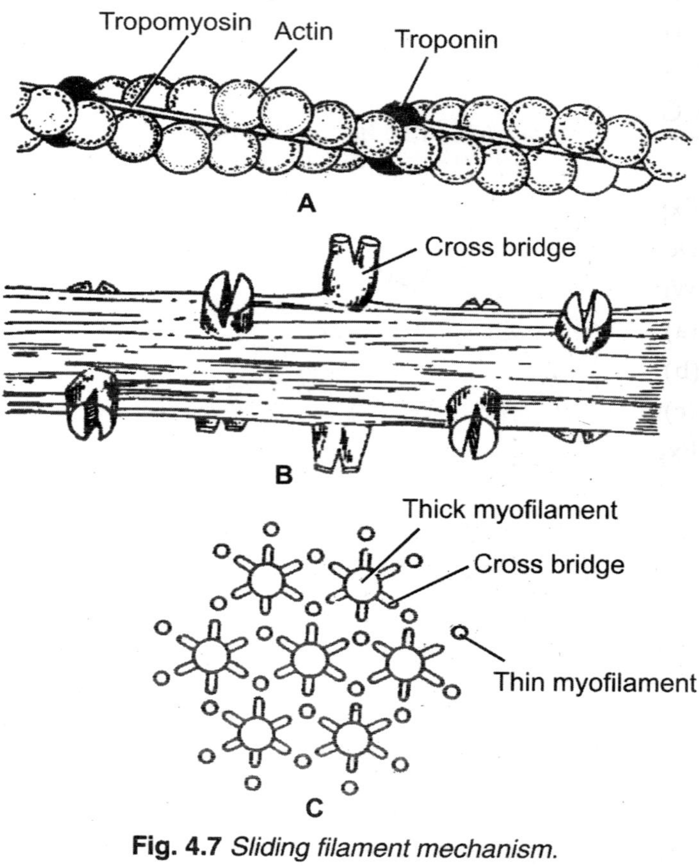

Fig. 4.7 *Sliding filament mechanism.*

(ii) Resting muscle length.

(iii) At short sarcomere lengths there is too much overlap, actins collide and interfere with each other, myosin hits Z-line.

(iv) At long sarcomere lengths too little overlap reduces number of potential crossbridges.

(v) At about normal resting length the maximal number of crossbridges form producing highest tension.

MUSCLE LENGTHENING

(i) Passive process, no active mechanism for returning muscle fibers to normal resting length.

(ii) Depends upon:

- (a) Elastic forces of extracellular fibers in tendons and connective tissues called series elastic elements.
- (b) Antagonistic muscle contraction.
- (c) Gravity.

STUDY QUESTIONS

1. Explain the different types of muscles.
2. Describe the structure of a muscle fiber.
3. Write short notes on:
   - (a) Sliding Filament Mechanism
   - (b) Muscle Contraction
   - (c) Muscle Twitch
4. Explain histology of skeletal muscle.

5

CHAPTER

The Integumentary System

INTRODUCTION

The integumentary system consists of the skin, hair, nails, the subcutaneous tissue below the skin, and assorted glands. The most obvious function of the integumentary system is the protection that the skin gives to underlying tissues. The skin not only keeps most harmful substances out, but also prevents the loss of fluids.

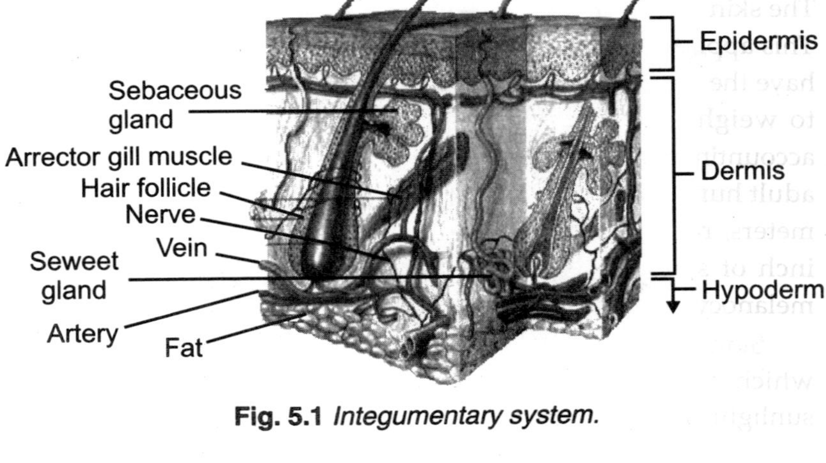

Fig. 5.1 *Integumentary system.*

TYPES OF GLANDS

There are four types of glands in the integumentary system:

(i) *Sudoriferous glands:* Sudoriferous glands are sweat producing glands. These are important to help maintain body temperature.

(ii) *Sebaceous glands:* Sebaceous glands are oil producing glands which help inhibit bacteria, keep us waterproof and prevent our hair and skin from drying out.

(iii) *Ceruminous glands:* Ceruminous glands produce earwax which keeps the outer surface of the eardrum pliable and prevents drying.

(iv) *Mammary glands*: Mammary glands produce milk.

A major function of the subcutaneous tissue is to connect the skin to underlying tissues such as muscles. Hair on the scalp provides insulation from cold for the head. The hair of eyelashes and eyebrows helps keep dust and perspiration out of the eyes, and the hair in our nostrils helps keep dust out of the nasal cavities. Any other hair on our bodies no longer serves a function, but is an evolutionary remnant. Nails protect the tips of fingers and toes from mechanical injury. Fingernails give the fingers greater ability to pick up small objects.

SKIN

Skin is considered one of the most important parts of the body. The skin is often known as "the largest organ in the human body". This applies to exterior surface, as it covers the body, appearing to have the largest surface area of all the organs. Moreover, it applies to weight, as it weighs more than any single internal organ, accounting for about 15 percent of body weight. For the average adult human, the skin has a surface area of between 1.5-2.0 square meters, most of it is between 2-3 mm thick. The average square inch of skin holds 650 sweat glands, 20 blood vessels, 60,000 melanocytes, and more than a thousand nerve endings.

Skin has pigmentation, melanin, provided by melanocytes, which absorbs some of the potentially dangerous radiation in sunlight. It also contains DNA repair enzymes which reverse UV damage, and people who lack the genes for these enzymes suffer high rates of skin cancer. One form predominantly produced by UV light, malignant melanoma, is particularly invasive, causing it to spread quickly, and can often be deadly. Human skin pigmentation varies among populations in a striking manner. This has sometimes led to the classification of people(s) on the basis of skin colour.

Damaged skin will try to heal by forming scar tissue, often giving rise to discolouration and depigmentation of the skin.

The use of natural or synthetic cosmetics to treat the appearance of the face and condition of the skin (such as pore control and black head cleansing) is common among many cultures.

STRUCTURE OF SKIN

The integumentary system consists of the *skin* and *accessory structures* such as hair, nails and glands. Skin is composed of the epidermis and the dermis. Below these layers lies the hypodermis or subcutaneous adipose layer, which is not usually classified as a layer of skin.

EPIDERMIS

The outermost epidermis consists of stratified squamous keratinizing epithelium with an underlying basement membrane. It contains no blood vessels, and is nourished by diffusion from the dermis. There are four types of cells that compose the epidermis. These cells are as follow:

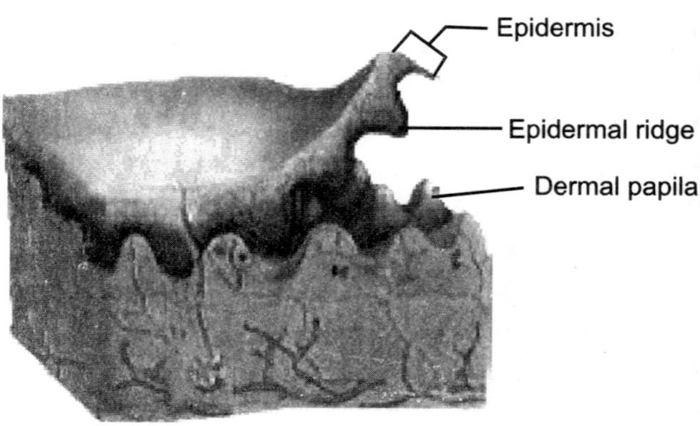

Fig. 5.2 *Structure of skin.*

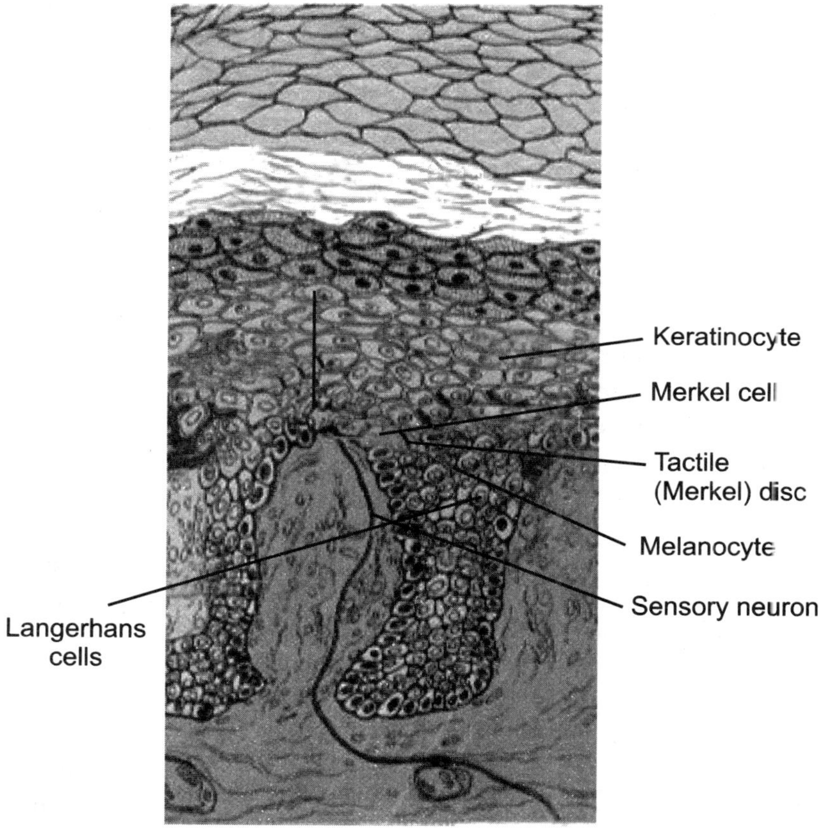

Fig. 5.3 *Anatomical structure of skin.*

Keratinocytes: Comprise approximately 90% of all epidermal cells. These cells produce a protein mixture known as keratin which helps waterproof and protect the skin.

Melanocytes: Comprise approximately 8% of all epidermal cells. These cells produce a group of pigments known as melanin which are responsible for skin, hair and eye colour.

Langerhans cells: These cells arise from the bone marrow and migrate to the epidermis. These cells play an important role in the immune response.

Merkel cells: These cells are located in the deepest regions of the epidermis and are associated with sensory neurons and are thought to function in the sensation of touch.

The epidermis can be further subdivided into the following strata (beginning with the outermost layer): *corneum, lucidum, granulosum, spinosum, and basale*. Cells are formed through mitosis at the innermost layers. They move up the strata changing shape and composition as they differentiate, inducing expression of new types of keratin genes. They eventually reach the corneum and become sloughed off (desquamation). This process is called *keratinization* and takes place within about 30 days. This layer of skin is responsible for keeping water in the body and keeping other harmful chemicals and pathogens out. Blood capillaries are found beneath the epidermis, and are linked to an arteriole and a venule. Arterial shunt vessels may bypass the network in ears, the nose and fingertips.

DERMIS

The dermis lies below the epidermis and contains a number of structures including blood vessels, nerves, hair follicles, smooth muscle, glands and lymphatic tissue. It consists of loose connective tissue otherwise called areolar connective tissue – collagen, elastin and reticular fibers are present. Erector muscles, attached between the hair papilla and epidermis, can contract, resulting in the hair fiber pulled upright and consequentially goose bumps. The main cell types are fibroblasts, adipocytes (fat storage) and macrophages. Sebaceous glands are exocrine glands which produce, a mixture of lipids and waxy substances: lubrication, water-proofing, softening and antibactericidal actions are among the many functions of sebum. Sweat glands open up via a duct onto the skin by a pore.

The dermis is made of an irregular type of fibrous connective tissue consisting of collagen and elastin fibers. It can be split into the papillary and reticular layers. The papillary layer is outermost and extends into the epidermis to supply it with vessels. It is composed of loosely arranged fibers. Papillary ridges make up the lines of the hands giving us fingerprints. The reticular layer is more dense and is continuous with the hypodermis. It contains the bulk of the structures (such as sweat glands). The reticular layer is composed of irregularly arranged fibers and resists stretching.

HYPODERMIS

The hypodermis is not part of the skin, and lies below the dermis. Its purpose is to attach the skin to underlying bone and muscle as well as supplying it with blood vessels and nerves. It consists of loose connective tissue and elastin. The main cell types are fibroblasts, macrophages and adipocytes (the hypodermis contains 50% of body fat). Fat serves as padding and insulation for the body.

FUNCTIONS OF SKIN

In medicine, the branch concerned with the skin is called dermatology.

(i) *Protection*: Skin gives an anatomical barrier between the internal and external environment in bodily defense. Langerhans cells in the skin are part of the immune system.

(ii) *Sensation*: Skin contains a variety of nerve endings that react to heat, cold, touch, pressure, vibration, and tissue injury.

(iii) *Heat regulation*: The skin contains a blood supply far greater than its requirements which allows precise control of energy loss by radiation, convection and conduction. Dilated blood vessels increase perfusion and heat loss while constricted vessels greatly reduce cutaneous blood flow and conserve heat. Erector pili muscles are significant in animals.

(iv) *Control of evaporation*: The skin provides a relatively dry and impermeable barrier to fluid loss. Loss of this function contributes to the massive fluid loss in burns.

(v) *Excretion*: The concentration of urea is 1/130th that of urine. Excretion by sweating is at most a secondary function to temperature regulation.

ACCESSORY STRUCTURES

The accessory structures of the integumentary system include hair, nails, and glands.

HAIR

A hair is divided into the shaft which is the aspect of the hair that protrudes above the surface of the skin and the root which is the aspect of the hair that is beneath the surface of the skin. The base of the root is expanded and is known as the hair bulb.

A hair is composed of numerous columns of dead yet keratinized cells held tightly together in three concentric layers known as the medulla, cortex and cuticle.

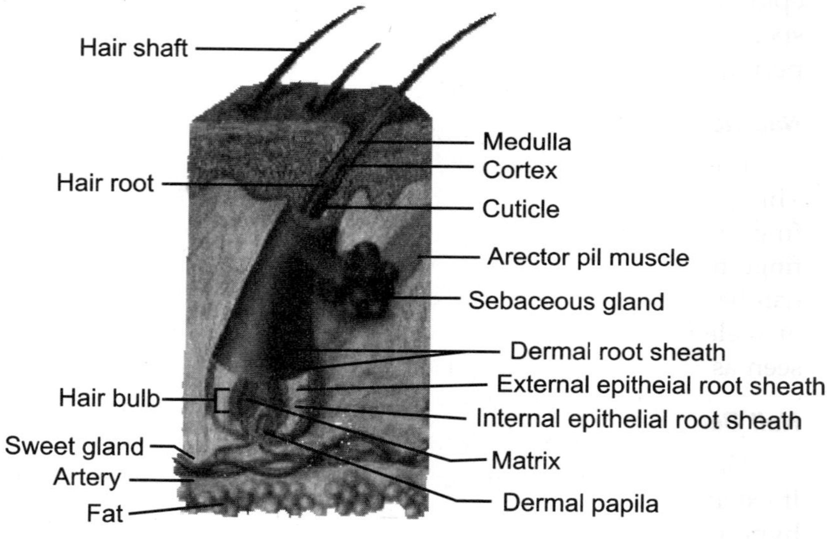

Fig. 5.4 *Structure of hair.*

Types of hair

Humans have three different types of hair:

(i) Lanugo, the fine hair that covers nearly the entire body of embryos.

(ii) Vellus hair, the short, fine, "peach fuzz" body hair that grows in most places on the human body in both sexes.

(iii) Terminal hair, the fully developed hair, which is generally longer, coarser, thicker, and darker than vellus hair.

NAILS

The fingernail is an important structure made of keratin. The fingernail generally serve two purposes. It serves as a protective plate and enhances sensation of the fingertip. The protection function of the fingernail is commonly known, but the sensation function is equally important. The fingertip has many nerve endings in it allowing us to receive volumes of information about objects we touch. The nail acts as a counterforce to the fingertip providing even more sensory input when an object is touched.

Nail Structure

Nails are plates of hard, tightly packed keratinized cells of epidermis. The structure we know of as the nail is divided into six specific parts — the root, nail bed, nail plate, eponychium (cuticle), perionychium, and hyponychium.

Nail Root

The root of the fingernail is also known as the germinal matrix. This portion of the nail is actually beneath the skin behind the fingernail and extends several millimeters into the finger. The fingernail root produces most of the volume of the nail and the nail bed. This portion of the nail does not have any melanocytes, or melanin producing cells. The edge of the germinal matrix is seen as a white, crescent shaped structure called the lunula.

Nail Bed

The nail bed is part of the nail matrix called the sterile matrix. It extends from the edge of the germinal matrix, or lunula, to the hyponychium. The nail bed contains the blood vessels, nerves, and melanocytes, or melanin-producing cells. As the nail is produced by the root, it streams down along the nail bed, which adds material to the undersurface of the nail making it thicker. It is important for normal nail growth that the nail bed be smooth. If it is not, the nail may split or develop grooves that can be cosmetically unappealing.

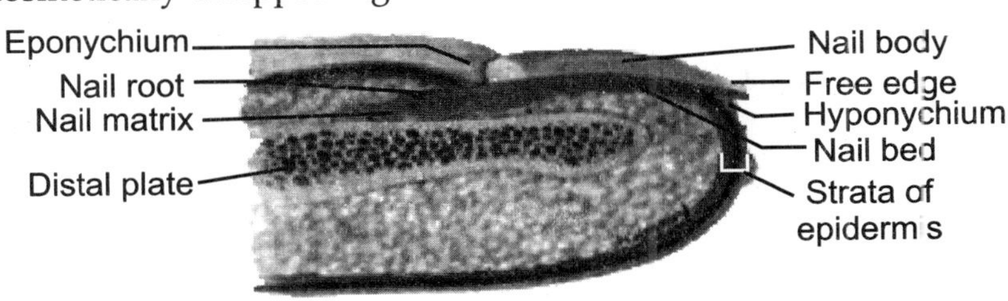

Fig. 5.5 *Structure of nail.*

Nail Plate

The nail plate is the actual fingernail, made of translucent keratin. The pink appearance of the nail comes from the blood vessels underneath the nail. The underneath surface of the nail plate has grooves along the length of the nail that help anchor it to the nail bed.

Eponychium

The cuticle of the fingernail is also called the eponychium. The cuticle is situated between the skin of the finger and the nail plate fusing these structures together and providing a waterproof barrier.

Perionychium

The perioncyhium is the skin that overlies the nail plate on its sides. It is also known as the paronychial edge. The perionychium is the site of hangnails, ingrown nails, and an infection of the skin called *paronychia*.

Hyponychium

The hyponychium is the area between the nail plate and the fingertip. It is the junction between the free edge of the nail and the skin of the fingertip, also providing a waterproof barrier.

GLANDS

The two major glands of the skin are the sebaceous and sweat glands.

Sweat Glands

There are approximately 3 to 4 million sweat glands in the human body. Sweat gland labeled as "sudoriferous gland" at center right. In humans, there are two kinds of sweat glands which are typically divided into two types, *eccrine* and *apocrine*, based on their structure and location.

Eccrine

Eccrine sweat glands are distributed over the entire body surface but are particularly abundant on the palms of hands, soles of feet, and on the forehead. These produce sweat that is composed chiefly of water with various salts. These glands are used for body temperature regulation.

Eccrine sweat glands are coiled tubular glands derived from the outer layer of skin but extending into the inner layer. They are distributed over almost the entire surface of the body in humans and many other species, but are lacking in some marine and fur-bearing species. The sweat glands are controlled by sympathetic cholinergic nerves which are controlled by a center in the hypothalamus. The hypothalamus senses core temperature directly, and also has input from temperature receptors in the skin and modifies the sweat output, along with other thermoregulatory processes.

Human eccrine sweat is composed chiefly of water with various salts and organic compounds in solution. It contains minute amounts of fatty materials, urea, and other wastes. The concentration of sodium varies from 35–65 mmol/l and is lower in people acclimatised to a hot environment. The sweat of other species generally differ in composition.

Apocrine

Apocrine glands occur during the early to mid puberty ages approximately around the age of 15 and release more than normal amounts of sweat for approximately a month and subsequently regulate and release normal amounts of sweat after a certain period of time. Apocrine sweat glands produce sweat that contains fatty materials. These glands are mainly present in the armpits and around the genital area and their activity is the main cause of sweat odor, due to the bacteria that breakdown the organic compounds in the sweat from these glands. Emotional stress increases the production of sweat from the apocrine glands, or more precisely. The sweat already present in the tubule is squeezed out. Apocrine sweat glands essentially serve as scent glands.

In some areas of the body, these sweat glands are modified to produce wholly different secretions, however, including the cerumen (wax) of the outer ear. Other glands, such as mammary glands, are greatly enlarged and modified to produce milk.

Sebaceous Glands

The sebaceous glands are glands found in the skin of mammals. They secrete an oily substance called *sebum* that is made of fat (lipids) and the debris of dead fat-producing cells. These glands exist in humans throughout the skin except in the palms of the hands and soles of the feet. Sebum acts to protect and waterproof hair and skin, and keep them from becoming dry, brittle, and cracked. It can also inhibit the growth of microorganisms on skin.

Sebaceous glands can usually be found in hair-covered areas where they are connected to hair follicles to deposit sebum on the hairs, and bring it to the skin surface along the hair shaft. The structure consisting of hair, hair follicle and sebaceous gland is also known as pilosebaceous unit. Sebaceous glands are also found in non haired areas of lips, eyelids, penis, labia minora and nipples; here the sebum reaches the surface through ducts. In the glands, sebum is produced within specialized cells and is released as these cells burst; sebaceous glands are thus classified as holocrine glands.

Sebum is odorless, but its bacterial breakdown can produce odors. Sebum is the cause of some people experiencing "oily" hair if it is not washed for several days. Earwax is partly sebum, as is mucopurulent discharge, the dry substance accumulating in the corners of the eye after sleeping.

A hair follicle with associated structures. The composition of sebum varies from species to species; in humans, the lipid content consists of about 25% wax monoesters, 41% triglycerides, 16% free fatty acids, and 12% squalene.

The activity of the sebaceous glands increases during puberty because of heightened levels of androgens.

Sebaceous glands are involved in skin problems such as acne and keratosis pilaris. A blocked sebaceous gland can result in a sebaceous cyst. The prescription drug isotretinoin significantly reduces the amount of sebum produced by the sebaceous glands, and is used to treat acne. The extreme use (up to 10 times doctor prescribed amounts) of anabolic steroids by bodybuilders to prevent weight loss tend to stimulate the sebaceous glands which can cause acne.

The sebaceous glands of a human fetus in utero secrete a substance called Vernix caseosa, a "waxy" or "cheesy" white substance coating the skin of newborns.

The preputial glands of mice and rats are large modified sebaceous glands that produce pheromones.

Ceruminous glands

Wet-type human earwax on a cotton swab. Earwax, also known by the medical term *cerumen,* is a yellowish, waxy substance secreted in the ear canal of humans and many other mammals. It plays a vital role in the human ear canal, assisting in cleaning and lubrication, and also provides some protection from bacteria, fungus, and insects. A comprehensive review of the physiology and pathophysiology of cerumen can be found in Roeser and Ballachanda. Excess or impacted cerumen can press against the eardrum and/or occlude the external auditory canal and impair hearing.

Lubrication

Lubrication prevents desiccation and itching of the skin within the ear canal (known as asteatosis). The lubricative properties arise from the high lipid content of the sebum produced by the sebaceous glands. In wet-type cerumen at least, these lipids include cholesterol, squalene, and many long-chain fatty acids and alcohols.

Antibacterial and Antifungal Roles

While studies conducted up until the 1960s found little evidence supporting an antibacterial role for cerumen, more recent studies have found that cerumen provides some bactericidal protection against some strains of bacteria. Cerumen has been found to be effective in reducing the viability of a wide range of bacteria (sometimes by up to 99%), including haemophilus influenzae, staphylococcus aureus, and many variants of Escherichia coli. The growth of two fungi commonly present in otomycosis was also significantly inhibited by human cerumen. These antimicrobial properties are due principally to the presence of saturated fatty acids, lysozyme and, especially, to the relatively low pH of cerumen (typically around 6.1 in normal individuals).

Mammary Glands

Mammary glands are the organs that, in the female mammal, produce milk for the sustenance of the young. These exocrine glands are enlarged and modified sweat glands and are the characteristic of mammals which gave the class its name.

Structure

The basic components of the mammary gland are the alveoli (hollow cavities, a few millimetres large) lined with milk-secreting epithelial cells and surrounded by myoepithelial cells. These alveoli join up to form groups known as lobules, and each lobule has a lactiferous duct that drains into openings in the nipple. The myoepithelial cells can contract, similar to muscle cells, and thereby push the milk from the alveoli through the lactiferous ducts towards the nipple, where it collects in widenings (sinuses) of the ducts. A suckling baby essentially squeezes the milk out of these sinuses.

Dissection of a lactating breast.

1—Fat

2—Lactiferous duct/lobule

3—Lobule

4—Connective tissue

5—Sinus of lactiferous duct

6—Lactiferous duct

One distinguishes between a simple mammary gland, which consists of all the milk-secreting tissue leading to a single lactiferous duct, and a complex mammary gland, which consists of all the simple mammary glands serving one nipple.

Humans normally have two complex mammary glands, one in each breast, and each complex mammary gland consists of 10-20 simple glands. (The presence of more than two nipples is known as polythelia and the presence of more than two complex mammary glands as polymastia.)

The development of mammary glands is controlled by hormones. The mammary glands exist in both sexes, but they are rudimentary until puberty when in response to ovarian hormones, they begin to develop in the female. Estrogen promotes formation, while testosterone inhibits it.

At the time of birth, the baby has lactiferous ducts but no alveoli. Little branching occurs before puberty when ovarian estrogens stimulate branching differentiation of the ducts into spherical masses of cells that will become alveoli. True secretory alveoli only develop in pregnancy, where rising levels of estrogen and progesterone cause further branching and differentiation of the duct cells, together with an increase in adipose tissue and a richer blood flow.

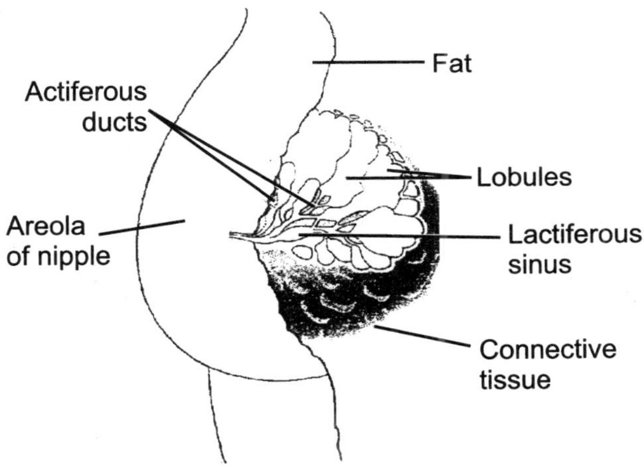

Fig.5.6 *Structure of breast.*

Colostrum is secreted in late pregnancy and for the first few days after giving birth. True milk secretion (lactation) begins a few days later due to a reduction in circulating progesterone and the presence of the hormone prolactin. The suckling of the baby causes the release of the hormone oxytocin which stimulates contraction of the myoepithelial cells.

HOMEOSTASIS

As a whole, the integumentary system plays a big part in maintaining homeostasis. The integumentary system is the outermost organ system of the body and many of its functions are related to this location. The skin protects the body against pathogens and chemicals, minimizes loss or entry of water, and blocks the harmful effects of sunlight. Sensory receptors in the skin provide information about the external environment, helping the skin regulate body temperature in response to environmental changes and helping the body react to pain and other tactile stimuli. The large surface area of the skin makes it ideal for temperature regulation. The rate of heat loss can be regulated by the amount of blood flowing through the the blood vessels in the dermis close to the surface of the skin. When the body temperature rises, as for example during exercise, sympathetic tone is reduced and this brings about dilation of the blood vessels supplying the skin. The increase in skin blood flow allows heat to be lost more rapidly so that body temperature does not rise above the normal homeostatic range. The rate of heat loss can also be boosted by the production of sweat, which takes up additional heat as it evaporates. Conversely, if heat production is less than required, the dermal vessels constrict, sweating stops, and heat is conserved by the body.

INTEGUMENTARY SYSTEM DISORDERS

ACNE

Acne is a skin disease marked by pimples on the face, chest, and back. The most common skin disease, acne affects an estimated 17 to 28 million people in the United States. Although it can strike people at any age, acne usually begins at puberty and worsens during adolescence.

At puberty, increased levels of androgens (male hormones) cause the sebaceous glands to secrete an excessive amount of sebum into hair follicles. The excess sebum combines with dead, sticky skin cells to form a hard plug that blocks the follicle. Bacteria that normally lives on the skin then invades the blocked follicle. Weakened, the follicle bursts open, releasing the sebum, bacteria, skin cells, and white blood cells into the surrounding tissues.

Treatment for acne depends on whether the condition is mild, moderate, or severe. The goal is to reduce sebum production, remove dead skin cells, and kill skin bacteria. In very mild cases, keeping the skin clean by washing with a mild soap is recommended. In other cases, medications applied directly to the skin or taken orally may be prescribed in combination with gentle cleansing.

ATHLETE'S FOOT

Athlete's foot is a common fungus infection in which the skin between the toes becomes itchy and sore, cracking and peeling away. Properly known as tinea pedis, the infection received its common name because the infection causing fungi grow well in warm, damp areas such as in and around swimming pools, showers, and locker rooms (areas commonly used by athletes).

The fungi that cause athlete's foot are unusual in that they live exclusively on dead body tissue (hair, the outer layer of skin, and nails). Researchers do not know exactly why some people develop the condition and others do not. It is known that sweaty feet, tight shoes, and the failure to dry feet well after swimming or bathing all contribute to the growth of the fungus.

Symptoms of athlete's foot include itchy, sore skin on the toes, with scaling, cracking, inflammation, and blisters. If the blisters break, raw patches of tissue may be exposed. If the infection spreads, itching and burning may increase.

Athlete's foot usually responds well to treatment. Simple cases are treated with antifungal creams or sprays. In more severe cases, an oral antifungal medication may be prescribed.

BURNS

There are few threats more serious to the skin than burns. Burns are injuries to tissues caused by intense heat, electricity, UV radiation (sunburn), or certain chemicals (such as acids). When skin is burned and cells are destroyed, the body readily loses its precious supply of fluids. Dehydration can follow, leading to a shutdown of the kidneys, a life-threatening condition. Infection of the dead tissue by bacteria and viruses occurs one to two days after skin has been burned. Infection is the leading cause of death in burn victims. Burns are classified according to their severity or depth: first-, second-, or third-degree burns.

First-degree burns occur when only the epidermis is damaged. The burned area is painful, the outer skin is reddened, and slight swelling may be present. Sunburns are usually first-degree burns. Although they may cause discomfort, these minor burns are usually not serious and heal within a few days.

Second-degree burns occur when the epidermis and the upper region of the dermis are damaged. The burned area is red, painful, and may have a wet, shiny appearance because of exposed tissue. Blisters may form. These moderate burns take longer to heal. If the blisters are not broken and care is taken to prevent infection, the burned skin may regenerate or regrow without permanent scars.

Third-degree burns occur when the entire depth of skin is destroyed. Because nerve endings have been destroyed, the burned area has no sensitivity. The area may be blackened or gray-white in colour. Muscle tissue and bone underneath may be damaged. In these serious to critical burns, regeneration of the skin is not possible. Skin grafting—taking a piece of skin from an unburned portion of the burn victim's body and transplanting it to the burned area—must be done to cover the exposed tissues. Third-degree burns take weeks to heal and will leave permanent scarring.

DERMATITIS

Dermatitis is any inflammation of the skin. There are many types of dermatitis and most are characterized by a pink or red rash that itches. Two common types are contact dermatitis and seborrheic dermatitis.

Contact dermatitis is an allergic reaction to something that irritates the skin. It usually appears within forty-eight hours after touching or brushing against a substance to which the skin is sensitive. The resin in poison ivy, poison oak, and poison sumac is the most common source of contact dermatitis. The skin of some people may also be irritated by certain flowers, herbs, and vegetables. Chemical irritants that can cause contact dermatitis include chlorine, cleaners, detergents and soaps, fabric softeners, perfumes, glues, and topical medications (those applied on the skin). Contact dermatitis can be treated with medicated creams or ointments and oral antihistamines and antibiotics.

ARTIFICIAL SKIN

Artificial skin, the synthetic or manmade equivalent of human skin, was first developed in the 1970s. Since then, the lives of many severely burned people have been saved through the use of artificial skin.

In the 1970s, John F. Burke, chief of trauma services at Massachusetts General Hospital in Boston, and Ioannis V. Yannas, chemistry professor at Massachusetts Institute of Technology in Cambridge, teamed upto develop some type of human skin replacement. In their research, the two men found that collagen fibers (protein found in human skin) and a long sugar molecule (called a polymer) could be combined to forrn a porous material that resembles skin. They then created a kind of artificial skin using polymers from shark cartilage and collagen from cowhide.

Burke and Yannas soon discovered that artificial skin acts like a framework onto which new skin tissue and blood vessels grow. As the new skin grows, the cowhide and shark substances from the artificial skin are broken down and absorbed by the body.

In 1979, Burke and Yannas used their artificial skin on their first patient, a woman who had suffered burns over half her body. After peeling away her burned skin, Burke applied a layer of artificial skin and, where possible, grafted or added on some of her own unburned skin. Three weeks later, the woman's new skin, the same colour as her unburned skin, was growing at an amazingly healthy rate.

With continued research and development, synthetic skin may become a more common treatment for burns and other serious skin disorders.

Seborrheic dermatitis, known commonly as seborrhea, appears as red, inflammed skin covered by greasy or dry scales that may be white, yellow, or gray. These scaly lesions appear usually on the scalp, hairline, and face. Dandruff is a mild form of seborrheic dermatitis. Medical researchers do not know the exact cause of this skin disease. They believe that a high-fat diet, alcohol, stress, oily skin, infrequent shampooing, and weather extremes (hot or cold) may play some role. The disease may be treated with special shampoos that help soften and remove the scaly lesions. In more severe cases, medicated creams or shampoos containing coal tar may be prescribed.

PSORIASIS

Psoriasis is a chronic (long-term) skin disease characterized by inflamed lesions with silvery-white scabs of dead skin. The disease affects roughly four million people in the United States, women slightly more than men. It is most common in fair-skinned people. Normal skin cells mature and replace dead skin cells every twenty-eight to thirty days. Psoriasis causes skin cells to mature in less than a week. Because the body cannot shed old skin as rapidly as new cells are rising to the surface, raised patches of dead skin develop. These patches are seen on the arms, back, chest, elbows, legs, folds between the buttocks, and scalp.

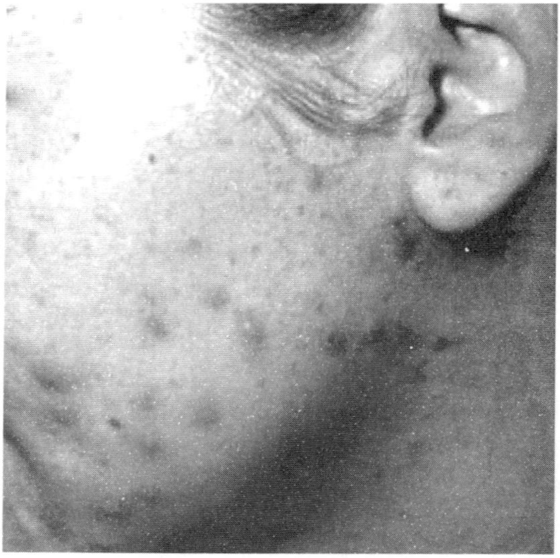

Fig. 5.7. *Psoriasis.*

The cause of psoriasis is unknown. In some cases, it may be hereditary or inherited. Attacks of psoriasis can be triggered by injury or infection, stress, hormonal changes, exposure to cold temperature, or steroids and other medications. The treatment for psoriasis depends on its severity. Steroid creams and ointments are commonly used to treat mild or moderate psoriasis. If the case is more severe, these medications may be used in conjunction with ultraviolet light B (UVB) treatments. Strong medications are reserved for those individuals suffering from extreme cases of psoriasis.

SKIN CANCER

Skin cancer is the growth of abnormal skin cells capable of invading and destroying other cells. Skin cancer is the single most common type of cancer in humans. The cause of most skin cancers or carcinomas is unknown, but overexposure to ultraviolet radiation in sunlight is a risk factor.

Basal cell carcinoma is the most common form of skin cancer, accounting for about 75 percent of cases. It is also the least malignant or cancerous (tending to grow and spread throughout the body). In this form of skin cancer, basal cells in the epidermis are altered so they no longer produce keratin. They also spread, invading the dermis and subcutaneous layer. Shiny, dome-shaped lesions develop most often on sunexposed areas of the face. The next most common areas affected are the ears, the backs of the hands, the shoulders, and the arms. When the lesion is removed surgically, 99 percent of patients recover fully.

Squamous cell carcinoma affects the cells of the second deepest layer of the epidermis. Like basal cell carcinoma, this type of skin cancer also involves skin exposed to the sun: face, ears, hands, and arms. The cancer presents itself as a small, scaling, raised bump on the skin with a crusting center. It grows rapidly and spreads to adjacent lymph nodes if not removed. If the lesion is caught early and removed surgically or through radiation, the patient has a good chance of recovering completely.

Malignant melanoma accounts for about 5 percent of all skin cancers, but it is the most serious type. It is a cancer of the melanocytes, cells in the lower epidermis that produce melanin. In their early stages, melanomas resemble moles. Soon, they appear as an expanding brown to black patch. In addition to invading surrounding tissues, the cancer spreads aggressively to other parts of the body, especially the lungs and liver. Overexposure to the sun may be a cause of melanomas, but the greatest risk factor seems to be genetic. Early discovery of the melanoma is key to survival. The primary treatment for this skin cancer is the surgical removal of the tumor or diseased area of skin. When the melanoma has spread to other parts of the body, it is generally considered incurable.

VITILIGO

Vitiligo is a skin disorder in which the loss of melanocytes (cells that produce the colour pigment melanin) results in patches of smooth, milky white skin. This often inherited disorder affects about 1 to 2 percent of the world's population. Although it is more easily observed in people with darker skin, it affects all races. It can begin at any age, but in 50 percent of the cases it starts before the age of twenty.

Medical researchers do not know the exact cause of the disorder. Some theorize that nerve endings in the skin may release a chemical that destroys melanocytes. Others believe that the melanocytes simply self-destruct. Still others think that vitiligo is a type of autoimmune disease, in which the body targets and destroys its own cells and tissues.

Vitiligo cannot be cured, but it can be managed. Cosmetics can be applied to blend the white areas with the surrounding normal skin. Sunscreens are useful to prevent the burning of affected areas and to prevent normal skin around the patches from becoming darker.

WARTS

Warts are small growths caused by a viral infection of the skin or mucous membrane. The virus infects the surface layer. Warts are contagious. They can easily pass from person to person. They can also pass from one area of the body to another on the same person. Affecting about 7 to 10 percent of the population, warts are particularly common among children, young adults, and women. Common warts include hand warts, foot warts, and flat warts. Hand warts grow around the nails, on the fingers, and on the backs of the hands. They appear mostly in areas where the skin is broken.

Foot warts (also called plantar warts) usually appear on the ball of the foot, the heel, or the flat part of the toes. Foot warts do not stick up above the surface like hand warts. If left untreated, they can grow in size and spread into clusters of several warts. If located on a pressure point of the foot, these warts can be painful.

Flat warts are smaller and smoother than other warts. They grow in great numbers and can erupt anywhere on the body. In children, they appear especially on the face. Many non-prescription wart remedies are available that will remove simple warts from hands and fingers. Physicians use stronger chemical medications to treat warts that are larger or do not respond to over-the-counter treatments. Freezing warts with liquid nitrogen or burning them with an electric needle are advanced treatment methods.

TATTOOS: BODY ART OR MUTILATION

Tattoos are relatively permanent marks or designs made on the skin. Tattoo comes from the Tahitian word *tattau,* meaning "to mark." The process of tattooing is accomplished by injecting coloured pigment into small deep holes made in the skin. The modern method of tattooing employs an electric needle to inject the pigment.

People have been decorating their bodies with pictures of animals, flowers, supernatural creatures, and various designs for thousands of years. Egyptian mummies dating from 3035 B.C. have been discovered with ornate designs of flowers tattooed on their skin. Many ancient cultures believed that a tattoo of an animal could capture the mystical spirit of that animal and magically link the wearer to the animal depicted.

While many cultures have revered tattoos, many others have considered them vulgar and offensive. For as long as people have applied tattoos to their skin, they have sought ways to remove them.

In modern times, tattoos can be removed medically through one of four ways. If the tattoo is small, it can be surgically cut off and the skin sewn back together. In a method called dermabrasion, the tattoo is "sanded" with a rotary abrasive instrument until the layers of skin peel. Another method that uses abrasion is called salabrasion. In this procedure, which is centuries old, salt water is applied to the tattoo and then it is vigorously rubbed with some sort of sanding device until the tattoo pigments are dispersed. All three of these methods leave some sort of scarring, but the last method, laser surgery, does not. Pulses of light from a laser are directed onto the tattoo, breaking up its pigments. The pigments are then removed over the next few weeks by the body's defense cells.

STUDY QUESTIONS

1. Explain in detailed the structure of skin.
2. Write short notes on:
   (a) Colour of the Skin
   (b) Hair Follicle
   (c) Sebaceous Gland
   (d) Thermohomeostasis.
3. Describe the accessory organs of the skin.

6

CHAPTER

Human Blood Group

BLOOD

The primary function of blood is to supply oxygen and nutrients as well as constitutional elements to tissues and to remove waste products. Blood also enables hormones and other substances to be transported between tissues and organs. Problems with blood composition or circulation can lead to downstream tissue malfunction. Blood is also involved in maintaining homeostasis by acting as a medium for transferring heat to the skin and by acting as a buffer system for bodily pH.

The blood is circulated through the lungs and body by the pumping action of the heart. The right ventricle pressurizes the blood to send it through the capillaries of the lungs, while the left ventricle repressurizes the blood to send it throughout the body. Pressure is essentially lost in the capillaries, hence gravity and especially the actions of skeletal muscles are needed to return the blood to the heart.

BLOOD COMPONENTS OR COMPOSITION

Blood may be transfused as whole blood or as one of its components. Because patients seldom require all of the components of *whole blood,* it makes sense to transfuse only that portion which is needed by a patient for a specific condition or disease. The treatment, referred to as "blood component therapy", allows several patients to benefit from one unit of donated whole blood. Up to four components may be derived from one unit of blood.

Whole blood is a living tissue that circulates through the heart, arteries, veins and capillaries carrying nourishment, electrolytes, hormones, vitamins, antibodies, heat and oxygen to the body's tissues. Whole blood contains red blood cells, white blood cells and platelets suspended in a proteinaceous fluid called plasma.

RED BLOOD CELLS

Red blood cells are perhaps the most recognisable component of whole blood. Red cells contain haemoglobin, a complex iron-containing protein that carries oxygen throughout the body and gives blood its red colour. Manufactured in the bone marrow, red blood cells are continuously being produced and broken down. They live for approximately 120 days in the circulatory system and are eventually removed by the spleen.

Patients who benefit most from transfusions of red blood cells include those with chronic anaemia resulting from disorders such as kidney failure, malignancies or gastrointestinal bleeding and those with acute blood loss resulting from trauma or surgery. Donated red blood cells normally have a life of 35 days or may be treated and frozen for extended storage for up to 10 years. Red blood cells can be donated through an allogeneic donation (whole blood).

Functions

The main function is the transportation of oxygen throughout the body and the ability of the blood to carry out carbondioxide which is called carbamino – hemoglobin. Maintaining the balance of blood is important. The balance can be measured by the acid and base levels in the blood. This is called pH. Normal pH of blood ranges between 7.35-7.45; this normal blood is called Alkaline (less acidic than water). A drop in pH is called Acidic. This condition is also called Acidosis. A jump in pH higher than 7.45 is called

"Alkalosis". To maintain the homeostasis (or balance,) the blood has tiny molecules within the RBC that help prevent drops or increases from happening.

Red blood cells are broken down and hemoglobin is released. The globin part of the hemoglobin is broken down into amino acid components, which in turn is recycled by the body. The iron is recovered and returned to the bone marrow to be reused. The heme portion of the molecule experiences a chemical change and then gets excreted as bile pigment (bilirubin) by the liver. Heme portion after being broken down contributes to the colour of faeces and your skin colour changing after being bruised.

WHITE BLOOD CELLS

White blood cells are vital to prevent and fight infection. White blood cells are made in the bone marrow and their life span varies from a few hours to many weeks. White blood cells are essential to protect us from infection, but they are not often transfused because they are difficult to collect and their life span is so short.

Functions

White blood cells (leukocytes) are also known as "WBC's". White blood cells are made in the bone marrow but they also divide in the blood and lymphatic systems. They are commonly amoeboid cells that move or feed by means of temporary projections, called pseudopods (false feet), and escape the circulatory system through the capillary beds. The different types of WBC's are Basophils, Eosinophils, Eeutrophils, Monocytes, B- and T-cell lymphocytes. Neutrophils, Eosinophils, and Basophils are all granular leukocytes. Lymphocytes and Monocytes are agranular leukocytes. Basophils store and synthesize histamine which is important in allergic reactions. They enter the tissues and become "mass cells" which help blood flow to injured tissues by the release of histamine. Eosinophils are chemotaxic and kill parasites. Neutrophils are the first to act when there is an infection and are also the most abundant white blood cells. Neutrophils fight bacteria and viruses by phagocytosis which mean they engulf pathogens that may cause infection. The life span of a Neutrophil is only about 12-48 hours.

Monocytes are the biggest of the white blood cells and are responsible for rallying the cells to defend the body. Monocytes carry out phagocytosis and are also called macrophages. Lymphocytes help with our immune response. There are two Lymphocytes: the B- and T-Lymphocytes. B-Lymphocytes produce antibodies that find and mark pathogens for destruction. T-Lymphocytes kill anything that they deem abnormal to the body.

WBC's are classified by phenotype which can be identified by looking at the WBC's under a microscope. The granular phenotype are able to stain blue. The agranular phenotype are able to stain red. Neutrophils make up 50-70% of granular cells, Eosinophils make up 2-4%, and Basophils 0-1%. Monocytes make up 2-8% of Agranular cells. B- and T-Lymphocytes make up 20-30%. As you can see, there is a great deal of differentiation between WBC's. These special cells help our bodies defend themselves against pathogens. Not only do they help our immune system but they remove toxins, wastes, and abnormal or damaged cells. Thus, we can say that WBC's main function is being phagocytic which means to engulf or swallow cells.

PLATELETS

Platelets are very small cellular components that help the clotting process by sticking to the lining of blood vessels. Platelets are made in the bone marrow and survive in the circulatory system for an average of 9 to 10 days before being removed from the body by the spleen. The platelet is vital to life, because it helps prevent both massive blood loss resulting from trauma and blood vessel leakage that would otherwise occur in the course of normal day-to-day activity.

PLASMA

Plasma which makes up 45-55% of blood volume. Formed cellular elements (red and white blood cells, and platelets) which combine to make the remaining blood volume. Plasma, which is 90% water, constitutes about 55% of blood volume. Plasma contains:

Albumin: The chief protein constituent.

Fibrinogen: Responsible in part, for the clotting of blood.

Globulins: Including antibodies and other clotting proteins.

Plasma serves a variety of functions, from maintaining a satisfactory blood pressure and volume to supplying critical proteins for blood clotting and immunity. It also serves as the medium of exchange for vital minerals such as sodium and potassium.

BLOOD COMPONENT USE

Whole blood can be processed into the following components:

(i) *Fresh frozen plasma*: Used to treat patients who have bleeding problems.

(ii) *Platelets*: For control of haemorrhage, often in patients with leukaemia.

(iii) *Cryoprecipitate*: Contains blood clotting substitutes for seriously ill patients.

(iv) *White cells*: Occasionally used for patients who are not producing their own white cells.

(v) *Red blood cells*: Used for the treatment of anaemia and bleeding after trauma and surgery.

(vi) *Frozen red cells*: Used for long term storage of rare blood groups.

(vii) *Filtered red cells*: For patients who have antibodies against white cells.

BLOOD CIRCULATION FROM THE HEART TO THE LUNGS

Gas Exchange

Oxygen (O_2) is the most immediate need of every cell and is carried throughout the body by the blood circulation. Oxygen is used at the cellular level as the final electron acceptor in the electron transport chain (the primary method of generating ATP for cellular reactions). Oxygen is carried in the blood bound to hemoglobin molecules within red blood cells. Hemoglobin binds oxygen when passing through the alveoli of the lungs and releases oxygen in the warmer, more acidic environment of bodily tissues.

Carbon dioxide (CO_2) is removed from tissues by blood and released into the air via the lungs. Carbon dioxide is produced by cells as they undergo the processes of cellular respiration (particularly the Kreb's cycle). The molecules are produced from carbons that were originally part of glucose. Most of the carbon dioxide combines with water and is carried in the plasma as bicarbonate ions. An excess of carbon dioxide (through exercise, or from holding ones breath) quickly shifts the blood pH to being more acidic (acidosis). Chemoreceptors in the brain and major blood vessels detect this shift and stimulate the breathing center of the brain (the medulla oblongata). Hence, as CO_2 levels build up and the blood becomes more acidic, we involuntarily breathe faster, thus lowering CO_2 levels and stabilizing blood pH. In contrast, a person who is hyperventilating (such as during a panic attack) will release too much CO_2 and the blood will become too alkaline (alkalosis).

HEMOSTASIS (COAGULATION OR CLOTTING)

Hemostasis is the natural process of stopping blood flow or loss of blood following an injury (hemo = blood; stasis = standing). It has three stages:

(1) vascular spasm, vasoconstriction, or intense contraction of blood vessels,

(2) formation of a platelet plug, and

(3) blood clotting or coagulation.

Once the flow of blood has been stopped, tissue repair can begin.

Vascular spasm or vasoconsriction: In a normal individual, immediately after a blood vessel has been cut and endothelial cells are damaged, vasoconstriction occurs, thus slowing blood flow to the area. Smooth muscle in the vessel wall goes through spasms or intense contractions that constrict the vessel. If the vessels are small, spasms compress the inner walls together and may be able to stop the bleeding completely. If the vessels are medium to large-sized, the spasms slow down immediate outflow of blood, lessening the damage but still preparing the vessel for the later steps of hemostasis. These vascular spasms usually last for about 30 minutes, long enough for the next two stages of hemostasis to take place.

Formation of a Platelet Plug

Within 20 seconds of an injury, coagulation is initiated. Contrary to popular belief, clotting of a cut on the skin is not initiated by air or drying out, but by platelets adhering to and activated by collagen in the blood vessels endothelium. The activated platelets then release the contents of their granules, which contain a variety of substances that stimulate further platelet activation and enhance the hemostatic process.

When the lining of a blood vessel breaks and endothelial cells are damaged, revealing collagen proteins in the vessel wall, platelets swell, grow spikey extensions, and start clumping together. They start to stick to each other and the walls of the vessel. This continues as more platelets congregate and undergo these same transformations. This process results in a platelet plug that seals the injured area. If the injury is small, a platelet plug may be able to form and close it within several seconds. If the damage is more serious, the next step of blood clotting will take place. Platelets contain secretory granules. When they stick to the proteins in the vessel walls, they degranulate, thus releasing their products, which include ADP (adenosine diphosphate), serotonin, and thromboxane A2.

A Blood Clot Forms

If the platelet plug is not enough to stop the bleeding, the third stage of hemostasis begins: the formation of a blood clot. First, blood changes from a liquid to a gel. At least 12 substances called clotting factors take part in a series of chemical reactions that eventually create a mesh of protein fibers within the blood. Each of the clotting factors has a very specific function. We will discuss just three of the substances here: prothrombin, thrombin, and fibrinogen. Prothrombin and fibrinogin are proteins that are produced and deposited in the blood by the liver.

Prothrombin: When blood vessels are damaged, vessels and nearby platelets are stimulated to release a substance called prothrombin activator, which in turn activates the conversion of prothrombin, a plasma protein, into an enzyme called *thrombin*. This reaction requires calcium ions.

Thrombin: Thrombin facilitates the conversion of a soluble plasma protein called fibrinogen into long insoluble fibers or threads of the protein fibrin.

Fibrin: Fibrin threads wind around the platelet plug at the damaged area of the blood vessel, forming an interlocking network of fibers and a framework for the clot. This net of fibers traps and helps hold platelets, blood cells and other molecules tight to the site of injury, functioning as the initial clot. This temporary fibrin clot can form in less than a minute, and usually does a good job of reducing the blood flow. Next, platelets in the clot begin to shrink, tightening the clot and drawing together the vessel walls. Usually, this whole process of clot formation and tightening takes less than an half hour.

The use of adsorbent chemicals, such as zeolites, and other hemostatic agents, are also being explored for use in sealing severe injuries quickly.

BLOOD GROUPS

Blood groups are complex chemical systems found on the surface of blood cells. The two main blood group systems in transfusion practice are the ABO system and the Rh(D) type. Identification of the correct blood group is important to prevent reaction following transfusion.

Within the ABO system, people can be one of four groups: O, A, B or AB, while in the Rh(D) system they can be either Rh(D) positive or Rh(D) negative. Each system is inherited independently of the other. As a result, there are eight main blood groups.

ABO Blood Groups

Parents	*Possible children*
O & O	O
O & A	O or A
O & B	O or B
O & AB	A or B
A & A	O or A
A & A	O or A
A & B	O,A, B, or AB
A & AB	A, B or AB
B & B	O or B
B & AB	A, B or AB
AB & AB	A, B or AB

Fig. 6.1 *Compatibility of different blood groups.*

The Givers/Receivers above chart shows the compatibility of different blood groups. For example, an A negative patient may receive blood from an O negative or an A negative donor.

Rh(D) negative patients should not normally receive Rh(D) positive red cells, this is particularly important in women of childbearing age.

Type O negative donors are referred to as "the *universal donors*" because in an emergency their red cells can be transfused to people who have any blood type. Because any patient can receive type O negative blood, there is a particular need for O donors to give regularly.

INHERITANCE OF BLOOD GROUPS

Blood groups are inherited from our biological parents in the same way as eye colour and other genetic traits.

Within the ABO blood group system, the A and B genes are co-dominant, i.e., these will be expressed whenever the gene is present. The O gene is silent and only expressed when neither A nor B is present.

The Rh(D) group is also dominant and will be expressed if inherited from either parent. If the Rh(D) gene is not inherited from either biological parent, then the individual will be Rh(D) negative. The charts outline the possible ABO and Rh(D) group combinations of parents and the possible blood types of their biological children.

COMPATIBILITY IN BLOOD TRANSFUSIONS

Blood transfusions between donor and recipient of incompatible blood types can cause severe acute immunological reactions, hemolysis (RBC destruction), renal failure, shock, and sometimes death. Antibodies can be highly active and can attack RBCs and bind components of the complement system to cause massive hemolysis of the transfused blood.

A patient should ideally receive their own blood or type-specific blood products to minimize the chance of a transfusion reaction. If time allows, the risk will further be reduced by cross-matching blood, in addition to blood typing both recipient and donor. Cross-matching involves mixing a sample of the recipient's blood with a sample of the donor's blood and checking to see if the mixture agglutinates, or forms clumps. Blood bank technicians usually check for agglutination with a microscope, and if it occurs, that particular donor's blood cannot be transfused to that particular recipient. Blood transfusion is a potentially risky medical procedure and it is vital that all blood specimens are correctly identified, so in cross-matching labelling is standardized using a barcode system known as ISBT 128.

HEMOLYTIC DISEASE OF THE NEWBORN

Often a pregnant woman carries a fetus with a different blood type to herself, and sometimes the mother forms antibodies against the red blood cells of the fetus, leading to low fetal blood counts, a condition known as hemolytic disease of the newborn.

Hemolytic disease of the newborn (also known as HDN) is an alloimmune condition that develops in a fetus when the IgG antibodies produced by the mother and passing through the placenta include ones which attack the red blood cells in the fetal circulation. The red cells are broken down and the fetus can develop reticulocytosis and anemia. The fetal disease ranges from mild to very severe and fetal death from heart failure – hydrops fetalis – can occur. When the disease is moderate or severe many erythroblasts are present in the fetal blood and so these forms of the disease can be called erythroblastosis fetalis.

Before birth, options for treatment include intrauterine transfusion or early induction of labor when pulmonary maturity has been attained, fetal distress is present, or 35 to 37 weeks of gestation have passed. The mother may also undergo plasma exchange to reduce the circulating levels of antibody by as much as 75%.

After birth, treatment depends on the severity of the condition, but could include temperature stabilization and monitoring, phototherapy, transfusion with compatible packed red blood, exchange transfusion with a blood type compatible with both the infant and the mother, sodium bicarbonate for correction of acidosis and/or assisted ventilation.

Rh negative mothers who have had a pregnancy with or are pregnant with a Rh positive infant, are given Rh immune globulin (RhIG) also known as Rhogam, during pregnancy and after delivery to prevent sensitization to the D antigen. It works by binding any fetal red cells with the D antigen before the mother is able to produce an immune response and form anti-D IgG. A drawback to pre-partum administration of RhIG is that it causes a positive antibody screen when the mother is tested which is indistinguishable from immune reasons for antibody production.

DISEASES OF THE BLOOD

DISSEMINATED INTRAVASCULAR COAGULATION

Disseminated intravascular coagulation (DIC), also called consumptive coagulopathy, is a pathological process in the body where the blood starts to coagulate throughout the whole body. This depletes the body of its platelets and coagulation factors, and there is a paradoxically increased risk of hemorrhage. It occurs in critically ill patients, especially those with gramnegative sepsis (particularly meningococcal sepsis) and acute promyelocytic leukemia.

HEMOPHILIA

Hemophilia is a disease where there is low or no blood protein, causing an inability to produce blood clots. There are two types of Hemophilia: Type A, which is a deficiency in factor VIII and Type B (Christmas disease), a deficiency on factor IX. Because people with hemophilia do not have the ability to make blood clots, even a little cut may kill them, or the smallest bump or jar to the body could cause severe bruising that doesn't get better for months.

Hemophilia is passed down from mothers to their sons. Hemophilia is sometimes known as the "Royal Disease". This is because Queen Victoria, Queen of England (1837-1901), was a carrier of hemophilia. The hemophilia disease was passed down to her son Leopold who ended up dying at age 31. Queen Victoria also had two daughters who were carriers. These daughters passed hemophilia into the Spanish, German, and Russian royal families. One of the most famous stories is that of the Russian royal family. Alexandra, grand-daughter to Queen Victoria, married Nicholas (Tsar of Russia in the 1900s). Alexandra was a carrier of the disease and passed the disease to their first son, Tsarevich Alexi, who was heir to the throne of Russia. The family tried to keep their son's secret from the people, but Alexi suffered with serious bruises and extreme pain. The family found help from a monk named Rasputin. He kept their secret and gained a great deal of power over the family, making them think he was their only hope. During this time of great turmoil in Russia, Nicholas and Alexandra spent most of their attentions on their son, and not on the people. It wasn't long before the Bolshevik Revolution of 1917 began.

ANEMIA

Anemia or anaemia, from the Greek meaning "without blood", refers to a deficiency of red blood cells (RBC's) and/or hemoglobin. This results in a reduced ability of blood to transfer oxygen to the tissues, causing *hypoxia*. Since all human cells depend on oxygen for survival, varying degrees of anemia can have a wide range of clinical consequences. Hemoglobin (the oxygen-carrying protein in the red blood cells) has to be present to ensure adequate oxygenation of all body tissues and organs.

The three main classes of anemia include *excessive blood loss* (acutely such as a hemorrhage or chronically through low-volume loss), *excessive blood cell destruction* (hemolysis) or *deficient red blood cell production* (ineffective hematopoiesis). In menstruating women, dietary iron deficiency is a common cause of deficient red blood cell production.

SICKLE-CELL

Image of RBC's with sickle cell mutations. Sickle-cell disease is a general term for a group of genetic disorders caused by sickle hemoglobin (Hgb S or Hb S). In many forms of the disease, the red blood cells change shape upon deoxygenation because of polymerization of the abnormal sickle hemoglobin. This process damages the red blood cell membrane, and can cause the cells to become stuck in blood vessels. This deprives the downstream tissues of oxygen and causes ischemia and infarction. The disease is chronic and lifelong. Individuals are most often well, but their lives are punctuated by periodic painful attacks. In addition to periodic pain, there may be damage of internal organs, and/or stroke. Lifespan is often shortened with sufferers living to an average of 40 years. It is common in people from parts of the world where malaria is or was common, especially in sub-Saharan Africa or in descendants of those peoples.

Genetics: Sickle-cell disease is inherited in the autosomal recessive pattern, depicted above. The allele responsible for sickle cell anemia is autosomal recessive. A person who receives the defective gene from both father and mother develops the disease; a person who receives one defective and one healthy allele remains healthy, but can pass on the disease and is known as a carrier. If two parents who are carriers have a child, there is a 1-in-4 chance of their child developing the illness and a 1-in-2 chance of their child just being a carrier.

POLYCYTHEMIA

Polycythemia is a condition in which there is a net increase in the total circulating erythrocyte (red blood cell) mass of the body. There are several types of polycythemia.

Primary Polycythemia

In primary polycythemia, there may be 8 to 9 million and occasionally 11 million erythrocytes per cubic millimeter of blood (a normal range for adults is 4-5 million), and the hematocrit may be as high as 70 to 80%. In addition, the total blood volume can increase to as much as twice as normal. The entire vascular system can become markedly engorged with blood, and circulation times for blood throughout the body can increase up to twice the normal value. The increased numbers of erythrocytes can increase the viscosity of the blood to as much as five times normal. Capillaries can become plugged by the very viscous blood, and the flow of blood through the vessels tends to be extremely sluggish.

As a consequence of the above, people with untreated polycythemia are at a risk of various thrombotic events (deep venous thrombosis, pulmonary embolism), heart attack and stroke, and have a substantial risk of Budd-Chiari syndrome (hepatic vein thrombosis). The condition is considered chronic; no cure exists. Symptomatic treatment can normalize the blood count and most patients can live a normal life for years.

Secondary Polycythemia

Secondary polycythemia is caused by either appropriate or inappropriate increases in the production of erythropoietin that result in an increased production of erythrocytes. In secondary polycythemia, there may be 6 to 8 million and occasionally 9 million erythrocytes per cubic millimeter of blood. A type of secondary polycythemia in which the production of erythropoietin increases appropriately is called physiologic polycythemia. Physiologic polycythemia occurs in individuals living at high altitudes (4275 to 5200 meters), where oxygen availability is less than at sea level. Many athletes train at higher altitudes to take advantage of this effect — a legal form of blood doping. Actual polychthemia sufferers have been known to use their condition as an athletic advantage for greater stamina.

Other causes of secondary polycythemia include smoking, renal or liver tumors, or heart or lung diseases that result in hypoxia. Endocrine abnormalities, prominently including pheochromocytoma and adrenal adenoma with Cushing's syndrome, are also secondary causes. Athletes and bodybuilders who abuse anabolic steroids or erythropoietin may develop secondary polycythemia.

Relative Polycythemia

Relative polycythemia is an apparent rise of the erythrocyte level in the blood; however, the underlying cause is reduced blood plasma. Relative polycythemia is often caused by fluid loss i.e., burns, dehydration and stress polycythemia.

LEUKEMIA

Leukemia is a cancer of the blood or bone marrow characterized by an abnormal proliferation of blood cells, usually white blood cells (leukocytes). It is part of the broad group of diseases called hematological neoplasms. Damage to the bone marrow, by way of displacing the normal marrow cells with increasing numbers of malignant cells, results in a lack of blood platelets, which are important in the blood clotting process. This means people with leukemia may become bruised, bleed excessively, or develop pin-prick bleeds (petechiae).

White blood cells, which are involved in fighting pathogens, may be suppressed or dysfunctional, putting the patient at the risk of developing infections. The red blood cell deficiency leads to anaemia, which may cause dyspnea. All symptoms may also be attributable to other diseases; for diagnosis, blood tests and a bone marrow biopsy are required.

IMMUNITY

Immunity is the body's capability to repel foreign substances and cells. The non-specific responses are the first line of defense. Highly specific responses are the second line of defense and are tailored to an individual threat. The immune response includes both specific and non-specific components. Non-specific responses block the entry and spread of disease-causing agents. Antibody-mediated and cell-mediated responses are two types of specific response. The immune system is associated with defense against disease-causing agents, problems in transplants and blood transfusions, and diseases resulting from over-reaction (autoimmune, allergies) and under-reaction (AIDS).

GENERAL DEFENSES

Barriers to entry are the skin and mucous membranes. The skin is a passive barrier to infectious agents such as bacteria and viruses. The organisms living on the skin surface are unable to penetrate the layers of dead skin at the surface. Tears and saliva secrete enzymes that breakdown bacterial cell walls. Skin glands secrete chemicals that retard the growth of bacteria. Mucus membranes lining the respiratory, digestive, urinary, and reproductive tracts secrete mucus that forms another barrier. Physical barriers are the first line of defense.

When microorganisms penetrate skin or epithelium lining respiratory, digestive, or urinary tracts, inflammation results. Damaged cells release chemical signals such as histamine that increase capillary blood flow into the affected area (causing the areas to become heated and reddened). The heat makes the environment unfavourable for microbes, promotes healing, raises mobility of white blood cells, and increases the metabolic rate of nearby cells. Capillaries pass fluid into interstitial areas, causing the infected/injured area to swell. Clotting factors trigger formation of many small blood clots. Finally, monocytes (a type of white blood cell) clean up dead microbes, cells, and debris.

The inflammatory response is often strong enough to stop the spread of disease-causing agents such as viruses, bacteria, and fungi. The response begins with the release of chemical signals and ends with cleanup by monocytes. If this is not enough to stop the invaders, the complement system and immune response act.

Protective proteins that are produced in the liver include the complement system of proteins. The complement system proteins bind to a bacterium and open pores in its membrane through which fluids and salt move, swelling and bursting the cell.

The complement system directly kills microbes, supplements inflammatory response, and works with the immune response. It complements the actions of the immune system. Complement proteins are made in the liver and become active in a sequence (C1 activates C2, etc.). The final five proteins form a membrane-attack complex (MAC) that embeds itself into the plasma membrane of the attacker. Salts enter the invader, facilitating water to cross the membrane, swelling and bursting the microbe. Complement also functions in the immune response by tagging the outer surface of invaders for attack by phagocytes.

SPECIFIC DEFENSES

The immune system also generates specific responses to specific invaders. The immune system is more effective than the non-specific methods, and has a memory component that improves response time when an invader of the same type (or species) is again encountered.

Immunity results from the production of antibodies specific to a given antigen (antibody-generators, located on the surface of an invader). Antibodies bind to the antigens on invaders and kill or inactivate them in several ways. Most antibodies are themselves proteins or are a mix of protein and polysaccharides. Antigens can be any molecule that causes antibody production.

LYMPHOCYTES

White blood cells known as lymphocytes arise from by mitosis of stem cells in the bone marrow. Some lymphocytes migrate to the thymus and become T cells that circulate in the blood and are associated with the lymph nodes and spleen. B cells remain in the bone marrow and develop before moving into the circulatory and lymph systems. B cells produce antibodies.

ANTIBODY-MEDIATED (HUMORAL IMMUNITY)

Antibody-mediated (humoral) immunity is regulated by B cells and the antibodies they produce. Cell-mediated immunity is controlled by T cells. Antibody-mediated reactions defend against invading viruses and bacteria. Cell-mediated immunity concerns cells in the body that have been infected by viruses and bacteria, protect against parasites, fungi, and protozoans, and also kill cancerous body cells. Antibody-mediated *immunity stages* in this process are:

- antigen detection
- activation of helper T cells
- antibody production by B cells.

Each stage is directed by a specific cell type.

MACROPHAGES

Macrophages are white blood cells that continually search for foreign (non-self) antigenic molecules, viruses, or microbes. When found, the macrophages engulfs and destroys them. Small fragments of the antigen are displayed on the outer surface of the macrophage plasma membrane.

HELPER T CELLS

Helper T cells are macrophages that become activated when they encounter the antigens now displayed on the macrophage surface. Activated T cells identify and activate B cells.

B CELLS

B cells divide, forming plasma cells and B memory cells. Plasma cells make and release between 2000 and 20,000 antibody molecules per second into the blood for the next four or five days. B memory cells live for months or years, and are part of the immune memory system.

ANTIBODIES

Antibodies bind to specific antigens in a lock-and-key fashion, forming an antigen-antibody complex. Antibodies are a type of protein molecule known as immunoglobulins. There are five classes of immunoglobulins: IgG, IgA, IgD, IgE, and IgM.

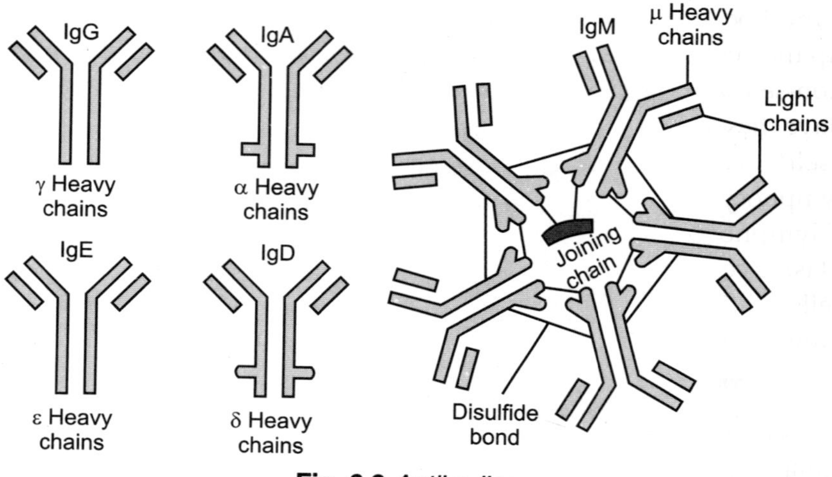

Fig. 6.2 *Antibodies.*

Antibodies are Y-shaped molecules composed of two identical long polypeptide (Heavy or H chains) and two identical short polypeptides (Light or L chains). Function of antibodies includes:

- Recognition and binding to antigens.
- Inactivation of the antigen.

A unique antigenic determinant recognizes and binds to a site on the antigen, leading to the destruction of the antigen in several ways. The ends of the Y are the antigen-combining site that is different for each antigen.

Helper T cells activate B cells that produce antibodies. Supressor T cells slow down and stop the immune response of B and T cells, serving as an off switch for the immune system. Cytotoxic (or killer) T cells destroy body cells infected with a virus or bacteria. Memory T cells remain in the body awaiting the reintroduction of the antigen.

A cell infected with a virus will display viral antigens on its plasma membrane. Killer T cells recognize the viral antigens and attach to that cell's plasma membrane. The T cells secrete proteins that punch holes in the infected cell's plasma membrane. The infected cell's cytoplasm leaks out, the cell dies, and is removed by phagocytes. Killer T cells may also bind to cells of transplanted organs.

The immune system is the major component of this defense. Lymphocytes, monocytes, lymph organs, and lymph vessels make up the system. The immune system is able to distinguish self from non-self. Antigens are chemicals on the surface of a cell. All cells have these. The immune system checks cells and identifies them as "self" or "non-self". Antibodies are proteins produced by certain lymphocytes in response to a specific antigen. B-lymphocytes and T-lymphocytes produce the antibodies. B-lymphocytes become plasma cells which then generate antibodies. T-lymphocytes attack cells which bear antigens they recognize. They also mediate the immune response.

THE IMMUNE SYSTEM AND MEMORY OF INFECTIONS

Secondary immunity, the resistance to certain diseases after having had them once, results from production of memory B and

T cells during the first exposure to the antigen. A second exposure to the same antigen produces a more massive and faster response. The secondary response is the basis for vaccination.

VACCINATION

Vaccination is a term derived from the Latin vacca (cow, after the cowpox material used by Edward Jenner in the first vaccination). A vaccine stimulates the antibody production and formation of memory cells without causing of the disease. Vaccines are made from killed pathogens or weakened strains that cause antibody production but not the disease. Recombinant DNA techniques can now be used to develop even safer vaccines.

The immune system can develop long-term immunity to some diseases. Man can use this to develop vaccines, which produce induced immunity. Active immunity develops after an illness or vaccine. Vaccines are weakened (or killed) viruses or bacteria that prompt the development of antibodies. Application of biotechnology allows development of vaccines that are the protein (antigen) which in no way can cause the disease. Passive immunity is the type of immunity when the individual is given antibodies to combat a specific disease. Passive immunity is short-lived.

BLOOD TYPES, RH, AND ANTIBODIES

There are 30 or more known antigens on the surface of blood cells. These form the blood groups or blood types. In a transfusion, the blood groups of the recipient and donor must be matched. If improperly matched, the recipient's immune system will produce antibodies causing clotting of the transfused cells, blocking circulation through capillaries and producing serious or even fatal results.

ABO blood types are determined by a gene, I (for isoagglutinin). There are three *alleles*, IA, IB and IO. Proteins produced by the A and B alleles are antigenic. Individuals with blood type A have the A antigen on the surface of their red blood cells, and antibodies to type B blood in their plasma. People with blood type B have the B antigen on their blood cells and antibodies against type A in their plasma. Individuals with type AB blood produce have antigens for A and B on their cell surfaces and no antibodies for either blood type A or B in their plasma. Type O individuals have no antigens on their red blood cells but antigens to both A and B are in their plasma.

People with type AB blood can receive blood of any type. Those with type O blood can donate to anyone. If a transfusion is made between an incompatible donor and recipient, the recipient's blood will undergo a cascade of events. Reaction of antigens on cells and antibodies in plasma will produce clumping that clogs capillaries, other cells burst, releasing hemoglobin that can crystallize in the kidney and lead to kidney failure.

The Rh (for the rhesus monkey in which it was discovered) blood group is made up of those Rh positive (Rh+) individuals who can make the Rh antigen and those Rh negative (Rh–) who cannot.

Hemolytic disease of the newborn (HDN) results from Rh incompatibility between an Rh– mother and Rh+ fetus. Rh+ blood from the fetus enters the mother's system during birth, causing her to produce Rh antibodies. The first child is usually not affected, however, subsequent Rh+ fetuses will cause a massive secondary reaction of the maternal immune system. To prevent HDN, Rh– mothers are given an Rh antibody during the first pregnancy with an Rh+ fetus and all subsequent Rh+ fetuses.

ORGAN TRANSPLANTS AND ANTIBODIES

Success of organ transplants and skin grafts requires a matching of histocompatibility antigens that occur on all cells in the body. Chromosome 6 contains a cluster of genes known as the *Human Leukocyte Antigen* complex (HLA) that are critical to the outcome of such procedures. The array of HLA alleles on either copy of our chromosome 6 is known as a *haplotype*.

The large number of alleles involved mean no two individuals, even in a family, will have the same identical haplotype. Identical twins have a 100% HLA match. The best matches are going to occur within a family. The preference order for transplants is identical twin > sibling > parent > unrelated donor. Chances of an unrelated donor matching the recipient range between 1 in

1,00,000-200,000. Matches across racial or ethnic lines are often more difficult. When HLA types are matched survival of transplanted organs dramatically increases.

ALLERGIES AND DISORDERS OF THE IMMUNE SYSTEM

The immune system can overreact, causing allergies or autoimmune diseases. Likewise, a suppressed, absent, or destroyed immune system can also result in disease and death.

Allergies result from immune system hypersensitivity to weak antigens that do not cause an immune response in most people. Allergens, substances that cause allergies, include dust, molds, pollen, cat dander, certain foods, and some medicines (such as penicillin). Up to 10% of the U.S. population suffer from at least one allergy.

After exposure to an allergen, some people make IgE antibodies as well as B and T memory cells. Subsequent exposure to the same allergen causes a massive secondary immune response that releases plenty of IgE antibodies. These bind to mast cells found usually in connective tissues surrounding blood vessels. Mast cells then release histamine, which starts the inflammatory response. In some individuals the histamine release causes life-threatening anaphylaxis or anaphylactic shock.

The immune system usually distinguishes "self" from "nonself". The immune system learns the difference between cells of the body and foreign invaders. Autoimmune diseases result when the immune system attacks and destroys cells and tissues of the body. Juvenile diabetes, Grave's disease, Multiple sclerosis, Systemic lupus erythematosus, and Rheumatoid arthritis are some of the autoimmune diseases.

Myasthenia gravis (MG) is a muscle weakness caused by destruction of muscle-nerve connections. Multiple sclerosis (MS) is caused by antibodies attacking the myelin of nerve cells. Systemic lupus erythematosis (SLE) has the person forming a series of antibodies to their own tissues, such as kidneys (the leading cause of death in SLE patients) and the DNA in their own cellular nuclei. In systemic lupus erythematosus (SLE), the immune system attacks connective tissues and major organs of the body. Rheumatoid arthritis; sufferers have damage to their joints. Some evidence supports Type I diabetes as an auto immune disease. Juvenile diabetes results from the destruction of insulin-producing cells in the pancreas.

Immunodeficiency diseases result from the lack or failure of one or more parts of the immune system. Affected individuals are susceptible to diseases that normally would not bother most people. Genetic disorders, Hodgkin's disease, cancer chemotherapy, and radiation therapy can cause immuno-deficiency diseases.

Severe Combined Immunodeficiency (SCID) results from a complete absence of the cell-mediated and antibody-mediated immune responses. Affected individuals suffer from a series of seemingly minor infections and usually die at an early age. A small group suffering from adenosine deaminase (ADA) deficiency, a type of SCID, are undergoing gene therapy to provide them with normal copies of the defective gene.

Acquired Immunodeficiency Syndrome (AIDS) is currently receiving the most attention among the immunodeficiency diseases. AIDS is a collection of disorders resulting from the destruction of T cells by the Human Immunodeficiency Virus (HIV), a retrovirus. When HIV replicates in the human T cells, it buds from the T cell plasma membrane encased in a coat derived from the T cell plasma membrane. HIV selectively infects and kills T4 helper cells. The viral RNA is converted into DNA by the enzyme reverse transcriptase; this DNA can become incorporated into a human chromosome for months or years.

When the infected T cell is needed in the immune response, the viral genes are activated and the virus replicates, killing the infected cell and producing a new round on T4 cell infection. Gradually, the number of T4 cells, the master on switch for the immune system, decline. The immune response grows less powerful, eventually failing. Premature death results from a series of rare diseases (such as fungal pneumonia and Kaposi's sarcoma, a rare cancer) that overwhelm the body and its compromised immune system.

STUDY QUESTIONS

1. What is blood? Explain the main components of blood.
2. How blood circulate from the heart to the lungs?
3. Explain the diffrent types of blood groups.
4. Write short note on Hemostasis.

■■■

7 CHAPTER

CARDIOVASCULAR SYSTEM

INTRODUCTION

The heart and circulatory system (also called the *cardiovascular system*) make up the network that delivers blood to the body's tissues. With each heartbeat, blood is sent throughout our bodies, carrying oxygen and nutrients to all of our cells. Each day, 2,000 gallons (more than 7,570 liters) of blood travel many times through about 60,000 miles (96,560 kilometers) of blood vessels that branch and cross, linking the cells of our organs and body parts. From the hard-working heart, to our thickest arteries, to capillaries so thin that they can only be seen through a microscope, the cardiovascular system is our body's lifeline.

The circulatory system works closely with other systems in our bodies. It supplies oxygen and nutrients to our bodies by working with the respiratory system. At the same time, the circulatory system helps carry waste and carbon dioxide out of the body. Hormones – produced by the endocrine system – are also transported through the blood in our circulatory system. As the body's chemical messengers, hormones transfer information and instructions from one set of cells to another.

The circulatory system is composed of the heart and blood vessels, including *arteries, veins,* and *capillaries*. Human body actually have *two* circulatory systems:

1. THE PULMONARY CIRCULATION

In the *pulmonary circulation,* blood low in oxygen but high in carbon dioxide is pumped out of the right ventricle into the pulmonary artery, which branches off in two directions. The right branch goes to the right lung, and *vice versa*. In the lungs, the branches divide further into capillaries. Blood flows more slowly through these tiny vessels, allowing time for gases to be exchanged between the capillary walls and the millions of *alveoli,* the tiny air sacs in the lung. During the process called oxygenation, oxygen is taken up by the bloodstream. Oxygen locks onto a molecule called hemoglobin in the red blood cells. The newly oxygenated blood leaves the lungs through the pulmonary veins and heads back to the heart. It enters the heart in the left atrium, then fills the left ventricle so it can be pumped into the systemic circulation.

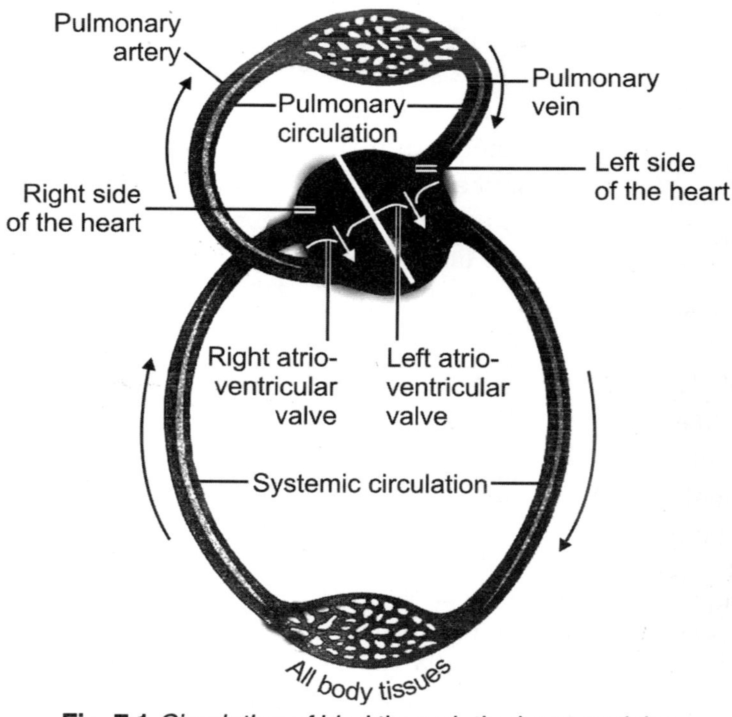

Fig. 7.1 *Circulation of blod through the heart and the pulmonary and systemic circulation.*

2. THE SYSTEMIC CIRCULATION

In the *systemic circulation,* blood travels out of the left ventricle, to the aorta, to every organ and tissue in the body, and then back to the right atrium. The arteries, capillaries, and veins of the systemic circulatory system are the channels through which this long journey takes place. Once in the arteries, blood flows to smaller arterioles and then to capillaries. While in the capillaries, the bloodstream delivers oxygen and nutrients to the body's cells and picks up waste materials. Blood then goes back through the capillaries into venules, and then to larger veins until it reaches the vena cavae. Blood from the head and arms returns to the heart through the superior vena cava, and blood from the lower parts of the body returns through the inferior vena cava. Both vena cavae deliver this oxygen-depleted blood into the right atrium. From here the blood exits to fill the right ventricle, ready to be pumped into the pulmonary circulation for more oxygen.

HEART

The heart is the key organ in the circulatory system. The heart weighs between 7 and 15 ounces (200 to 425 grams) and is a little larger than the size of your fist. By the end of a long life, a person's heart may have beat (expanded and contracted) more than 3.5 billion times. In fact, each day, the average heart beats 1,00,000 times, pumping about 2,000 gallons (7,571 litres) of blood. Human heart is located between your lungs in the middle of your chest, behind and slightly to the left of your breastbone (sternum). A double-layered membrane called the *pericardium* surrounds your heart like a sac. The outer layer of the pericardium surrounds the roots of your heart's major blood vessels and is attached by ligaments to your spinal column, diaphragm, and other parts of your body. The inner layer of the pericardium is attached to the heart muscle. A coating of fluid separates the two layers of membrane, letting the heart move as it beats, yet still be attached to your body.

The heart gets messages from the body that tell it when to pump more or less blood depending on a person's needs. When we are sleeping, it pumps just enough to provide for the lower amounts of oxygen needed by our bodies at rest. When we are exercising or frightened, the heart pumps faster to get more oxygen to our bodies.

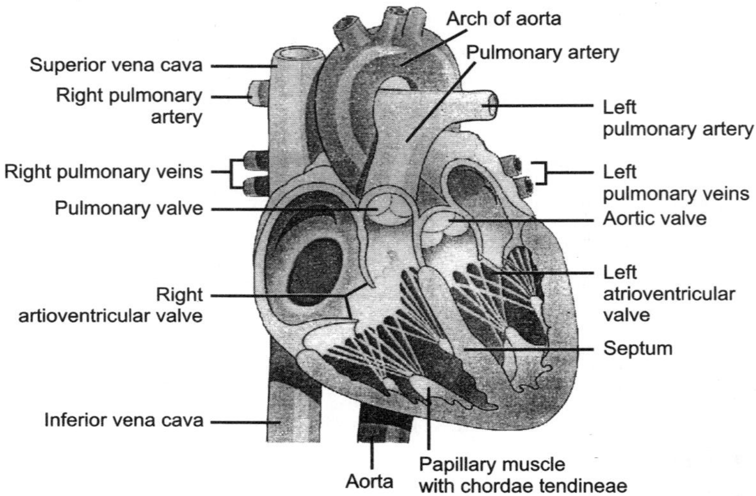

Fig. 7.2 *The interior of heart.*

STRUCTURE OF HEART

The heart wall is divided into three layers:

1. EPICARDIUM OR PERICARDIUM

The epicardium is the outer layer of the wall of the heart. It is composed of connective tissue covered by the epithelium. The epicardium is also known as the visceral pericardium. The pericardium is the fluid filled sac that surrounds the heart and the proximal ends of the aorta, vena cava, and the pulmonary artery. It provides an outer protective layer for the heart. The pericardium has several functions:

- Keeps the heart contained in the chest cavity.
- Prevents the heart from overexpanding when blood volume increases.
- Limits heart motion.

Pericardial Membranes

The pericardium is divided into three layers:

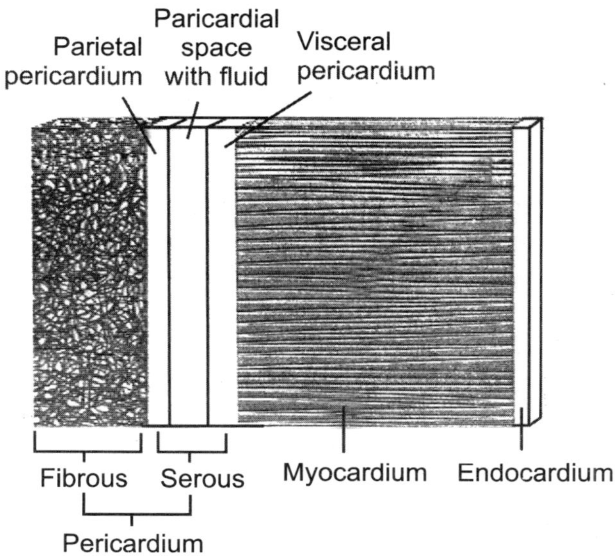

Fig. 7.3 *Layers of heart wall.*

- *Fibrous Pericardium:* The outer fibrous sac that covers the heart.
- *Parietal Pericardium:* Lies between the visceral pericardium and the fibrous pericardium. It provides an additional layer of insulation for the heart.
- *Visceral Pericardium:* Also called the epicardium, this is the outer layer of the wall of the heart.

Pericardial Cavity

The pericardial cavity lies between the visceral pericardium and the parietal pericardium.

2. MYOCARDIUM

Myocardium is the muscular middle layer of the wall of the heart. It is composed of spontaneously contracting cardiac muscle fibers which allow the heart to contract. It stimulates heart contractions to pump blood from the ventricles and relaxes the heart to allow the artria to receive blood.

3. ENDOCARDIUM

The endocardium is the inner layer of the heart. It consists of epithelial tissue and connective tissue. Its functions are:

- Lines the inner cavities of the heart, covers heart valves and is continuous with the inner lining of blood vessels.
- *Purkinje fibers* are located in the endocardium. They participate in the contraction of the heart muscle. Purkinje fibers are fiber branches that extend from the atrioventricular bundle. It relays cardiac impulses to the ventricular cells causing the ventricles to contract.

ANATOMY OF HEART

The heart has four chambers that are enclosed by thick, muscular walls. It lies between the lungs and just to the left of the middle of the chest cavity. The bottom part of the heart is divided into two chambers called the right and left ventricles, which pump blood out of the heart. A wall called the interventricular septum divides the ventricles.

The upper part of the heart is made up of the other two chambers of the heart, called the *right* and *left atria*. The right and left atria receive the blood entering the heart. A wall called the interatrial septum divides the atria, and they are separated from the ventricles by the *atrioventricular valve*. The tricuspid valve separates the *right atrium* from the *right ventricle,* and the mitral valve separates the left atrium and the left ventricle.

Two other heart valves separate the ventricles and the large blood vessels that carry blood leaving the heart. These valves are called the *pulmonic valve,* which separates the right ventricle from the pulmonary artery leading to the lungs, and the *aortic valve,* which separates the left ventricle from the aorta, the body's largest blood vessel.

THE HEART VALVES

Four types of valves regulate blood flow through your heart:

- The *tricuspid valve* regulates blood flow between the right atrium and right ventricle.
- The *pulmonary valve* controls blood flow from the right ventricle into the pulmonary arteries, which carry blood to your lungs to pick up oxygen.

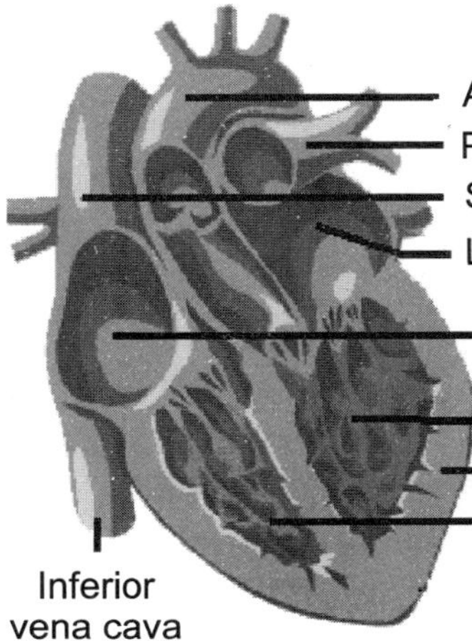

Fig. 7.4 *The heart valves.*

- The *mitral valve* lets oxygen-rich blood from your lungs pass from the left atrium into the left ventricle.
- The *aortic valve* opens the way for oxygen-rich blood to pass from the left ventricle into the aorta, your body's largest artery, where it is delivered to the rest of your body.

THE CONDUCTION SYSTEM

A unique electrical system in the heart causes it to beat in its regular rhythm. The heart's electrical system controls all the events that occur when your heart pumps blood. The electrical system also is called the *cardiac conduction system*. It is made up of three main parts:

- The ***sinoatrial* (SA) node** located in the right atrium of heart. The *sinoatrial* or *SA node.* The SA node is sometimes called the heart's *"natural pacemaker."* An electrical impulse from this natural pacemaker travels through the muscle fibers of the atria and ventricles, causing them to contract a small area of tissue in the wall of the right atrium, sends out an electrical signal to start the contracting of the heart muscle.
- The ***atrioventricular (AV)*** node located on the interatrial septum close to the tricuspid valve. These electrical impulses cause the atria to contract first; they then travel down to the *atrioventricular* or *AV node,* which acts as a kind of relay station.

From here the electrical signal travels through the right and left ventricles, causing them to contract and force blood out into the major arteries.

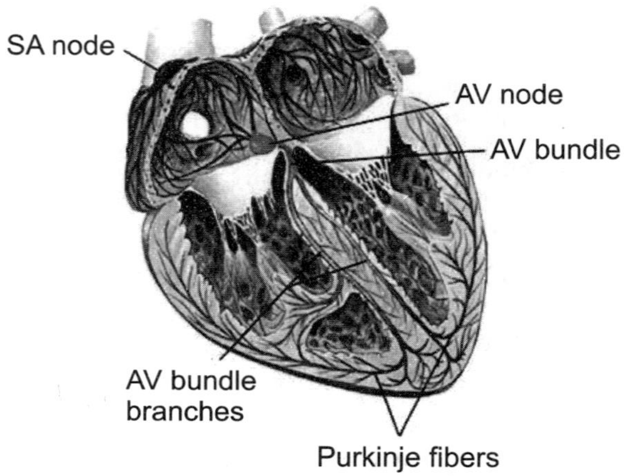

Fig. 7.5 *Cardiac conduction system of heart.*

- The ***His-Purkinje system*** located along the walls of heart's ventricles. This is a mass of specialised fibres from the AV node. The AV bundle crosses the fibrous ring that separate atria and ventricles then, at the upper end of the ventricular septum, it divides into *right and left bundle branches.*

The AV bundle, bundle branches and Purkinje fibres convey electrical impulses from AV node to the apex of themyocardium where the wave of ventricular contraction begins, then sweeps upwards and outwards, pumping blood into the pulmonary artery and aorta.

THE HEARTBEAT

A heartbeat is a two-part pumping action that takes about a second. As blood collects in the upper chambers (the right and left atria), the heart's natural pacemaker (the *SA node*) sends out an electrical signal that causes the atria to contract. This contraction pushes blood through the tricuspid and mitral valves into the resting lower chambers (the right and left ventricles). This part of the two-part pumping phase (the longer of the two) is called ***diastole***.

The second part of the pumping phase begins when the ventricles are full of blood. The electrical signals from the SA node travel along a pathway of cells to the ventricles, causing them to contract. This is called ***systole***. As the ***tricuspid*** and ***mitral valves*** shut tight to prevent a back flow of blood, the pulmonary and aortic valves are pushed open. While blood is pushed from the right ventricle into the lungs to pick up oxygen, oxygen-rich blood flows from the left ventricle to the heart and other parts of the body.

After blood moves into the pulmonary artery and the aorta, the ventricles relax, and the pulmonary and aortic valves close. The lower pressure in the ventricles causes the tricuspid and mitral valves to open, and the cycle begins again. This series of contractions is repeated over and over again, increasing during times of exertion and decreasing while you are at rest. The heart normally beats about 60 to 80 times a minute when you are at rest, but this can vary. As you get older, your resting heart rate rises. Also, it is usually lower in people who are physically fit.

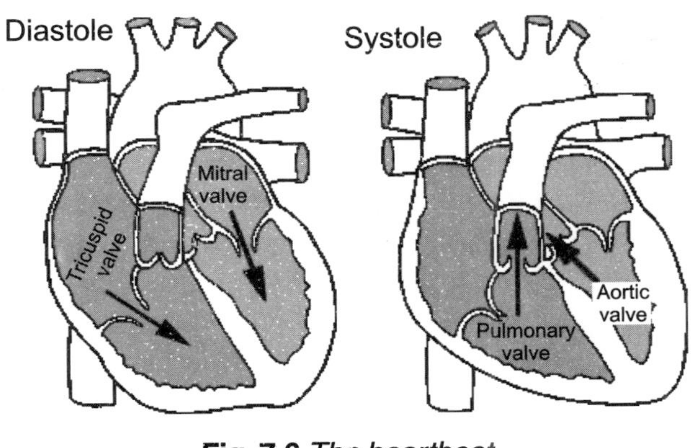

Fig. 7.6 *The heartbeat.*

Your heart does not work alone, though. Your brain tracks the conditions around you—climate, stress, and level of physical activity—and adjusts your cardiovascular system to meet those needs. The human heart is a muscle designed to remain strong and reliable for a hundred years or longer. By reducing your risk factors for cardiovascular disease, you may help your heart stay healthy longer.

HEART SOUND "LUB-DUB"

A healthy heart makes a "lub-dub" sound with each beat. One complete heartbeat makes up a *cardiac cycle,* which consists of two phases. In the first phase, the ventricles contract (this is called *systole,* sending blood into the pulmonary and systemic circulation. To prevent the flow of blood backwards into the atria during systole, the atrioventricular valves close, creating the first ("***lub***") sound.

When the ventricles finish contracting, the aortic and pulmonic valves close to prevent blood from flowing back into the ventricles. This is what creates the second sound (the "***dub***"). Then the ventricles relax (this is called *diastole*) and fill with blood from the atria, which makes up the second phase of the *cardiac cycle.*

The *atrioventricular* and *semilunar valves* prevent backflow as the heart contracts. Defects in any of these that allow some blood to leak backwards cause distinctive sounds through a *stethoscope,* thus are called *heart murmurs.*

A baby's heart starts beating when it is about four weeks old (the mother's period is two weeks late, and she's just beginning to suspect she might be pregnant). A newborn's heart rate is around 135 to 140 beats per minute (bpm). By age 15 to 30, the rate decreases to about 65-75 bpm, then speeds up slightly as the person ages. The pulse is a wave of contraction of the artery walls (which roughly corresponds to the heart rate) as blood is forced into the arteries. Pulse is usually measured using the radial artery (the one along the radius). To find your pulse, rest your right arm in the palm of your left hand. Curl the fingers of your left hand up around the thumb side of your right wrist. Place several fingers of your left hand along and just to the outside (thumb side) of the tendon that runs along your wrist. With gentle pressure, you should be able to feel your pulse.

An ***electrocardiogram (ECG)*** measures changes in electrical potential across the heart, and can detect the contraction pulses that pass over the surface of the heart. There are three slow, negative changes, known as P, R, and T as shown in Figure 7.7. Positive deflections are the Q and S waves. The P wave represents the contraction impulse of the atria, the T wave the ventricular contraction. ECGs are useful in diagnosing heart abnormalities.

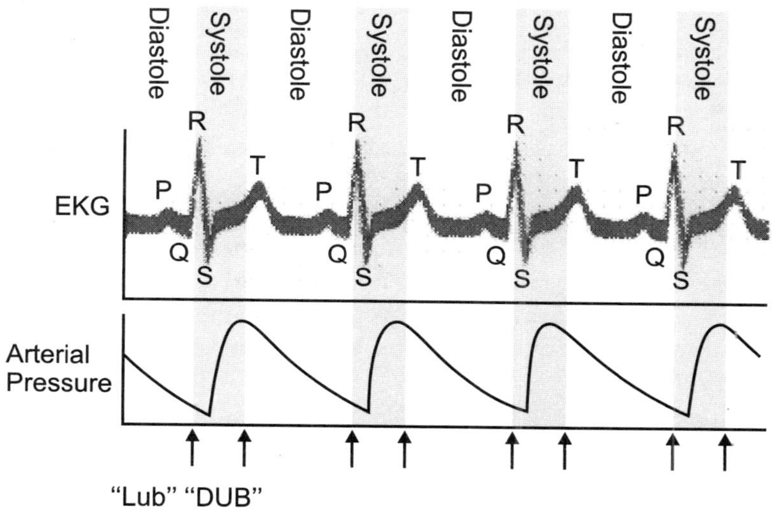

Fig. 7.7 *The EKG.*

BLOOD VESSELS

Blood vessels carrying blood away from the heart are called ***arteries***. They are the thickest blood vessels, with muscular walls that contract to keep the blood moving away from the heart and through the body. In the systemic circulation, oxygen-rich blood is pumped from the heart into the aorta. This huge artery curves up and back from the left ventricle, then heads down in front of the spinal column into the abdomen. Two *coronary arteries* branch off at the beginning of the aorta and divide into a network of smaller arteries that provide oxygen and nourishment to the muscles of the heart.

Unlike the aorta, the body's other main artery, the *pulmonary artery*, carries oxygen-poor blood. From the right ventricle, the pulmonary artery divides into right and left branches, on the way to the lungs where blood picks up oxygen. Arterial walls have three layers:

- The ***endothelium*** is on the inside and provides a smooth lining for blood to flow over as it moves through the artery.

- The ***media*** is the middle part of the artery, made up of a layer of muscle and elastic tissue.
- The ***adventitia*** is the tough covering that protects the outside of the artery.

As they get farther from the heart, the arteries branch out into *arterioles*, which are smaller and less flexible.

Blood vessels that carry blood back to the heart are called ***veins***. They are not as muscular as arteries, but they contain valves that prevent blood from flowing backward. Veins have the same three layers that arteries do, but they are thinner and less flexible. The two largest veins are the *superior* and *inferior vena cavae.* The terms superior and inferior do not mean that one vein is better than the other, but that they are located above (superior) and below (inferior) the heart.

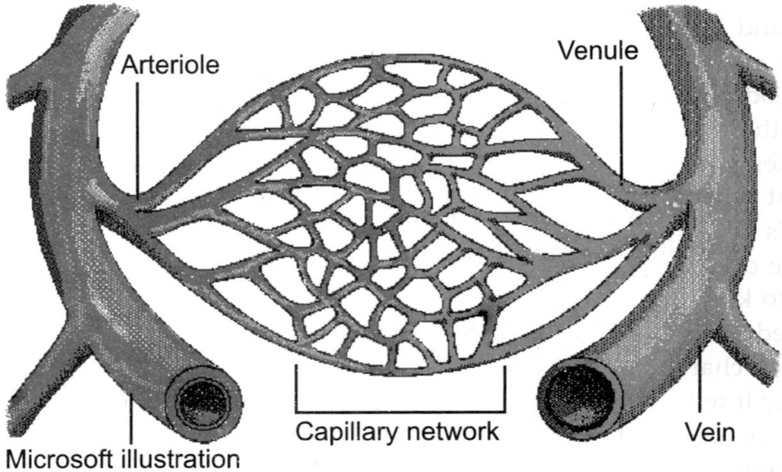

Fig. 7.8 *Blood vessel.*

A network of tiny ***capillaries*** connects the arteries and veins. Even though they are tiny, the capillaries are one of the most important parts of the circulatory system because it is through them that nutrients and oxygen are delivered to the cells. In addition, waste products such as carbon dioxide are also removed by the capillaries.

BLOOD PRESSURE

Blood pressure is maximum during systole, when the heart is pushing, and minimum during diastole, when the heart is relaxed.

In a living person, the blood pressure doesn't go to zero because the thick, elastic artery walls exert pressure on the blood. A sphygmomanometer is the instrument used to determine BP. The artery used to determine BP is the brachial artery, which runs down the upper arm, splitting into the radial and ulnar arteries near the elbow. The cuff of the sphygmomanometer is wrapped around the arm just above the elbow and pumped up to block off blood flow (the pressure exerted by the cuff is higher than the systolic pressure). The pressure in the cuff is gradually decreased, and when it equals the person's systolic pressure, the heart can force blood under the cuff, and a sound is heard as the pulses of blood surge under the cuff. As the pressure in the cuff is lowered, when it equals the diastolic pressure, blood can flow freely, so the sound disappears (not enough pressure is exerted by cuff to restrict blood flow). Thus, by listening for the first sound, and when the sound becomes faint, while watching the pressure indicator on the sphygomomanometer, it is possible to determine someone's blood pressure. Typically, when you go to the doctor's office, one of the first things that is done to you is that someone (a nurse?) takes your blood pressure. I have frequently had the experience that when I ask what the results were, I initially get the answer "It's OK." Here's a tip: you, not they, are in charge of your health. The only way you can educate yourself to how your body works is to keep re-asking the question until you get a real answer. You need to know the actual numbers to be able to evaluate if things have changed or are good or bad. Be persistent and eventually they'll tell you what your BP is.

A neonate's BP is around 80/45 mm Hg meaning that the systolic pressure is equivalent to air pressure that will support a column of mercury 80 millimeters high in a barometer, and the diastolic is equivalent to the air pressure that will support a column of mercury 45 millimeters high. For adults in their 20s, 120/80 mm Hg is considered average for a male and 115/75 mm Hg for a female, thus the accepted average is said to be 120/80 mm Hg. With age, the arteries become less elastic (due in part to undesirable lipid deposits in their walls), so the BP rises. Hypertension is when the BP is too high. There are two ways this could happen: either the systolic pressure is greater than 145 to 160 mm Hg and/or the diastolic is greater than 90 to 100. Major contributing factors include the amounts of salt, cholesterol (and other lipids), and sugar in one's diet and the amount of exercise the person gets. Frequently, diuretics are prescribed to try to remove water from the person's blood, thus lowering the blood volume and hopefully thereby, the BP. However, many diuretics also remove potassium (and other beneficial minerals?) from the person's system, and if serum potassium levels are not carefully monitored and go to low, this could cause a heart attack!

THE LYMPHATIC SYSTEM

The lymphatic system is composed of lymph vessels, lymph nodes, and organs. The functions of this system include the absorbtion of excess fluid and its return to the blood stream, absorption of fat (in the villi of the small intestine) and the immune system function.

Lymph vessels are closely associated with the circulatory system vessels. Larger lymph vessels are similar to veins. Lymph capillaries are scatted throughout the body. Contraction of skeletal muscle causes movement of the lymph fluid through valves.

Lymph organs include the *bone marrow, lymph nodes, spleen,* and *thymus*. Bone marrow contains tissue that produces lymphocytes. B-lymphocytes (B-cells) mature in the bone marrow. T-lymphocytes (T-cells) mature in the thymus gland. Other blood cells such as monocytes and leukocytes are produced in the bone marrow. *Lymph nodes* are areas of concentrated lymphocytes and macrophages along the lymphatic veins. The spleen is similar to the lymph node except that it is larger and filled with blood. The spleen serves as a reservoir for blood, and filters or purifies the blood and lymph fluid that flows through it. If the spleen is damaged or removed, the individual is more susceptible to infections. The thymus secretes a hormone, thymosin, that causes pre-T-ells to mature (in the thymus) into T-cells.

THE VASCULAR SYSTEM

Two main routes for circulation are the *pulmonary* (to and from the lungs) and the *systemic* (to and from the body). Pulmonary arteries carry blood from the heart to the lungs. In the lungs gas exchange occurs. Pulmonary veins carry blood from lungs to heart. The aorta is the main artery of systemic circuit.

The vena cavae are the main veins of the systemic circuit. Coronary arteries deliver oxygenated blood, food, etc. to the heart.

Animals often have a portal system, which begins and ends in capillaries, such as between the digestive tract and the liver.

Fish pump blood from the heart to their gills, where gas exchange occurs, and then on to the rest of the body. Mammals pump blood to the lungs for gas exchange, then back to the heart for pumping out to the systemic circulation. Blood flows in only one direction.

PULSE

In medicine, a person's pulse is the throbbing of their arteries as an effect of the heart beat. When the heart contracts, blood is ejected into the aorta and the aorta stretches. At this point, the wave of distention (pulse wave) is pronounced but relatively slow-moving (3–6 m/s). As it travels towards the peripheral blood vessels, it gradually diminishes and becomes faster. In the large arterial branches, its velocity is 7–10 m/s; in the small arteries, it is 15–35 m/s. The pressure pulse is transmitted fifteen or more times more rapidly than the blood flow.

Pulse is also used to denote the frequency of the heart beat, usually measured in beats per minute. In most people, the pulse is an accurate measure of heart rate. Under certain circumstances, including *arrhythmias*, some of the heart beats are ineffective, and the aorta is not stretched enough to create a palpable pressure wave.

The pulse is too irregular and the heart rate can be (much) higher than the pulse rate. In this case, the heart rate should be determined by auscultation of the heart apex, in which case it is not the pulse. The pulse deficit (difference between heart beats and pulsations at the periphery) should be determined by simultaneous palpation at the radial artery and auscultation at the heart apex.

A normal pulse rate for a healthy adult, while resting, can range from 60 to 100 beats per minute (bpm), although well conditioned athletes may have a healthy pulse rate lower than 60 bpm. Bradycardia occurs when the pulse rate is below 60 per minute, whereas tachycardia occurs when the rate is above 100 bpm.

During sleep, this can drop to as low as 40 bpm; during strenuous exercise, it can rise as high as 150–200 bpm. Generally, pulse rates are higher in infants and young children. The resting heart rate for an infant is usually close to an adult's pulse rate during strenuous exercise (average 110 bpm for an infant).

Pulses are manually palpated with fingers. When palpating the carotid artery, the femoral artery or the brachial artery, the thumb may be used.

However, the thumb has its own pulse which can interfere with detecting the patient's pulse at other points, where two or three fingers should be used. Fingers or thumb must be placed near an artery and pressed gently against a firm structure, usually a bone, in order to feel the pulse.

STUDY QUESTIONS

1. Explain the structure of human heart. Describe the physiology of heartbeat.
2. What do you mean by blood vessels? Explain the types of blood vessels.
3. Explain in detailed the process of the circulation of blood.
3. Write short notes on:
   (a) S-A Node;
   (b) A-V Node;
   (c) Bundle of 'His'; and
   (d) ECG.

8

CHAPTER

The Respiratory System

INTRODUCTION

The Respiratory System is crucial to every human being. Without it, we would cease to live outside of the womb. Let us begin by taking a look at the structure of the respiratory system and how vital it is to life. During inhalation or exhalation air is pulled towards or away from the lungs, by several cavities, tubes, and openings. The organs of the respiratory system make sure that oxygen enters our bodies and carbon dioxide leaves our bodies. The respiratory tract is the path of air from the nose to the lungs. It is divided into two sections:

Upper Respiratory Tract are: the Nostrils, Nasal Cavities, Pharynx, Epiglottis, and the Larynx.

Lower Respiratory Tract consists of the Trachea, Bronchi, Bronchioles, and the Lungs. As air moves along the respiratory tract it is warmed, moistened and filtered.

STRUCTURE OF THE HUMAN RESPIRATORY SYSTEM

THE NOSE

Usually air will enter the respiratory system through the nostrils. The nostrils then lead to open spaces in the nose called the nasal passages. The nasal passages serve as a moistener, a filter, and to warm-up the air before it reaches the lungs. The hairs existing within the nostrils prevents various foreign particles from entering. Different air passageways and the nasal passages are covered with a mucous membrane. Many of the cells which produce the cells that make up the membrane contain cilia. Others secrete a type a sticky fluid called mucus. The mucus and cilia collect dust, bacteria, and other particles in the air. The mucus also helps in moistening the air. Under the mucous membrane there are a large number of capillaries. The blood within these capillaries helps to warm the air as it passes through the nose. The nose serves three purposes. It warms, filters, and moistens the air before it reaches the lungs. You will obviously lose these special advantages if you breath through your mouth.

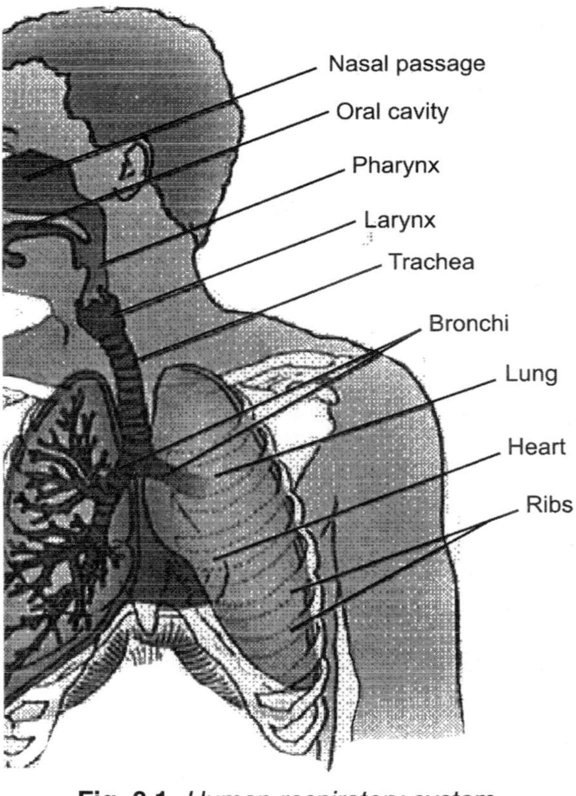

Fig. 8.1. *Human respiratory system.*

PHARYNX AND LARYNX

Air travels from the nasal passages to the pharynx, or more commonly known as the throat. When the air leaves the pharynx it passes into the larynx, or the voice box. The voice box is constructed mainly of crtilage, which is a flexible connective tissue. The vocal chords are two pairs of membranes that are stretched across the inside of the larynx. As the air is exspired, the vocal chords vibrate. Humans can control the vibrations of the vocal chords, which enables us to make sounds. Food and liquids are blocked from entering the opening of the larynx by the epiglottis to prvent people from choking during swallowing.

TRACHEA

The larynx goes directly into the trachea or the windpipe. The trachea is a tube approximately 12 centimeters in length and 2.5 centimeters wide. The trachea is kept open by rings of cartilage within its walls. Similar to the nasal passages, the trachea is covered with a ciliated mucous membrane. Usually the cilia move mucus and trapped foreign matter to the pharynx. After that, they leave the air passages and are normally swallowed. The respiratory system cannot deal with tabacco smoke very keenly. Smoking stops the cilia from moving. Just one cigarette slows their motion for about 20 minutes. The tabacco smoke increases the amount of mucus in the air passages. When smokers cough, their body is attempting to dispose of the extra mucus.

BRONCHI

Around the center of the chest, the trachea divides into two cartilage-ringed tubes called bronchi. Also, this section of the respiratory system is lined with ciliated cells. The bronchi enter the lungs and spread into a tree-like fashion into smaller tubes called bronchial tubes.

BRONCHIOLES

The bronchial tubes divide and then subdivide. By doing this their walls become thinner and have less and less cartilage. Eventually, they become a tiny group of tubes called bronchioles.

ALVEOLI

Each bronchiole ends in a tiny air chamber that looks like a bunch of grapes. Each chamber contains many cup-shaped cavities known as alveoli. The walls of the alveoli, which are only about one cell thick, are the respiratory surface. They are thin, moist, and are surrounded by several numbers of capillaries. The exchange of oxygen and carbon-dioxide between blood and air occurs through these walls.

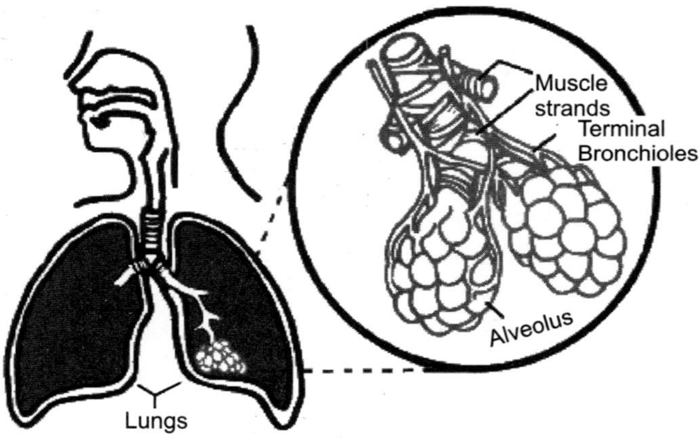

Fig. 8.2. *Alveoli.*

The estimation is that lungs contain about 300 million alveoli. Their total surface area would be about 70 square meters. That is 40 times the surface area of the skin. Smoking makes it difficult for oxygen to be taken through the alveoli. When the cigarette smoke is inhaled, about one-third of the particles will remain within the alveoli. There are too many particles from smoking or from other sources of air pollution which can damage the walls in the alveoli. This causes a certain tissue to form. This tissue reduces the working area of the respiratory surface and leads to the disease called *emphysema*.

INSPIRATION

Inspiration is initiated by contraction of the diaphragm and in some cases the intercostals muscles when they receive nervous impulses. During normal quiet breathing, the phrenic nerves stimulate the diaphragm to contract and move downward into the abdomen. This downward movement of the diaphragm enlarges the thorax. When necessary, the intercostal muscles also increase the thorax by contacting and drawing the ribs upward and outward.

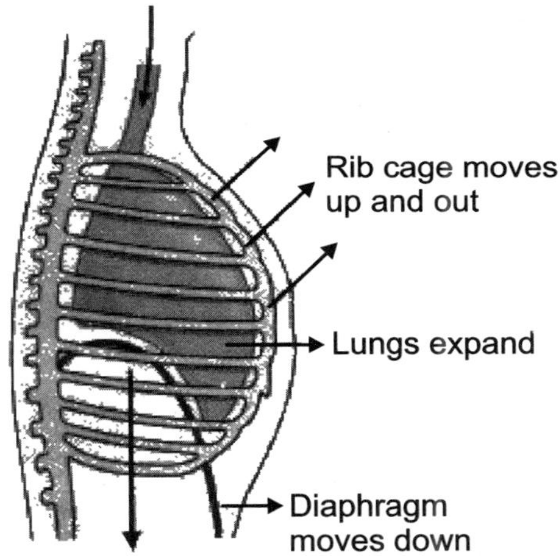

Fig. 8.3. *Inspiration.*

The active increase of the thorax changes the stability set up in a resting lung. As the thoracic wall moves away from lung which increases the space between the thoracic wall and lung and decreases the pressure in the intrapleural cavity. This decrease in pressure causes the pressure in the alveoli to become greater than the elastic recoil that is inherent in lung tissue. Thus, when contraction of the diaphragm and the intercostal muscles actively increase the size of the thorax, the lungs are passively forced to expand. This expansion increases the size of the alveoli which decreases pressure in the alveoli.

EXPIRATION

During quiet breathing, expiration is normally a passive process and does not require muscles to work. When the lungs are stretched and expanded, stretchy receptors within the alveoli send inhibitory nerve impulses to the medulla oblongata, causing it to stop sending signals to the rib cage and diaphragm to relax and rise. This elastic recoil causes the lungs and chest cavity to shrink and increase the air pressure within the lungs. This increased positive air pressure pushes the air out of the lungs. Expiration happens as the diaphragm relaxes. Although the respiratory system is primarily under involuntary control, and regulated by the medulla oblongata, we have some voluntary control over it also. This is due to the higher brain function of the cerebral cortex.

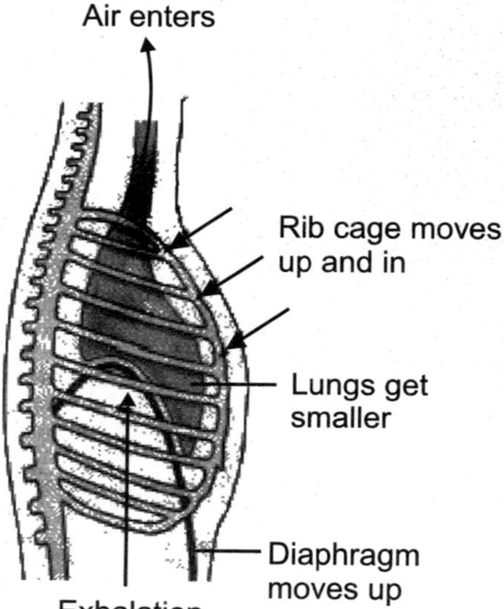

Fig. 8.4. *Expiration.*

When under physical or emotional stress, more frequent and deep breathing is needed, and both inspiration and expiration will work as active processes. Additional muscles in the rib cage forcefully contract and push more air out of the lungs. (This cannot occur during rest.) In addition to deeper breathing, when coughing or sneezing we exhale forcibly. Our abdominal muscles will contract suddenly (when there is an urge to cough or sneeze), raising the abdominal pressure. The rapid increase in pressure pushes the relaxed diaphragm up against the pleural cavity. This causes air to be forced out of the lungs. Another function of the respiratory system is to sing and to speak. Our exert of conscious control over our breathing is what allows us to speak and sing.

CELLULAR RESPIRATION

First, the oxygen must diffuse from the alveolus into the capillaries. It is able to do this because the capillaries are permeable to oxygen. After it is in the capillary, about 5% will be dissolved in the blood plasma. The other oxygen will bind to red blood cells. The red blood cells contain hemoglobin that carries oxygen. Blood with hemoglobin is able to transport 26 times more oxygen than plasma without hemoglobin. Our bodies would have to work much harder pumping more blood to supply our cells with oxygen without the help of hemoglobin. Once it diffuses by osmosis it combines with the hemoglobin to form oxyhemoglobin.

Now the blood carrying oxygen is pumped through the heart to the rest of the body. Oxygen will travel in the blood into arteries, arterioles, and eventually capillaries where it will be very close to body cells. Now with different conditions in temperature and pH (warmer and more acidic than in the lungs), and with pressure being exerted on the cells, the hemoglobin will give up the oxygen where it will diffuse to the cells to be used for cellular respiration, also called aerobic respiration. Cellular respiration is the process of moving energy from one chemical form (glucose) into another (ATP), since all cells use ATP for all metabolic reactions.

It is in the mitochondria of the cells where oxygen is actually consumed and carbon-dioxide produced. Oxygen is produced as it combines with hydrogen ions to form water at the end of the electron transport chain. As cells take apart the carbon molecules from glucose, these get released as carbon dioxide. Each body cell releases carbon dioxide into nearby capillaries by diffusion, because the level of carbon dioxide is higher in the body cells than in the blood. In the capillaries, some of the carbon-dioxide is dissolved in plasma and some is taken by the hemoglobin, but most enters the red blood cells where it binds with water to form carbonic acid. It travels to the capillaries surrounding the lung where a water molecule leaves, causing it to turn-back into carbon-dioxide. It then enters the lungs where it is exhaled into the atmosphere.

BREATHING AND LUNG MECHANICS

Ventilation is the exchange of air between the external environment and the alveoli. Air moves by bulk flow from an area of high pressure to low pressure. All pressures in the respiratory system are relative to atmospheric pressure (760 mmHg at sea level). Air will move in or out of the lungs depending on the pressure in the alveoli. The body changes the or pressure in the alveoli by changing the volume of the lungs. As volume increases pressure decreases and as volume decreases pressure increases. There are two phases of ventilation: inspiration and expiration. During each phase the body changes the lung dimensions to produce a flow of air either in or out of the lungs.

The body is able to change the dimensions of the lungs because of the relationship of the lungs to the thoracic wall. Each lung is completely enclosed in a sac called the pleural sac.

The parietal pleura is attached to the thoracic wall where as the visceral pleura is attached to the lung itself. In-between these two membranes is a thin layer of intrapleural fluid. The intrapleural fluid completely surrounds the lungs and lubricates the two surfaces so that they can slide across each other. Changing the pressure of this fluid also allows the lungs and the thoracic wall to move together during normal breathing. Much the way two glass slides with water in-between them are difficult to pull apart, such is the relationship of the lungs to the thoracic wall.

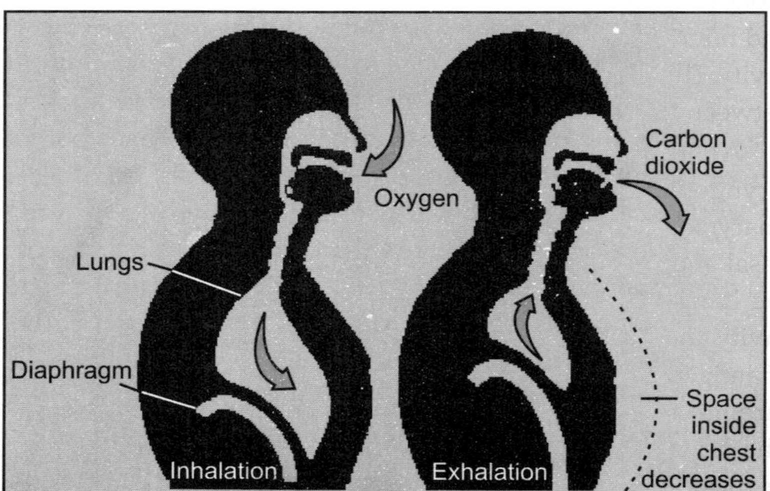

Fig. 8.5 *Breathing and lung mechanism.*

The rhythm of ventilation is also controlled by the "Respiratory Center" which is located largely in the medulla oblongata of the brain stem. This is part of the autonomic system and as such is not controlled voluntarily (one can increase or decrease breathing rate voluntarily, but that involves a different part of the brain). While resting, the respiratory center sends out action potentials that travel along the phrenic nerves into the diaphragm and the external intercostal muscles of the rib cage, causing inhalation. Relaxed exhalation occurs between impulses when the muscles relax. Normal adults have a breathing rate of 12-20 respirations per minute.

The Pathway of Air

When one breathes air in at sea level, the inhalation is composed of different gases. These gases and their quantities are Oxygen which makes up 21%, Nitrogen which is 78%, Carbon Dioxide with 0.04% and others with significantly smaller portions.

In the process of breathing, air enters into the nasal cavity through the nostrils and is filtered by coarse hairs (vibrissae) and mucous that are found there. The vibrissae filter macroparticles, which are particles of large size. Dust, pollen, smoke, and fine particles are trapped in the mucous that lines the nasal cavities (hollow spaces within the bones of the skull that warm, moisten, and filter the air). There are three bony projections inside the nasal cavity. The superior, middle, and inferior nasal chonchae. Air passes between these chonchae via the nasal meatuses.

Air then travels past the nasopharynx, oropharynx, and laryngopharynx, which are the three portions that make up the pharynx. The pharynx is a funnel-shaped tube that connects our nasal and oral cavities to the larynx. The tonsils which are part of the lymphatic system, form a ring at the connection of the oral cavity and the pharynx. Here, they protect against foreign invasion of antigens. Therefore, the respiratory tract aids the immune system through this protection. Then the air travels through the larynx. The larynx closes at the epiglottis to prevent the passage of food or drink as a protection to our trachea and lungs. The larynx is also our voicebox; it contains vocal cords, in which it produces sound. Sound is produced from the vibration of the vocal cords when air passes through them.

The trachea, which is also known as our *windpipe,* has ciliated cells and mucous secreting cells lining it, and is held open by C-shaped cartilage rings. One of its functions is similar to the larynx and nasal cavity, by way of protection from dust and other particles. The dust will adhere to the sticky mucous and the cilia helps propel it back up the trachea, to where it is either swallowed or coughed up. The mucociliary escalator extends from the top of the trachea all the way down to the bronchioles, through the trachea, the air is now able to pass into the bronchi.

LUNG CAPACITY

The normal volume moved in or out of the lungs during quiet breathing is called *tidal volume.* When we are in a relaxed state, only a small amount of air is brought in and out, about 500 ml. You can increase both the amount you inhale, and the amount you exhale, by breathing deeply. Breathing in very deeply is *inspiratory reserve volume* and can increase lung volume by 2900 ml, which is quite a bit more than the tidal volume of 500 ml. We can also increase expiration by contracting our thoracic and abdominal muscles. This is called *expiratory reserve volume* and is about 1400 ml of air. Vital capacity is the total of tidal, inspiratory reserve and expiratory reserve volumes; it is called *vital capacity* because it is vital for life, and the more air you can move, the better off you are. There are a number of illnesses that we will discuss later in the chapter that decrease vital capacity. Vital capacity can vary a little depending on how much we can increase inspiration by expanding our chest and lungs. Some air that we breathe never even reaches the lungs! Instead it fills our nasal cavities, trachea, bronchi, and bronchioles. These passages are not used in gas exchange so they are considered to be dead air space. To make sure that the inhaled air gets to the lungs, we need to breathe slowly and deeply. Even when we exhale deeply some air is still in the lungs (about 1000 ml) and is called residual volume. This air is not useful for gas exchange. There are certain types of diseases of the lung where residual volume builds up because the person cannot fully empty the lungs. This means that the vital capacity is also reduced because their lungs are filled with useless air.

CONTROL OF BREATHING

The respiratory center is gray matter in the pons and the upper medulla, which is responsible for rythemic respiration. This center can be divided into an inspiratory center and an expiratory center in the medulla, an apneustic center in the lower and midpons and a pneumotaxic center in the rostral-most part of the pons. This respiratory center is very sensitive to the pCO_2 in the arteries and to the pH level of the blood. The CO_2 can be brought back to the lungs in three different ways; dissolved in plasma, as carboxyhaemoglobin, or as carbonic acid. That particular form of acid is almost broken down immediately by carbonic hydrase into bicarbonate and hydrogen ions. This process is then reversed in the lungs, so that water and carbon dioxide are exhaled. The medulla oblongata reacts to both CO_2 and pH levels which triggers the breathing process, so that more oygen can enter the body to replace the oxygen that has been utilized. The medulla oblongata sends nural impulses down through the spinal chord and into the diaphragm. The impulse contracts down to the floor of the chest cavity, and at the same time there is a message sent to the chest muscles to expand causing a partial vacuum to be formed in the lungs. The partial vacuum will draw air into the lungs.

There are two other ways the Medulla Oblongata can be stimulated. The first type is when there is an oxygen debt (lack of oxygen reaching the muscles), and this produces lactic acid which lowers the pH level. The Medulla Oblongata is then stimulated. If the pH rises it begins a process known as the Bohr shift. The Bohr shift is affected when there are extremely high oxygen and carbon dioxide pressures present in the human body. This factor causes difficulty for the oxygen and carbon dioxide to attach to hemoglobin. When the body is exposed to higher altitudes the oxygen will not attach to the hemoglobin properly, causing the oxygen level to drop and the person will black out. This theory also applies to divers who go to great depths, and the pressure of the oxygen becomes poisonous. These pressures are known as

pO_2 and pCO_2, or partial pressures. The second type occurs when the major arteries in the body called the aortic and carotid bodies, sense a lack of oxygen within the blood and they send messages to the Medulla Oblongata.

PROBLEMS ASSOCIATED WITH THE RESPIRATORY TRACT AND BREATHING

The environment of the lung is very moist, which makes it a hospitable environment for bacteria. Many respiratory illnesses are the result of bacterial or viral infection of the lungs. Because we are constantly being exposed to harmful bacteria and viruses in our environment, our respiratory health can be adversely affected. There are a number of illnesses and diseases that can cause problems with breathing. Some are simple infections, and others are disorders that can be quite serious.

CARBON MONOXIDE POISONING

Caused when carbon monoxide binds to hemoglobin in place of oxygen. Carbon monoxide binds much tighter, without releasing, causing the hemoglobin to become unavailable to oxygen. The result can be fatal in a very short amount of time.

Mild Symptoms: Flu like symptoms, dizziness, fatigue, headaches, nausea, and irregular breathing.

Moderate Symptoms: Chest pain, rapid heart beat, difficulty thinking, blurred vision, shortness of breath and unsteadiness

Severe Symptoms: Seizures, palpitations, disorientation, irregular heart beat, low blood pressure, coma and death.

PULMONARY EMBOLISM

Blockage of the pulmonary artery (or one of its branches) by a blood clot, fat, air or clumped tumor cells. By far the most common form of pulmonary embolism is a thromboembolism, which occurs when a blood clot, generally a venous thrombus, becomes dislodged from its site of formation and embolizes to the arterial blood supply of one of the lungs.

Symptoms may include difficulty breathing, pain during breathing, and more rarely circulatory instability and death. Treatment, usually, is with **anticoagulant** medication.

UPPER RESPIRATORY TRACT INFECTIONS

The upper respiratory tract consists of our nasal cavities, pharynx, and larynx. Upper respiratory infections (URI) can spread from our nasal cavities to our sinuses, ears, and larynx. Sometimes a viral infection can lead to what is called a secondary bacterial infection. "Strep throat" is a primary bacterial infection and can lead to an upper respiratory infection that can be generalized or even systemic (affects the body as a whole). Antibiotics are not used to treat viral infections, but are successful in treating most bacterial infections, including strep throat. The symptoms of strep throat can be a high fever, severe sore throat, white patches on a dark red throat, and stomach ache.

SINUSITIS

An infection of the cranial sinuses is called sinusitis. Only about 1-3% of URI's are accompanied by sinusitis. This "sinus infection" develops when nasal congestion blocks off the tiny openings that lead to the sinuses. Some symptoms include: post nasal discharge, facial pain that worsens when bending forward, and sometimes even tooth pain can be a symptom. Successful treatment depends on restoring the proper drainage of the sinuses. Taking a hot shower or sleeping upright can be very helpful. Otherwise, using a spray decongestant or sometimes a prescribed antibiotic will be necessary.

OTITIS MEDIA

Otitis media in an infection of the *middle ear*. Even though the middle ear is not part of the respiratory tract, it is discussed here because it is often a complication seen in children who has a nasal infection. The infection can be spread by way of the auditory (Eustachian) tube that leads form the nasopharynx to the middle ear. The main symptom is usually pain. Sometimes though, vertigo, hearing loss, and dizziness may be present. Antibiotics can be prescribed and tubes are placed in the eardrum to prevent the buildup of pressure in the middle ear and the possibility of hearing loss.

Tonsillitis occurs when the tonsils become swollen and inflamed. The tonsils located in the posterior wall of the nasopharynx are often referred to as adenoids. If you suffer from tonsillitis frequently and breathing becomes difficult, they can be removed surgically in a procedure called a tonsillectomy.

LARYNGITIS

An infection of the larynx is called laryngitis. It is accompanied by hoarseness and being unable to speak in an audible voice. Usually, laryngitis disappears with treatment of the URI. Persistent hoarseness without a URI is a warning sign of cancer, and should be checked into by your physician.

LOWER RESPIRATORY TRACT DISORDERS

Lower respiratory tract disorders include infections, restrictive pulmonary disorders, obstructive pulmonary disorders, and lung cancer.

ACUTE BRONCHITIS

An infection that is located in the primary and secondary bronchi is called bronchitis. Most of the time, it is preceded by a viral URI that led to a secondary bacterial infection. Usually, a non-productive cough turns into a deep cough that will expectorate mucus and sometimes pus.

PNEUMONIA

A bacterial or viral infection in the lungs where the bronchi and the alveoli fill with a thick fluid. Usually it is preceded by influenza. Symptoms of pneumonia include high fever and chills, with headache and chest pain. Pneumonia can be located in several lobules of the lung and obviously, the more lobules involved, the more serious the infection. It can be caused by a bacteria that is usually held in check, but due to stress or reduced immunity has gained the upper hand.

PULMONARY FIBROSIS

Vital capacity is reduced in these types of disorders because the lungs have lost their elasticity. Inhaling particles such as sand, asbestos, coal dust, or fiberglass can lead to pulmonary fibrosis, a condition where fibrous tissue builds up in the lungs. This makes it so our lungs cannot inflate properly and are always tending toward deflation.

ASTHMA

Asthma is a respiratory disease of the bronchi and bronchioles. The symptoms include wheezing, shortness of breath, and sometimes a cough that will expel mucus. The airways are very sensitive to irritants which can include pollen, dust, animal danders, and tobacco. Even being out in cold air can be an irritant. When exposed to an irritant, the smooth muscle in the bronchioles undergoes spasms. Most asthma patients have at least some degree of bronchial inflammation that reduces the diameter of the airways and contributes to the seriousness of the attack. While asthma is not curable, it is treatable.

RESPIRATORY TUMOURS

Tumours of the respiratory system are either malignant or benign. Benign tumours are relatively rare causes of respiratory disease. Examples of benign tumours are: *pulmonary hamartoma,* congenital malformations such as pulmonary sequestration and congenital cystic adenomatoid malformation (CCAM).

Malignant Tumours

Malignant tumours, or cancers of the respiratory system, particularly lung cancers, are a major health problem responsible for 15% of all cancer diagnoses and 29% of all cancer deaths. The majority of respiratory system cancers are attributable to smoking tobacco.

The major types of respiratory system cancer are:

- Small cell lung cancer
- Non-small cell lung cancer
- Adenocarcinoma
- Squamous cell carcinoma
- Large cell undifferentiated carcinoma
- Other lung cancers (carcinoid, Kaposi's sarcoma, melanoma)
- Lymphoma
- Head and neck cancer
- Mesothelioma, usually caused by exposure to asbestos dust.

In addition, since many cancers spread via the bloodstream and the entire cardiac output passes through the lungs, it common for cancer metastases to occur the lung. Breast cancer may invade directly through local spread, and through lymph node metastases. After metastasis to the liver, colon cancer frequently metastasizes to the lung. Prostate cancer, germ cell cancer and renal cell carcinoma may also metastasize to the lung.

Treatment of respiratory system cancer depends on the type of cancer. Surgery (usually removal of part of the lung, a lobectomy or an entire lung, a pneumonectomy), chemotherapy and radiotherapy are all used. The chance of surviving lung cancer depends on the cancer stage at the time the cancer is diagnosed and is only about 14-17% overall. In the case of metastases to the lung, treatment can occasionally be curative but only in certain, rare circumstances.

PULMONARY VASCULAR DISEASES

Pulmonary vascular diseases are conditions that affect the pulmonary circulation. Examples of these conditions are:

Pulmonary embolism, a blood clot that forms in a vein, breaks free, travels through the heart and lodges in the lungs (thromboembolism). Large pulmonary emboli are fatal, causing sudden death. A number of other substances can also embolise to the lungs but they are much more rare: fat embolism (particularly after bony injury), amniotic fluid embolism (with complications of labour and delivery), air embolism (iatrogenic).

Pulmonary arterial hypertension, elevated pressure in the pulmonary arteries. It can be idiopathic or due to the effects of another disease, particularly COPD. This can lead to strain on the right side of the heart, a condition known as cor pulmonale.

Pulmonary edema, leakage of fluid from capillaries of the lung into the alveoli (or air spaces). It is usually due to congestive heart failure.

Pulmonary hemorrhage, inflammation and damage to capillaries in the lung resulting in blood leaking into the alveoli. This may cause blood to be coughed up. Pulmonary hemorrhage can be due to auto-immune disorders such as Wegener's granulomatosis and Goodpasture's syndrome.

RESPIRATORY DISTRESS SYNDROME

Pathophysiology

At birth the pressure needed to expand the lungs requires high inspiratory pressure. In the presence of normal surfactant levels the lungs retain as much as 40% of the residual volume after the first breath and thereafter will only require far lower inspiratory pressures. In the case of deficiency of surfactant the lungs will collapse between breaths, this makes the infant work hard and each breath is as hard as the first breath. If this goes on further the pulmonary capillary membranes become more permeable, letting in fibrin rich fluids between the alveolar spaces and in turn forms a hyaline membrane. The hyaline membrane is a barrier to gas exchange, this hyaline membrane then causes hypoxemia and carbon dioxide retention that in turn will further impair surfactant production.

Etiology

Type II alveolar cells produce surfactant and do not develop until the 25th to the 28th week of gestation, in this, respiratory distress syndrome is one of the most common respiratory disease in premature infants. Furthermore, surfactant deficiency and pulmonary immaturity together leads to alveolar collapse. Predisposing factors that contribute to poorly functioning type II alveolar cells in a premature baby are if the child is a preterm male, white infants, infants of mothers with diabetes, precipitous deliveries, cesarean section performed before the 38th week of gestation. Surfactant synthesis is influenced by hormones, this ranges form insulin and cortisol. Insulin inhibits surfactant production, explaining why infants of mothers with diabetes type I are at risk of development of respiratory distress syndrome. Cortisol can speed up maturation of type II cells and therefore production of surfactant. Finally, in the baby delivered by cesarean section are at greater risk of developing respiratory distress syndrome because the reduction of cortisol produced because the lack of stress that happens during vaginal delivery, hence cortisol increases in high stress and helps in the maturation of type II cells of the alveoli that cause surfactant.

Treatment

Today to prevent respiratory distress syndrome are animal sources and synthetic surfactants, and administrated through the airways by an endotracheal tube and the surfactant is suspended in a saline solution. Treatment is initiated post birth and in infants who are at high risk for respiratory distress syndrome.

SLEEP APNEA

CPAP is the most common treatment for obstructive sleep apnea. Sleep apnea or sleep apnoea is a sleep disorder characterized by pauses in breathing during sleep. These episodes, called apneas (literally, "without breath"), each last long enough so one or more breaths are missed, and occur repeatedly throughout sleep. The standard definition of any apneic event includes a minimum 10 second interval between breaths, with either a neurological arousal (3-second or greater shift in EEG frequency, measured at C3, C4, O1, or O2), or a blood oxygen desaturation of 3-4 percent or greater, or both arousal and desaturation. Sleep apnea is diagnosed with an overnight sleep test called polysomnogram. One method of treating central sleep apnea is with a special kind of CPAP, APAP, or VPAP machine with a Spontaneous Time (ST) feature. This machine forces the wearer to breathe a constant number of breaths per minute.

Continuous Positive Airway Pressure or (CPAP), in which a controlled air compressor generates an airstream at a constant pressure. This pressure is prescribed by the patient's physician, based on an overnight test or titration.

Nutrition for COPD (Chronic Obstructive Pulmonary Disease) Patients

Nutrition is particularly important for ventilator-dependent patient. When metabolizing macronutrients carbon dioxide and water are produced. The respiratory quotient (RQ) is a ratio of produced carbon dioxide to amount consumed. Carbohydrates metabolism produces the most amount of carbon dioxide so they have the highest (RQ). Fats produce the least amount of carbon dioxide along with proteins. Protein has a slightly higher RQ ratio. It is recommended that this kind of patient not exceed a 1.0 respiratory quotient (RQ). Lowering carbohydrates and supplementing fat or protein in the diet might not result in maintaining the desired outcome because, excess amounts fat or protein may also result in a respiratory quotient (RQ) higher than 1.0.

STUDY QUESTIONS

1. What is respiration? Explain the breathing mechanism in human being.
2. Describe the various parts of respiratory system.
3. Explain the process of artificial breathing.
4. Explain the process of lung air volumes.
5. Write short notes on:
   (a) Respiratory Distress Syndrome.
   (b) Transport of Respiratory Gases.
   (c) Regulation of Respiration.

CHAPTER 9

THE DIGESTIVE SYSTEM

INTRODUCTION

The digestive system is made up of the digestive tract—a series of hollow organs joined in a long, twisting tube from the mouth to the anus—and other organs that help the body breakdown and absorb food. Organs that make up the digestive tract are the mouth, oesophagus, stomach, small intestine, large intestine—also called the *colon*—rectum, and anus. Inside these hollow organs is a lining called the *mucosa*. In the mouth, stomach, and small intestine, the mucosa contains tiny glands that produce juices to help digest food. The digestive tract also contains a layer of smooth muscle that helps breakdown food and move it along the tract. Two "solid" digestive organs, the liver and the pancreas, produce digestive juices that reach the intestine through small tubes called *ducts*. The gallbladder stores the liver's digestive juices until they are needed in the intestine.

DIGESTIVE MECHANISM

The first step in the digestive system can actually begin before the food is even in your mouth. When you smell or see something that you just have to eat, you start to salivate in anticipation of eating, thus beginning the *digestive process*.

Food is the body's source of fuel. Nutrients in food give the body's cells the energy they need to operate. Before food can be used it has to be broken down into tiny little pieces, so it can be absorbed and used by the body. In humans, proteins need to be broken down into amino acids, starches into sugars, and fats into fatty acids and glycerol. During digestion two main processes occur at the same time.

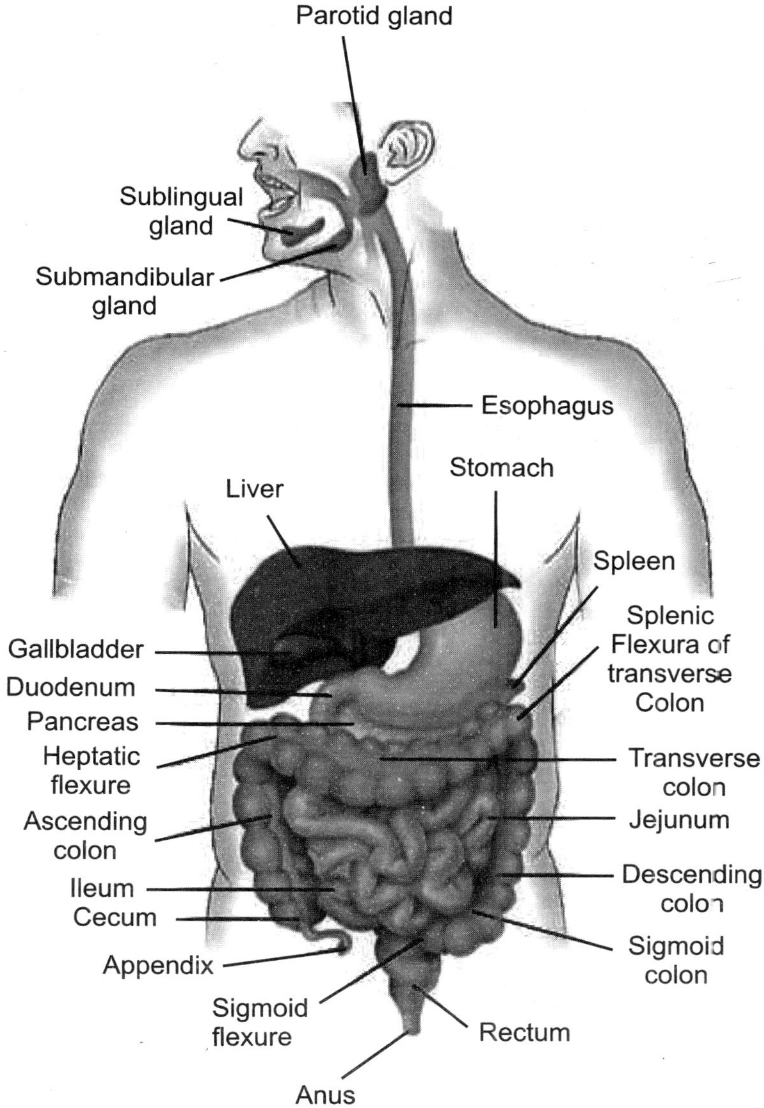

Fig. 9.1 *Human digestive system.*

Mechanical digestion: Larger pieces of food get broken down into smaller pieces while being prepared for chemical digestion. Mechanical digestion starts in the mouth and continues in to the stomach.

Chemical digestion: Several different enzymes breakdown macromolecules into smaller molecules that can be more efficiently absorbed. Chemical digestion starts with saliva and continues into the intestines.

STRUCTURE OF ALIMENTARY CANAL

The digestive system is made up by the alimentary canal, or the digestive tract, and other abdominal organs that play a part in digestion such as the liver and the pancreas. The alimentary canal is the long tube of organs that runs from the mouth (where the food enters) to the anus (where indigestible waste leaves). The average adult digestive tract is about thirty feet (30′) long. While in the digestive tract the food is really passing through the body rather than being in the body.

MOUTH

Mechanical digestion takes place in the *mouth,* where the saliva, teeth, and tongue all play an important role in this digestive process. A brain reflex triggers the flow of saliva when we see or even think about food. Saliva moistens the food while the teeth chew it up and make it easier to swallow. Amylase, which is the digestive enzyme found in saliva, starts to breakdown starch into simpler sugars before the food even leaves the mouth. The nervous pathway involved in salivary excretion requires stimulation of receptors in the mouth, sensory impulses to the brain stem, and parasympathetic impulses to salivary glands.

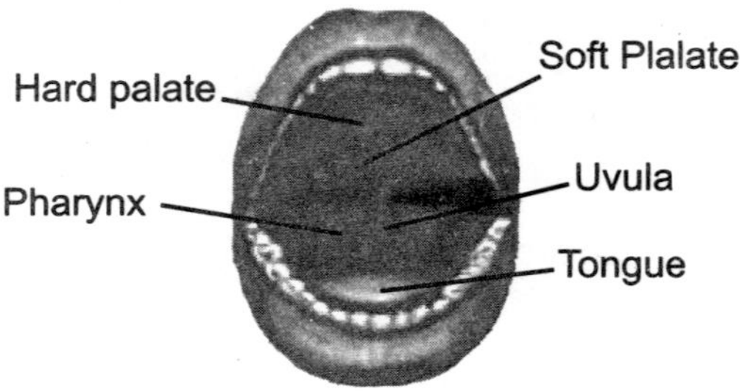

Fig. 9.2 *Mouth cavity.*

Saliva and Salivary Glands

The smallest taste, smell, and anticipation of food sends signals to the brain. The brain in turn sends messages to a system of salivary glands. Saliva is essentially made up of water and begins to soften up the food, so it can pass more smoothly down the throat. Besides water there is also a very special substance, an enzyme called pytalin , whose main task is to breakdown the food into simpler forms.

Saliva is produced in and secreted from salivary glands. The basic secretory units of salivary glands are clusters of cells called an acini. These cells secrete a fluid that contains water, electrolytes, mucus and enzymes, all of which flow out of the acinus into collecting ducts. Within the ducts, the composition of the secretion is altered. Much of the sodium is actively reabsorbed, potassium is secreted, and large quantities of bicarbonate ion are secreted. Bicarbonate secretion is of tremendous importance to ruminants because it, along with phosphate, provides a critical buffer that neutralizes the massive quantities of acid produced in the stomach. Small collecting ducts within salivary glands lead into larger ducts, eventually forming a single large duct that empties into the oral cavity.

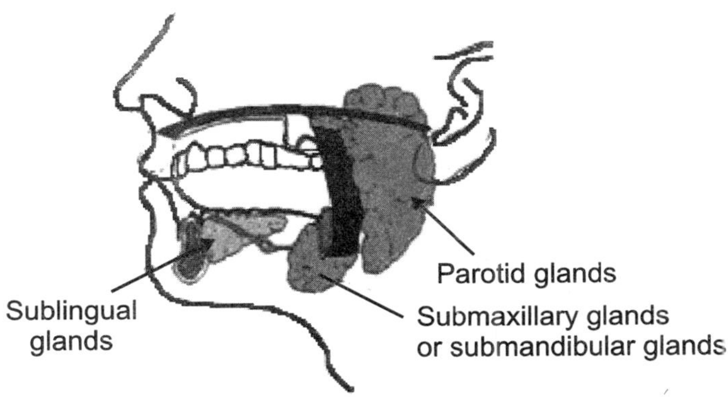

Fig. 9.3 *Salivary glands.*

Most animals have three major pairs of salivary glands that differ in the type of secretion they produce:

(i) Parotid glands produce a serous, watery secretion.

(ii) Submaxillary (mandibular) glands produce a mixed serous and mucous secretion.

(iii) Sublingual glands secrete a saliva that is predominantly mucous in character.

The basis for different glands secreting saliva of differing composition can be seen by examining salivary glands histologically. Two basic types of acinar epithelial cells exist:

(i) Serous cells, which secrete a watery fluid, essentially devoid of mucus.

(ii) Mucous cells, which produce a very mucus-rich secretion.

Acini in the parotid glands are almost exclusively of the serous type, while those in the sublingual glands are predominantly mucus cells. In the submaxillary glands, it is common to observe acini composed of both serous and mucus epithelial cells. In the histologic sections of canine salivary gland shown above, the cells stained pink are serous cells, while the white, foamy cells are mucus-secreting cells. Secretion of saliva is under control of the autonomic nervous system, which controls both the volume and type of saliva secreted. This is actually fairly interesting: a dog fed dry dog food produces saliva that is predominantly serous, while dogs on a meat diet secrete saliva with much more mucus. Parasympathetic stimulation from the brain, as was well demonstrated by Ivan Pavlov, results in greatly enhanced secretion, as well as increased blood flow to the salivary glands.

Teeth

The aftermath of the action of the teeth in digestion results in two outcomes: havoc and devastation. The teeth are gears to demolish chunks of food by a series of actions such as clamping, slashing, piercing, grinding and crushing. The teeth do the first drastic destruction to food in the digestive system. There are four types of teeth:

(i) *Canines* are pointy and sharp. They tear up food.

(ii) *Incisors* are shaped like tiny chisels with flat ends that are somewhat sharp. They cut and chop food.

(iii) *Premolars* have ridges, and are bigger and stronger than the canine and incisors. They grind and crush food.

(iv) *Molars* are the toughest of the bunch. They are strong and wide. They grind food.

Tongue

The tongue consists of four types of taste buds—salty, sweet, sour, and bitter—and is a very maneuverable and pliable arrangement of muscle. It helps to remove, and dislocate food particles in the teeth and shifts food around in the mouth in order to assist with the all important act of swallowing. The act of swallowing food, which at this place in the system is called a *bolus*,

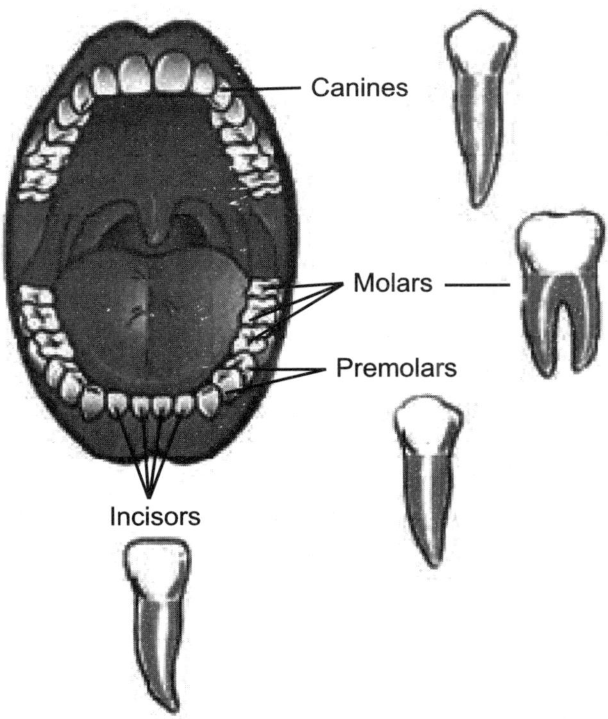

Fig. 9.4 *Structure of tooth.*

brings many organs into action. As the top of your tongue presses up against the hard palate, the roof of your mouth, food is shoved to the back of the mouth. This action in turn brings the soft palate and ursula (the place at the very back of the mouth where there is a teardrop shape located) into action. They keep the food from being misguided toward the nose. Once past the soft palate, the food is in the pharynx, a train station with two tracks, one leading to the trachea (windpipe), the other to the oesophagus (food tube). The epiglottis projects out from the trachea side and helps to admit free movement of air as it is swallowed and at the same time restricts entrance to the oesophagus. The larynx-hyper link, provides the epiglottis with most of its muscle for movement. It applies an upward force that helps to relax some tension on the esophagus, so that food enters where it is meant to go, down the esophagus and not down the windpipe.

Peristalsis

This mechanical action has to do with sets of muscles that cooperate to move both liquid and solid food along the digestive tract. In other word, it pushes food along your esophagus, stomach, and intestine. Gravitational pull is lessened in a sense when food enters the esophagus because of peristalsis. Peristalsis helps a person to swallow lying down or even standing on their head. Peristalsis has another essential task besides assisting in the movement of food through the body. It also helps to knead, agitate, and pound the solid residue that is left after the teeth or those without teeth, the gums, have done their best.

Digestive Sphincters

The gastrointestinal tract is supplied with a number of muscular valves. These control and direct the quantity of food that goes through the digestive tract and inhibits the back movement of partially digested food.

PHARYNX

Swallowing your food happens when the muscles in your tongue and mouth move the food into your pharynx. The pharynx, which is the passageway for food and air, is about five inches (5″) long. A small flap of skin called the *epiglottis* closes over the pharynx to prevent food from entering the trachea and thus choking. For swallowing to happen correctly a combination of 25 muscles must all work together at the same time. Salivary glands also produce an estimated three liters of saliva per day.

OESOPHAGUS

After passing through the throat, the food moves down a muscular tube in the chest called the *oesophagus*. Peristalsis (involuntary wavelike muscle contractions along the G.I. tract) moves the food from the esophagus and pushes it down into the stomach. At the end of the oesophagus there is a sphincter that allows food into the stomach then closes backup so the food cannot travel backup into the oesophagus.

General Histology of the Gut

The wall of the digestive tube from the mouth to the anus is composed of *four* basic layers or tunics.

(i) Tunica Serosa

Tunica serosa is the outermost covering of the digestive tube. In most of the digestive tract (stomach and intestines) it consists of a thin layer of loose connective tissue covered by mesothelium (a type of squamous epithelium that lines body cavities); within the peritoneal cavity, this structure is also referred to as visceral peritoneum. In the abdominal cavity, the serosa on each side of the tube fuses together to form a suspensory structure called mesentery, which houses vascular and nervous supplies to the digestive tract and is continuous with the lining of the cavity. In regions outside of the abdominal cavity where the digestive tube is essentially affixed to adjacent structures via its outer layer of connective tissue (esophagus and rectum), this tunic is referred to as tunica adventitia instead of tunica serosa.

(ii) Tunica Muscularis

Tunica muscularis endows the digestive tube with an ability to be motile. In most of the digestive tube, this tunic consists of two thick layers of smooth muscle. Muscle fibers in the inner layer are aligned circularly, whereas those in the outer layer have a longitudinal orientation. This combination of circular and longitudinal smooth muscle gives the tube an ability to perform complex movements that squeeze and propel ingesta in the lumen. Between the inner circular and outer longitudinal layers of smooth muscle is another critical component of the digestive tract's nervous system —the mycenteric plexus.

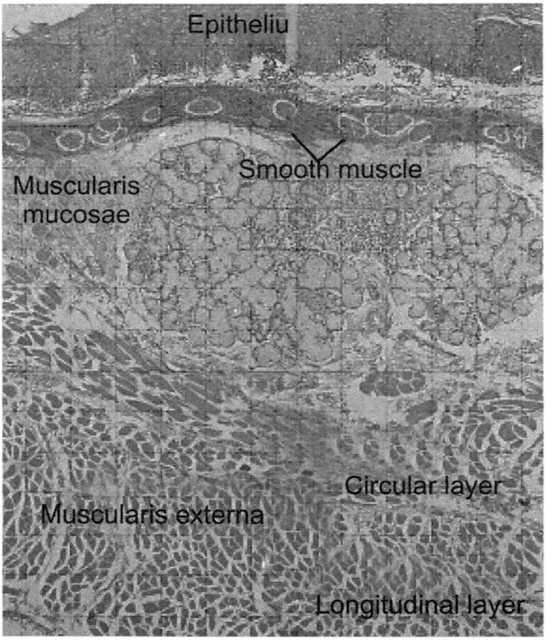

Fig. 9.5 *Histology of gut.*

(iii) Tunica Submucosa

Tunica submucosa lies immediately beneath the mucosa, and is a layer of loose to dense connective tissue containing blood and lymphatic vessels. The submucosa also contains the submucous plexus, a critical component of the digestive tract's nervous system which provides nervous control to the mucosa.

(iv) Tunica Mucosa

Tunica mucosa is the innermost layer of the digestive tube and lines the lumen. Among the four tunics, the mucosa is most variable in structure and function, endowing the tube with an ability to perform diverse and specialized digestive tasks along its length. Of critical importance in this regard are the epithelial cells that cover the mucosa and are thus in direct contact with the lumen. This epithelial cell sheet (lamina epithelialis) is distinctly different in different regions of the tract. Indeed, in most of the tract, several different cell types contribute to the epithelium, including cells dedicated to secretion, absorption or production of hormones.

STOMACH

The stomach lies between the esophagus and the first part of the small intestine (the duodenum). It is on the left side of the abdominal cavity; the fundus of the stomach lying against the diaphragm. Lying beneath the stomach is the pancreas. The stomach is divided into four sections, each of which has different cells and functions. The sections are:

(i) Cardiac region, where the contents of the esophagus empty into the stomach,

(ii) Fundus, formed by the upper curvature of the organ,

(iii) Body, the main central region, and

(iv) Pylorus or atrium, the lower section of the organ that facilitates emptying the contents into the small intestine.

Two smooth muscle valves, or sphincters, keep the contents of the stomach contained. They are the: (i) *Cardiac* or oesophageal sphincter, dividing the tract above, and (ii) *Pyloric* sphincter, dividing the stomach from the small intestine. The gastric juice, which is in the stomach, is highly acidic with a pH of 1-3. Gastric acid may cause or compound damage to the stomach wall or its layer of mucus, causing a peptic ulcer. On the inside of the stomach there are folds of skin call the gastric rugae. Gastric rugae make the stomach very extendable, especially after a very big meal.

Functions

It stores food and acid for digestion. Stomach muscles mix-up the food with enzymes and acids to make smaller digestible pieces. Acid is needed for digestion in the stomach and is secreted by chief cells. The gastric glands begin secreting before food enters the stomach due to the parasympathetic impulses of the vagas nerve. The stomach lining has glands that produce up to three quarts of this digestive fluid daily. The secretion of gastric juices occurs in three phases: cephalic, gastric, and intestinal. The cephalic phase is activated by the smell and taste of food and swallowing. The gastric phase is activated by the chemical effects of food and the distension of the stomach. The intestinal phase blocks the effect of the cephalic and gastric phases. Gastric juice also contains an enzyme named pepsin, which digests proteins, hydrochloric acid and mucus. Hydrochloric acid causes the stomach to maintain a pH of about 2, which helps kill off bacteria that comes into the digestive system via food.

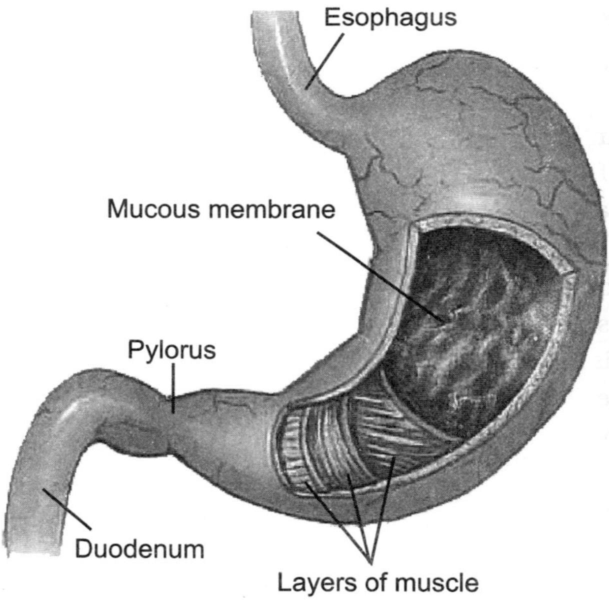

Fig. 9.6 *Stomach.*

Water, alcohol, salt, and simple sugars can be absorbed directly through the stomach wall. However, most substances in our food need a little more digestion and must travel into the intestines before they can be absorbed. When the stomach is empty it is about the size of one-fifth of a cup of fluid. When stretched and expanded, it can hold up to eight cups of food after a big meal.

Once mixed with digestive juices in the stomach the food is called *chyme*. The pyloric sphincter, a walnut shaped muscular tube at the stomach outlet, keeps chyme in the stomach until it reaches the right consistency to pass into the small intestine. The food leaves the stomach in small squirts rather than all at once.

Gastric Glands

There are many different gastric glands and they secret many different chemicals. Parietal cells secrete hydrochloric acid; chief cells secrete pepsinogen; goblet cells secrete mucus; argentaffin cells secrete serotonin and histamine; and G cells secrete the hormone gastrin.

Disorders of the Stomach

Disorders of the stomach are common. There can be a lot of different causes with a variety of symptoms. The strength of the inner lining of the stomach needs a careful balance of acid and mucus. If there is not enough mucus in the stomach, ulcers, abdominal pain, indigestion, heartburn, nausea and vomiting could all be caused by the extra acid.

Erosions, ulcers, and tumours can cause bleeding. When blood is in the stomach it starts the digestive process and turns black. When this happens, the person can have black stool or vomit. Some ulcers can bleed very slowly so the person won't recognize the loss of blood. Over time, the iron in your body will run out, which in turn, will cause anaemia.

There isn't a known diet to prevent against getting ulcers. A balanced, healthy diet is always recommended. Smoking can also be a cause of problems in the stomach. Tobacco increases acid production and damages the lining of the stomach. It is not a proven fact that stress alone can cause an ulcer.

SMALL INTESTINE

The small intestine is up to 6 meters long and is 2-3 centimetres wide. The small intestine is the site where most of the chemical and mechanical digestion is carried out. Tiny projections called *villi* line the small intestine which absorbs digested food into the capillaries. Most of the food absorption takes place in the jejunum and the ileum.

Functions

The functions of a small intestine is, the digestion of proteins into peptides and amino acids principally occurs in the stomach but some also occurs in the small intestine. Peptides are degraded into amino acids; lipids (fats) are degraded into fatty acids and glycerol; and carbohydrates are degraded into simple sugars.

Parts of the Small Intestine

The three main parts of the small intestine are: the *Duodenum*, the Jejunum, and the Ileum.

(i) The Duodenum

The upper part, the duodenum, is the most active in digestion. Secretions from the liver and pancreas are used for digestion in the duodenum. Epithelial cells of the duodenum secrete a watery mucus. It is the first and shortest part of the small intestine. It begins with the duodenal bulb and ends at the ligament of Treitz. The duodenum is almost entirely retro peritoneal. The duodenum is also where the bile and *pancreatic juices* enter the intestine.

(ii) The Jejunum

The jejunum is a part of the small bowel, located between the distal end of duodenum and the proximal part of ileum. The jejunum and the ileum are suspended by an extensive mesentery giving the bowel great mobility within the abdomen. The inner surface of the jejunum, its mucous membrane, is covered in projections called villi, which increase the surface area of tissue available to absorb nutrients from the gut contents. It is different from the ileum due to fewer goblet cells and generally lacks Preyer's patches.

(iii) The Ileum

Its function is to absorb vitamin B_{12} and bile salts. The wall itself is made up of folds, each of which has many tiny finger-like projections known as *villi,* on its surface. In turn, the epithelial cells which line these villi possess even larger numbers of micro villi. The cells that line the ileum contain the protease and carbohydrate enzymes responsible for the final stages of protein and carbohydrate digestion. These enzymes are present in the cytoplasm of the epithelial cells. The villi contain large numbers of capillaries which take the amino acids and glucose produced by digestion to the hepatic portal vein and the liver.

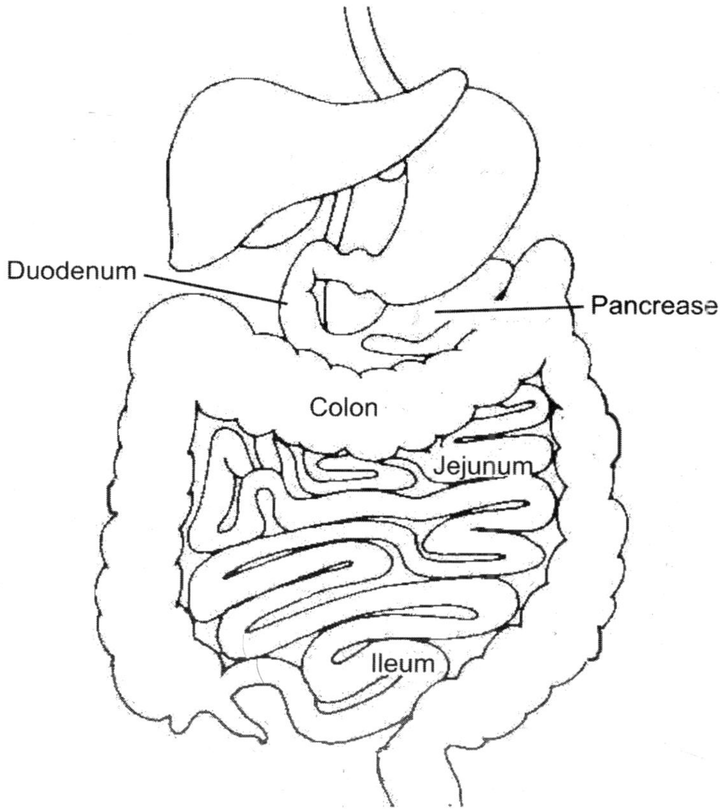

Fig. 9.7 *Parts of the small intestine.*

LARGE INTESTINE

The large intestine (colon) extends from the end of the ileum to the anus. It is about 5 feet long, being one-fifth of the whole extent of the intestinal canal. It's caliber is largest at the commencement at the cecum, and gradually diminishes as far as the rectum, where there is a dilatation of considerable size just above the anal canal. It differs from the small intestine in by the greater caliber, more fixed position, sacculated form, and in possessing certain appendages to its external coat, the appendices epicolic. Further, its longitudinal muscular fibers do not form a continuous layer around the gut, but are arranged in three longitudinal bands or taniae.

The large intestine is divided into the *cecum, colon, rectum,* and *anal canal*. In its course, describes an arch which surrounds the convolutions of the small intestine. It commences in the right iliac region, in a dilated part, the cecum. It ascends through the right lumbar and hypochondriac regions to the under surface of the liver; here it takes a bend, the right colic flexure, to the left and passes transversely across the abdomen on the confines of the epigastric and umbilical regions, to the left hypochondriac region; it then bends again, the left colic flexure, and descends through the left lumbar and iliac regions to the pelvis, where it forms a bend called the sigmoid flexure; from this it is continued along the posterior wall of the pelvis to the anus.

PANCREAS, LIVER, AND GALLBLADDER

The pancreas, liver, and gallbladder are essential for digestion. The pancreas produces enzymes that help digest proteins, fats, and carbohydrates, the liver produces bile that helps the body absorb fat, and the gallbladder stores the bile until it is needed. The enzymes and bile travel through special channels called ducts and into the small intestine where they help breakdown the food.

PANCREAS

The pancreas is located posterior to the stomach and in close association with the duodenum. In humans, the pancreas is a 6-10 inch elongated organ in the abdomen located retro peritoneal. It is often described as having three regions: a head, body and tail. The pancreatic head abuts the second part of the duodenum while the tail extends towards the spleen. The pancreatic duct runs the length of the pancreas and empties into the second part of the duodenum at the *ampulla of Vater*. The common bile duct commonly joins the pancreatic duct at or near this point.

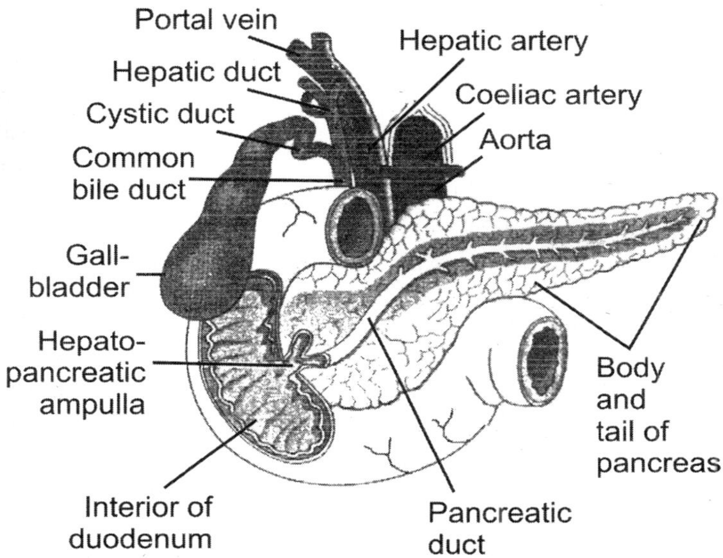

Fig. 9.8 *The pancreas in relation to the duodenum and biliary tract; part of the anterior wall of the duodenum has been removed.*

The pancreas is supplied arterially by the pancreaticoduodenal arteries, themselves branches of the superior mesenteric artery of the hepatic artery (branch of celiac trunk from the abdominal aorta). The superior mesenteric artery provides the inferior pancreaticoduodenal arteries while the gastroduodenal artery (one of the terminal branches of the hepatic artery) provides the superior pancreaticoduodenal artery. Venous drainage is via the pancreatic duodenal veins which end up in the portal vein. The splenic vein passed posterior to the pancreas but is said to not drain the pancreas itself. The portal vein is formed by the union of the superior mesenteric vein and splenic vein posterior to the body of the pancreas. In some people (as many as 40%), the inferior mesenteric vein also joins with the splenic vein behind the pancreas, in others it simply joins with the superior mesenteric vein instead.

The function of the pancreas is to produce enzymes that break down all categories of digestible foods (*exocrine pancreas*) and secrete hormones that affect carbohydrates metabolism (*endocrinc pancreas*).

(i) Exocrine Pancrease

The pancrease is composed of pancreatic exocrine cells, whose ducts are arranged in clusters called *acini* (singular acinus). The cells are filled with secretory granules containing the precursor digestive enzymes (mainly trypsinogen, chymotrypsinogen, pancreatic lipase, and amylase) that are secreted into the lumen of the acinus. These granules are termed zymogen granules (zymogen referring to the inactive precursor enzymes.) It is important to synthesize inactive enzymes in the pancreas to avoid auto degradation, which can lead to pancreatitis.

The pancrease is near the liver, and is the main source of enzymes for digesting fats (lipids) and proteins — the intestinal walls have enzymes that will digest polysaccharides. Pancreatic secretions from ductal cells contain bicarbonate ions and are alkaline in order to neutralize the acidic chyme that the stomach churns out. Control of the exocrine function of the pancreas are via the hormone gastrin, cholecystokinin and secretin, which are hormones secreted by cells in the stomach and duodenum, in response to distension and/or food and which causes secretion of pancreatic juices.

The two major proteases which the pancreas are *trypsinogen* and *chymotrypsinogen*. These *zymogens* are inactivated forms of trypsin and chymotrypsin. Once released in the intestine, the enzyme enterokinase present in the intestinal mucosa activates trypsinogen by cleaving it to form trypsin. The free trypsin then cleaves the rest of the trypsinogen and chymotrypsinogen to their active forms. Pancreatic secretions accumulate in intralobular ducts that drain the main pancreatic duct, which drains directly into the duodenum. Due to the importance of its enzyme contents, injuring the pancreas is a very dangerous situation. A puncture of the pancreas tends to require careful medical intervention.

(ii) Endocrine Pancrease

Scattered among the acini are the endocrine cells of the pancreas, in groups called the islets of Langerhans. They are: Insulin-producing beta cells (50-80% of the islet cells) Glucagon-releasing alpha cells (15-20%) Somatostatin-producing delta cells (3-10%) Pancreatic polypeptide-containing PP cells (remaining%).

The islets are a compact collection of endocrine cells arranged in clusters and cords and are crisscrossed by a dense network of capillaries. The capillaries of the islets are lined by layers of endocrine cells in direct contact with vessels, and most endocrine cells are in direct contact with blood vessels, by either cytoplasmic processes or by direct apposition.

LIVER

The liver plays a major role in metabolism and has a number of functions in the body including glycogen storage, plasma protein synthesis, and drug detoxification. It also produces bile, which is important in digestion. It performs and regulates a wide variety of high-volume biochemical reaction requiring specialized tissues. The liver normally weighs between 1.3-3.0 kilograms and is a soft, pinkish-brown "boomerang shaped" organ. It is the second largest organ (the largest being the skin) and the largest gland within the human body. Its anatomical position in the body is immediately under the diaphragm on the right side of the upper abdomen. The liver lies on the right side of the stomach and makes a kind of bed for the gallbladder.

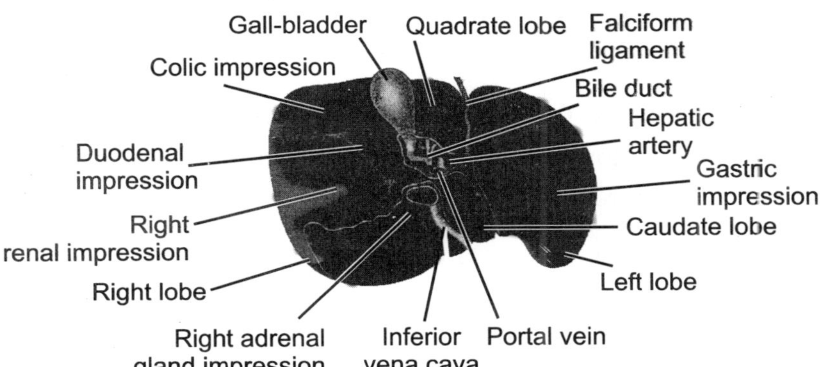

Fig. 9.9 *The liver, turned up show the posterior surface.*

The liver is supplied by two main blood vessels on its right lobe: the hepatic artery and the portal vein. The hepatic artery normally comes off the celiac trunk. The portal vein brings venous blood from the spleen, pancreas, and small intestine, so that the liver can process the nutrients and byproducts of food digestion. The hepatic veins drain directly into the inferior vena cava. The bile produced in the liver is collected in bile canaliculi, which merge from bile ducts. These eventually drain into the right and left hepatic ducts, which in turn merge to form the common hepatic duct. The cystic duct (from the gallbladder) joins with the common hepatic duct to form the common bile duct. Bile can either drain directly into the duodenum via the common bile duct or be temporarily stored in the gallbladder via the cystic duct. The common bile duct and the pancreatic duct enter the duodenum together at the ampulla of Vater. The branching's of the bile ducts resemble those of a tree, and indeed term "biliary tree" is commonly used in this setting.

Functions of the Liver

The various functions of the liver are carried out by the liver cells or hepatocytes. The liver produces and excretes bile required for dissolving fats. Some of the bile drains directly into the duodenum, and some is stored in the gallbladder. The liver performs several roles in carbohydrate metabolism:

(i) Gluconeogenesis (the formation of glucose from certain amino acids, lactate or glycerol).
(ii) Glycogenolysis (the formation of glucose from glycogen).
(iii) Glycogenesis (the formation of glycogen from glucose).
(iv) The breakdown of insulin and other hormones.
(v) The liver is responsible for the mainstay of protein metabolism.

Role of Liver in Lipid Metabolism

The liver also performs several roles in lipid metabolism:

(i) Cholesterol synthesis.
(ii) The production of triglycerides (fats).
(iii) The liver produces coagulation factors I (fibrinogen), II (prothrombin), V, VII, IX, X and XI, as well as protein C, protein S and antithrombin.

(iv) The liver breaks down haemoglobin, creating metabolites that are added to bile as pigment.

(v) The liver breaks down toxic substances and most medicinal products in a process called drug metabolism. This sometimes results in toxication, when the metabolite is more toxic than its precursor.

(vi) The liver converts ammonia to urea.

(vii) The liver stores a multitude of substances, including glucose in the form of glycogen, vitamin B_{12}, iron, and copper.

(viii) In the first trimester fetus, the liver is the main site of red blood cell production. By the 32nd weeks of gestation, the bone marrow has almost completely taken over that task.

(ix) The liver is responsible for immunological effects the reticuloendothelial system if the liver contains many immunologically active cells, acting as a 'sieve' for antigens carried to it via the portal system.

GALLBLADDER

The gallbladder is a-pear shaped organ that stores about 50 ml of bile (or "gall") until the body needs it for digestion. The gallbladder is about 7-10 cm long in humans and is dark green in appearance due to its contents (bile), not its tissue. It is connected to the liver and the duodenum by biliary tract.

The gallbladder is connected to the main bile duct through the gallbladder duct (cystic duct). The main biliary tract runs from the liver to the duodenum, and the cystic duct is effectively a "cul de sac", serving as entrance and exit to the gallbladder. The surface marking of the gallbladder is the intersection of the midclavicular line (MCL) and the trans pyloric plane, at the tip of the ninth rib. The blood supply is by the cystic artery and vein, which runs parallel to the cystic duct. The cystic artery is highly variable, and this is of clinical relevance since it must be clipped and cut during a cholecystectomy.

The gallbladder stores bile, which is released when food containing fat enters the digestive tract, stimulating the secretion of cholecystokinin (CCK). The bile emulsifies fats and neutralizes acids in partly digested food. After being stored in the gallbladder, the bile becomes more concentrated than when it left the liver, increasing its potency and intensifying its effect in fats.

ANUS

The human anus is situated between the buttocks, posterior to the perineum. It has two anal sphincters, one internal, the other external. These hold the anus closed until defecation occurs. One sphincter consists of smooth muscle and its action is involuntary; the other consists of striated muscle and its action is voluntary. Role of the anus is when the rectum is full, the increase in intra-rectal pressure forces the walls of the anal canal apart allowing the faecal matter to enter the canal. The rectum shortens as material is forced into the anal canal and peristaltic waves propel the faeces out of the rectum. The internal and external sphincters of the anus allow the faeces to be passed by muscles pulling the anus up over the exiting faeces.

ABSORPTION

The process of absorption happens in specialised structures called *villi*. These are tiny finger-like projections that push out into the digested food passing along the small intestine. They give a large surface area for the absorption to take place and make it more efficient. Each villus contains a good network of capillaries to pick up the nutrients and the cells are specialised to quickly absorb molecules by diffusion, osmosis and active transport.

The small intestine is the major site for digestion and absorption of nutrients. The pancreas secretes digestive enzymes and stomach acid-neutralizing bicarbonate. The liver produces bile, which is stored in the gall bladder before entering the bile duct into the duodenum.

Digestion of carbohydrates, proteins, and fat continues in the small intestine. Starch and glycogen are brokendown into maltose by small intestine enzymes. Proteases are enzymes secreted by the pancreas that continue the breakdown of protein into small peptide fragments and amino acids.

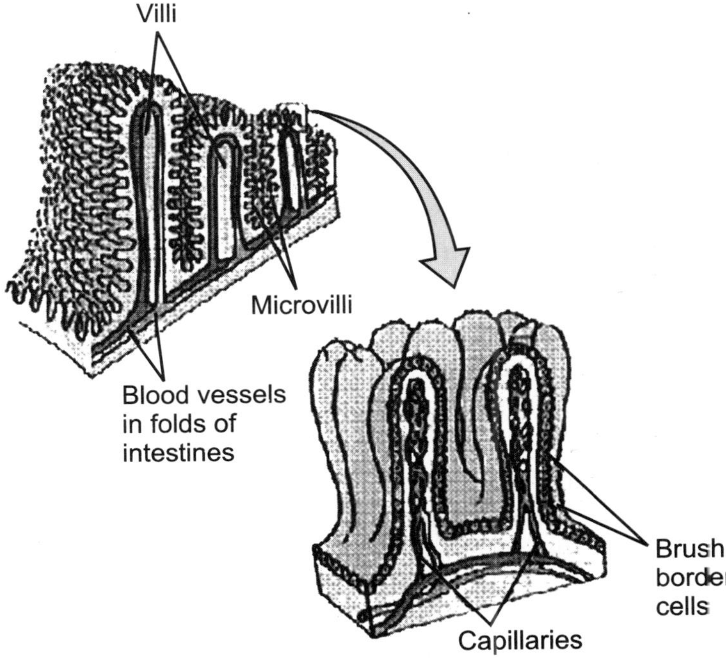

Fig. 9.10 *Absorption.*

Bile emulsifies fats, facilitating their breakdown into progressively smaller fat globules until they can be acted upon by lipases. Bile contains cholesterol, phospholipids, bilirubin, and a mix of salts. Fats are completely digested in the small intestine, unlike carbohydrates and proteins.

Most absorption occurs in the duodenum and jejunum. The inner surface of the intestine has circular folds that more than triple the surface area for absorption. Villi covered with epithelial cells increase the surface area by another factor of 10. The epithelial cells are lined with microvilli that further increase the surface area; a 6 metre long tube has a surface area of 300 square metres.

Each villus has a surface that is adjacent to the inside of the small intestinal opening covered in microvilli that form on top of an epithelial cell known as a *brush border*. Each villus has a capillary network supplied by a small arteriole. Absorbed substances pass through the brush border into the capillary, usually by passive transport.

Maltose, sucrose, and lactose are the main carbohydrates present in the small intestine; they are absorbed by the *microvilli*. Starch is broken down into two-glucose units (maltose) elsewhere. Enzymes in the cells convert these disaccharides into monosaccharides that then leave the cell and enter the capillary. Lactose intolerance results from the genetic lack of the enzyme lactase produced by the intestinal cells.

Peptide fragments and amino acids cross the epithelial cell membranes by active transport. Inside the cell they are broken into amino acids that then enter the capillary. Gluten enteropathy is the inability to absorb gluten, a protein found in wheat. Fat digestion is usually completed by the time the food reaches the ileum (lower third) of the small intestine. Bile salts are in turn absorbed in the ileum and are recycled by the liver and gallbladder. Fats pass from the epithelial cells to the small lymph vessel that also runs through the villus.

NUTRIENT ABSORPTION

Digested molecules of food, as well as water and minerals from the diet, are absorbed from the cavity of the upper small intestine. The absorbed materials cross the mucosa into the blood, mainly, and are carried off in the bloodstream to other parts of the body for storage or further chemical change. As previously noted, this part of the process varies with different types of nutrients.

CARBOHYDRATES

An average American adult eats about half a pound of carbohydrate each day. Some of our most common foods contain mostly carbohydrates. Examples are bread, potatoes, pastries, candy, rice, cornflakes, fruits, and vegetables. Many of these foods contain both starch, which can be digested, and fiber, which the body cannot digest.

The digestible carbohydrates are broken into simpler molecules by enzymes in the saliva, in juice produced by the pancreas, and in the lining of the small intestine. Starch is digested in two steps: First, an enzyme in the saliva and pancreatic juice breaks the starch into molecules called maltose; then an enzyme in the lining of the small intestine (maltase) splits the maltose into glucose molecules that can be absorbed into the blood. Glucose is carried through the bloodstream to the liver, where it is stored or used to provide energy for the work of the body.

Table sugar is another carbohydrate that must be digested to be useful. An enzyme in the lining of the small intestine digests table sugar into glucose and fructose, each of which can be absorbed from the intestinal cavity into the blood. Milk contains yet another type of sugar, lactose, which is changed into absorbable molecules by an enzyme called lactase, also found in the intestinal lining.

PROTEIN

Foods such as meat, eggs, and beans consist of giant molecules of protein that must be digested by enzymes before they can be used to build and repair body tissues. An enzyme in the juice of the stomach starts the digestion of swallowed protein.

Further digestion of the protein is completed in the small intestine. Here, several enzymes from the pancreatic juice and the lining of the intestine carry out the breakdown of huge protein molecules into small molecules called amino acids. These small molecules can be absorbed from the hollow of the small intestine into the blood and then be carried to all parts of the body to build the walls and other parts of cells.

FATS

Fat molecules are a rich source of energy for the body. The first step in digestion of a fat such as butter is to dissolve it into the watery content of the intestinal cavity. The bile acids produced by the liver act as natural detergents to dissolve fat in water and allow the enzymes to break the large fat molecules into smaller molecules, some of which are fatty acids and cholesterol.

The bile acids combine with the fatty acids and cholesterol and help these molecules to move into the cells of the mucosa. In these cells the small molecules are formed back into large molecules, most of which pass into vessels (called lymphatics) near the intestine. These small vessels carry the reformed fat to the veins of the chest, and the blood carries the fat to storage depots in different parts of the body.

VITAMINS

The large, hollow organs of the digestive system contain muscle that enables their walls to move. The movement of organ walls can propel food and liquid and also can mix the contents within each organ. Typical movement of the esophagus, stomach, and intestine is called peristalsis. The action of peristalsis looks like an ocean wave moving through the muscle. The muscle of the organ produces a narrowing and then propels the narrowed portion slowly down the length of the organ. These waves of narrowing push the food and fluid in front of them through each hollow organ.

WATER AND SALT

Most of the material absorbed from the cavity of the small intestine is water in which salt is dissolved. The salt and water come from the food and liquid we swallow and the juices secreted by the many digestive glands. In a healthy adult, more than a gallon of water containing over an ounce of salt is absorbed from the intestine every 24 hours.

FOOD AND FEEDING

Food supplies the animal with energy for all animal activities. To provide the materials for growth and repair of cells. To provide materials for production of hormones and enzymes. To provide raw materials for milk, egg and wool production etc.

THE MAJOR FOOD GROUPS

Food can either be Carbohydrate, Lipid (Fats and Oils), Protein, Vitamins or Mineral, as well as water. Green plants can make their own food in a process known as *Photosynthesis*. Therefore, plants are known as autotrophs. Animals have to ingest their food and cannot make all their food needs. Animals are known as heterotrophs.

CARBOHYDRATES

The main sources of carbohydrates in our diet are starches and sugars. Carbohydrates are made up of carbon, hydrogen and oxygen molecules with the common formula Cx $(H_2O)x$. Carbohydrates are classified by their number of sugar units and are called either monosaccharides, disaccharides or polysaccharides.

(i) Monosaccharides

Are glucose, fructose and galactose. All have the formula $C_6H_{12}O_6$ but arranged differently.

(ii) Disaccharides

Contain two sugar units:

Maltose – Glucose + Glucose

Lactose – Glucose + Galactose

Sucrose – Glucose + Fructose

(iii) Polysaccharides

Starches, cellulose, chitin etc. Humans and pigs cannot digest cellulose. However cattle and horses (and other ruminants) can, by a symbiotic relationship with bacteria in their stomachs. Carbohydrates are used in the body for energy or structure.

PROTEINS

The main sources are lean meat, egg white, fish, milk, pulse and nuts. Contain the elements carbon, hydrogen, oxygen and nitrogen (sometimes sulphur) proteins are made up of units called amino acids. There are over 80 known amino acids, but only 26 occur in proteins. These amino acids form long chains which come together as a protein molecule.

A typical protein molecule has 500+ amino acids. Some amino acids can be made by our body and these are called *non-essential amino acids*. Other amino acids can only be brought into our bodies by ingestion. These are known as *essential amino acids*. There are no essential amino acids for ruminants. Proteins are used in the body for growth and repair of cells.

LIPIDS (FATS AND OILS)

Sources of fats are obvious – butter, oils, nuts, milk and general fatty foods. Contain the elements carbon, hydrogen and oxygen. A molecule of fat is made up of one molecule of glycerol with three fatty acids chemically attached. Fats provide energy to the body (twice as much as carbohydrates), insulation and contain vitamins.

VITAMINS

Vitamins have many functions in the body. Vitamins mainly act as co-enzymes, which means they trigger enzymes to work.

MINERALS

Minerals have no energy value but are used in the body for many different reasons.

- — Osmo-regulation.
- — Acid-base balance (pH balance).
- — Formation of enzymes, pigments and hormones.
- — Triggers or activators in different reactions.

WATER

Water has no value but is essential for all bodily functions. Our bodies are made up of 75% water. Waters main function is as a medium where other food items are stored and moved. Of course, our blood is made of nearly all water, so it is vital that the human body gets 3–4 pints of water a day.

DISORDERS OF DIGESTIVE SYSTEM

ACUTE APPENDICITIS

An exemplary case of acute appendicitis in a 10-year-old boy. The organ is enlarged and sausage-like (botuliform). This longitudinal section shows the angry red inflamed mucosa with its irregular luminal surface. Diagnosed and removed early in the course of the disease, this appendix does not show late complications, like transmural necrosis, perforation, and abscess formation.

APPENDICITIS

Appendicitis is the inflammation of the appendix, the finger-like pouch that extends from the cecum. The most common symptoms are abdominal pain, loss of appetite, fever, and vomiting. Kids and teenagers are the most common victims of appendicitis and must be corrected by surgery. While mild cases may resolve without treatment, most require removal of the inflamed appendix, either by laparotomy or laparoscopy. Untreated, mortality is high, mainly due to peritonitis and shock.

CELIAC DISEASE

Celiac disease is a disorder in which a person's digestive system is damaged by the response of the immune system to a protein called gluten, which is found in *rye*, wheat, and *barley*, and also in foods like breakfast cereal and pizza crust. People that have celiac disease experience abdominal pain, diarrhea, bloating, exhaustion, and depression when they eat foods with gluten in them. They also have difficulty digesting their food. Celiac disease runs in families and becomes active after some sort of stress, like viral infections or surgery. The symptoms can be managed by following a gluten free diet. Doctors can diagnose this condition by taking a full medical history or with a blood test.

GASTRITIS AND PEPTIC ULCERS

Usually the stomach and the duodenum are resistant to irritation because of the strong acids produced by the stomach. But sometimes a bacteria called *Helicobacter pylori* or the chronic use of drugs or certain medications, weakens the mucous layer that coats the stomach and the duodenum, allowing acid to get through the sensitive lining beneath. This can cause irritation and inflammation of the lining of the stomach, which is called *gastritis*, or cause peptic ulcers, which are holes or sores that form in the lining of the stomach and duodenum and cause pain and bleeding. Medications are the best way to treat this condition.

GASTROINTESTINAL INFECTIONS

Gastrointestinal infections can be caused by bacteria such as Campylobacter, Salmonella, E. coli, or Shigella. They can also be caused by viruses or by intestinal parasites like amebiasis and giardiasis. The most common symptoms of gastrointestinal infections abdominal pain and cramps, diarrhea, and vomiting.

These conditions usually go away on their own and do not need medical attention.

INFLAMMATORY BOWEL DISEASE

Inflammatory bowel disease is the chronic inflammation of the intestines, which usually affect older kids, teens and adults. There are two major types, ulcerative colitis and Crohn's disease and indeterminate colitis, which occurs in 10-15% of patients. Ulcerative colitis usually affects just the rectum and small intestine, while Crohn's disease can affect the whole gastrointestinal tract from mouth to anus along with some other parts of the body. Patients with these diseases also suffer from extraintestinal symptoms including joint pain and red eye, which can signal a flare of the disease. These diseases are treated with medications and if necessary, intravenous or IV feeding, or in the more serious cases, surgery to remove the damaged areas of the intestines.

HEPATITIS

Hepatitis is a viral condition that inflames a person's liver which can cause it to lose its ability to function. Viral hepatitis, like hepatitis A, B, and C, is extremely contagious. Hepatitis A, which is a mild form of hepatitis, can be treated at home, but more serious cases that involve liver damage, might require hospitalization.

CHOLECYSTITIS

Acute or chronic inflammation if the gallbladder causes abdominal pain. 90% of cases of acute cholecystitis are caused by the presence of gallstones. The actual inflammation is due to secondary infection with bacteria of an obstructed gallbladder, with the obstruction caused by the gallstones. Gallbladder conditions are very rare in kids and teenagers but can occur when the kid or teenager has sickle cell anaemia or in kids being treated with long term medications.

FOOD ALLERGIES

Food allergies occur when the immune system thinks that a certain protein in any kind of food is a foreign object and will try to fight against it. Only about eight percent of children and two percent of adults actually have a food allergy. A person can be allergic to any kind of food, but the most common food allergies are from nuts, cow's milk, eggs, soya, fish, and shellfish. Most people who have a food allergy are allergic to less than four different foods.

The most common signs of food allergies are hives, swelling, itchy skin, itchiness, tingling or swelling in the mouth, coughing, trouble breathing, diarrhea, and vomiting. The two most common chronic illneses that are associated with food allergies are eczema and asthma. Food allergies can be fatal if they cause the reaction called anaphylaxis. This reaction makes it hard for the person to breathe. This can be treated by an epinephrine injection.

CONSTIPATION

Not everyone is on the same schedule for having a bowel movement. Depending on the person, a "normal" schedule can range anywhere from three times a day to three times a week. If you start having bowel movements less than your own personal schedule, then you might be getting the signs of constipation.

Constipation is when you have trouble having bowel movements. The stool is very hard making it hard to pass and causing a person to strain. You may even feel like you have to have a bowel movement even after you have already had one.

When you digest food, the waste products go through your intestines by the muscles contracting. When in the large intestine, most of the water and salt from the waste products are reabsorbed because they are needed by the body for our everyday functions, you can become constipated if too much water is absorbed, or if waste products move too slowly.

Not getting enough fluids, a low fiber diet, age, not being physically active, depression, stress and pregnancy can all be causes of constipation. Medications and narcotics can also cause a person to get constipated. Chronic constipation may be a symptom of a liver problem such as a urea cycle disorder.

The best way for a person to treat constipation is to make sure that you are getting enough fluids as well as fiber in your diet. By doing this, the bulk of your stool is increased and also makes the stool softer, so that it can move through your intestines more easily. Being more active and increasing your daily exercise also helps keep you regulated.

STUDY QUESTIONS

1. Explain the histology of gut.
2. Describe the process of absorbtion.
3. Discuss the process of digestion.
4. Write short notes on:
   (a) Faeces.
   (b) Defecation.
   (c) Enzymes.
   (e) Bile and bile juice.

■■■

10

CHAPTER

THE EXCRETORY SYSTEM

INTRODUCTION

The *Excretory* or *Urinary System* is a group of organs in the body concerned with filtering out excess fluid and other substances from the bloodstream. The substances are filtered out from the body in the form of urine. Urine is a liquid produced by the kidneys, collected in the bladder and excreted through the urethra. Urine is used to extract excess minerals or vitamins as well as blood corpuscles from the body. The urinary organs include the kidneys, ureters, bladder, and urethra. The urinary system works with the other systems of the body to help maintain homeostasis. The kidneys are the main organs of homeostasis because they maintain the acid base balance and the water salt balance of the blood.

FUNCTIONS OF THE EXCRETORY OR URINARY SYSTEM

One of the major functions of the Urinary system is the process of excretion. Excretion is the process of eliminating, from an organism, waste products of metabolism and other materials that are of no use. The urinary system maintains an appropriate fluid volume by regulating the amount of water that is excreted in the urine. Other aspects of its function include regulating the concentrations of various electrolytes in the body fluids and maintaining normal pH of the blood. Several body organs carry out excretion, but the kidneys are the most important excretory organ. The primary function of the kidneys is to maintain a stable internal environment (homeostasis) for optimal cell and tissue metabolism. They do this by separating urea, mineral salts, toxins, and other waste products from the blood. They also do the job of conserving water, salts, and electrolytes. At least one kidney must function properly for life to be maintained. Six important roles of the kidneys are:

(i) *Regulation of plasma ionic composition*: Ions such as sodium, potassium, calcium, magnesium, chloride, bicarbonate, and phosphates are regulated by the amount that the kidney excretes.

(ii) *Regulation ofplasma osmolarity*: The kidneys regulate osmolarity because they have direct control over how many ions and how much water a person excretes.

(iii) *Regulation of plasma volume*: Your kidneys are so important they even have an effect on your blood pressure. The kidneys control plasma volume by controlling how much water a person excretes. The plasma volume has a direct effect on the total blood volume, which has a direct effect on your blood pressure. Salts such as NaCl can cause osmosis, the diffusion of water into the blood.

(iv) *Regulation ofplasma hydrogen ion concentration (pH):* The kidneys partner up with the lungs and they together control the pH. The kidneys have a major role because they control the amount of bicarbonate excreted or held onto. The kidneys help maintain the blood pHmainly by excreting hydrogen ions and reabsorbing bicarbonate ions as needed.

(v) *Removal of metabolic waste products and foreign substances from the plasma*: One of the most important things the kidneys excrete is nitrogenous waste. As the liver breaks down amino acids it also releases ammonia. The liver then quickly combines that ammonia with carbon dioxide, creating urea which is the primary nitrogenous end product of metabolism in humans. The liver turns the ammonia into urea because it is much less toxic. We can also excrete some ammonia, creatinine and uric acid. The creatinine comes from the metabolic breakdown of creatine phospate (a high-energy phosphate in muscles). Uric acid comes from the breakdown of necloetides. Uric acid is insoluble and too much uric acid in the blood will build up and form crystals that can collect in the joints and cause gout.

(vi) *Secretion of hormones*: The endocrine system has assistance from the kidney's when releasing hormones. Renin is released by the kidneys. Renin leads to the secretion of aldosterone which is released from the adrenal cortex. Aldosterone promotes the kidneys to reabsorb the sodium (Na^+) ions. The kidneys also secrete erythropoietin when the blood doesn't have the capacity to carry oxygen. Erythropoietin stimulates red blood cell production. The vitamin D from the skin is also activated with help from the kidneys. Calcium (Ca^+) absorption from the digestive tract is promoted by vitamin D.

GROSS STRUCTURE OF KIDNEY

The kidneys are a pair of bean-shaped, reddish brown organs about the size of your fist. They are covered by the *renal capsule,* which is a tough capsule of *fibrous* connective tissue. Adhering to the surface of each kidney is two layers of fat to help cushion them. The kidneys are located at the rear wall of the abdominal cavity just above the waistline, and are protected by the rib-cage. They are considered retroperitoneal, which means they lie behind the peritoneum. There are three major regions of the kidney:

Renal Cortex

The outer, granulated layer is the renal cortex.

Renal Medulla

The inner radially striated layer is the *renal medulla*. This contains pyramid shaped tissue called the *renal pyramids,* separated by *renal columns.*

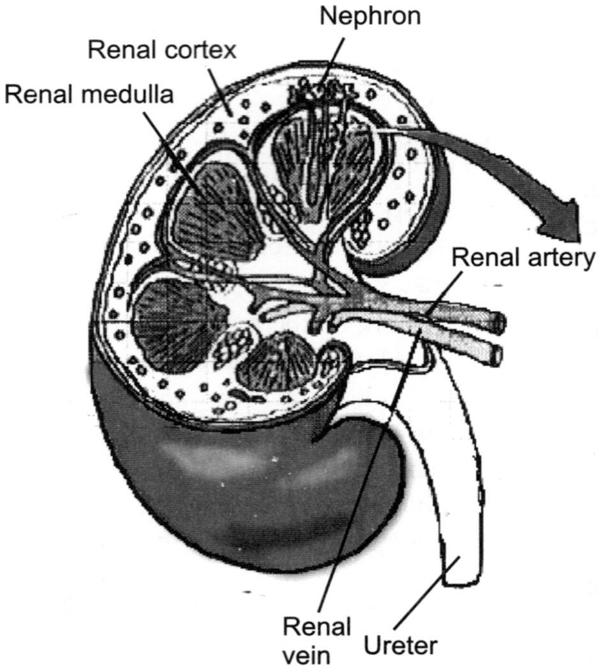

Fig. 10.1 *Structure of kidney.*

Renal Pelvis

The ureters are continuous with the renal pelvis and is the very center of the kidney.

Renal Vein

The renal veins are veins that drain the kidney. They connect the kidney to the inferior vena cava. Because the inferior vena cava is on the right half of the body, the left renal vein is generally the longer of the two. Unlike the right renal vein, the left renal vein often receives the left gonadal vein (left testicular vein in males, left ovarian vein in females). It frequently receives the left suprarenal vein as well.

Renal Artery

The renal arteries normally arise off the abdominal aorta and supply the kidneys with blood. The arterial supply of the kidneys are variable and there may be one or more renal arteries supplying each kidney. Due to the position of the aorta, the inferior vena cava and the kidneys in the body, the right renal artery is normally longer than the left renal artery. The right renal artery normally crosses posteriorly to the inferior vena cava. The renal arteries carry a large portion of the total blood flow to the kidneys. Up to a third of the total cardiac output can pass through the renal arteries to be filtered by the kidneys.

Ureters

The ureters are two tubes that drain urine from the kidneys to the bladder. Each ureter is a muscular tube about 10 inches (25 cm) long. Muscles in the walls of the ureters send the urine in small spurts into the bladder, (a collapsible sac found on the forward part of the cavity of the bony pelvis that allows temporary storage of urine). After the urine enters the bladder from the ureters, small folds in the bladder mucosa act like valves peventing backward flow of the urine. The outlet of the bladder is controlled by a sphincter muscle. A full bladder stimulates sensory nerves in the bladder wall that relax the sphincter and allow release of the urine. However, relaxation of the sphincter is also in part a learned response under voluntary control. The released urine enters the urethra.

NEPHRONS

A nephron is the basic structural and functional unit of the kidney. The nephron consists of a cup-shaped *Bowman's capsule* containing *capillaries* and the *glomerulus,* and a long *renal tube.*

Bowman's capsule and glomerulus together constitute the *Malpighian corpuscles* or *renal corpuscles.* These corpuscles were first described by *Morcello Malpighi* in 1966.

Blood flows into the kidney through the *renal artery,* which branches into capillaries associated with the glomerulus. Arterial pressure causes water and solutes from the blood to filter into the capsule. Fluid flows through the *proximal tubule,* which include the *loop of Henle,* and then into the *distal tubule.* The distal tubule empties into a *collecting duct.*

Each nephron has its own supply of blood from two capillary regions from the renal artery. Each nephron is composed of an initial filtering component (the *renal corpuscle*) and a tubule specialized for reabsorption and secretion (the *renal tubule*). The renal corpuscle filters out large solutes from the blood, delivering water and small solutes to the renal tubule for modification.

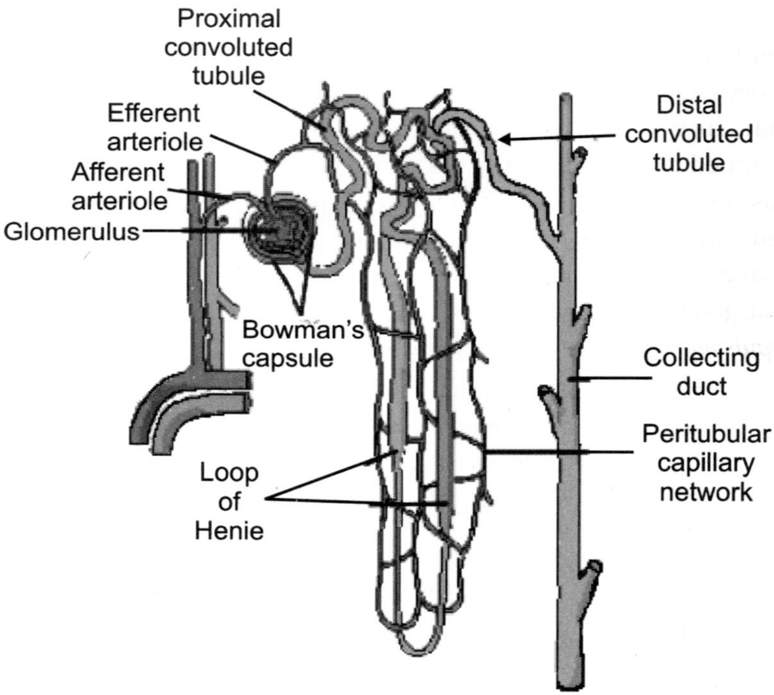

Fig. 10.2 *Structure of nephron.*

Functions of Nephron

The chief function of nephron is to regulate water and soluble substances by filtering the blood, reabsorbing what is needed and excreting the rest as urine. Nephrons eliminate wastes from the body, regulate blood volume and pressure, control levels of electrolytes and metabolites, and regulate blood pH. Its functions are vital to life and are regulated by the endocrine system by hormones such as antidiuretic hormone, aldosterone, and parathyroid hormone.

MICROSCOPIC STRUCTURE OF NEPHRON

1. GLOMERULAR CAPSULE OR BOWMAN'S CAPSULE

Bowman's capsule (also called the *glomerular capsule*) surrounds the glomerulus and is composed of visceral (simple squamous epithelial cells) (inner) and parietal (simple squamous epithelial cells) (outer) layers. The visceral layer lies just beneath the thickened glomerular basement membrane and is made of podocytes which send foot processes over the length of the glomerulus. Foot processes interdigitate with one another forming filtration slits that, in contrast to those in the glomerular endothelium, are spanned by diaphragms. The size of the filtration slits restricts the passage of large molecules (e.g., albumin) and cells (e.g., red blood cells and platelets). In addition, foot processes have a negatively-charged coat (glycocalyx) that limits the filtration of negatively-charged molecules, such as albumin. This action is called *electrostatic repulsion*.

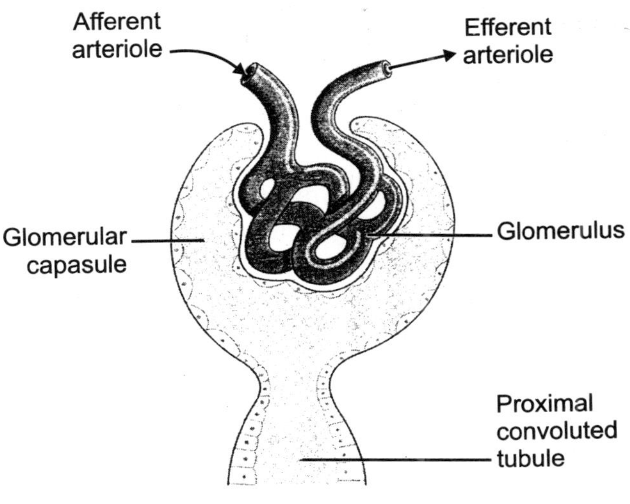

Fig. 10.3 *The glomerulus and glumerular capsule.*

The parietal layer of Bowman's capsule is lined by a single layer of squamous epithelium. Between the visceral and parietal layers is Bowman's space, into which the filtrate enters after passing through the podocytes' filtration slits. It is here that smooth muscle cells and macrophages lie between the capillaries and provide support for them. Unlike the visceral layer, the parietal layer does not function in filtration. Rather, the filtration barrier is formed by three components: the diaphragms of the filtration slits, the thick glomerular basement membrane, and the glycocalyx secreted by podocytes. 99% of glomerular filtrate will ultimately be reabsorbed.

The *process of filtration of the blood in the Bowman's capsule* is *ultrafiltration* (or glomerular filtration), and the normal rate of filtration is 125 ml/min, equivalent to ten times the blood volume daily. Measuring the glomerular filtration rate (GFR) is a diagnostic test of kidney function. A decreased GFR may be a sign of renal failure. Conditions that can effect GFR include: arterial pressure, afferent arteriole constriction, efferent arteriole constriction, plasma protein concentration and colloid osmotic pressure.

Any proteins that are roughly 30 kilodaltons or under can pass freely through the membrane. Although, there is some extra hindrance for negatively charged molecules due to the negative charge of the basement membrane and the podocytes. Any small molecules such as water, glucose, salt (NaCl), amino acids, and urea pass freely into Bowman's space, but cells, platelets and large proteins do not. As a result, the filtrate leaving the Bowman's capsule is very similar to blood plasma in composition as it passes into the proximal convoluted tubule. Together, the glomerulus and Bowman's capsule are called the renal corpuscle.

(a) Glomerulus

The glomerulus is a capillary tuft that receives its blood supply from an afferent arteriole of the renal circulation. The glomerular blood pressure provides the driving force for fluid and solutes to be filtered out of the blood and into the space made by Bowman's capsule. The remainder of the blood not filtered into the glomerulus passes into the narrower efferent arteriole. It then moves into the vasa recta, which are collecting capillaries intertwined with the convoluted tubules through the interstitial space, where the reabsorbed substances will also enter. This then combines with efferent venules from other nephrons into the renal vein, and rejoins with the main bloodstream.

(b) Afferent/Efferent Arterioles

The afferent arteriole supplies blood to the glomerulus. A group of specialized cells known as juxtaglomerular cells are located around the afferent arteriole where it enters the renal corpuscle. The efferent arteriole drains the glomerulus. Between the two arterioles lies specialized cells called the macula densa. The juxtaglomerular cells and the macula densa collectively form the juxtaglomerular apparatus. It is in the juxtaglomerular apparatus cells that the enzyme renin is formed and stored. Renin is released in response to decreased blood pressure in the afferent arterioles, decreased sodium chloride in the distal convoluted tubule and sympathetic nerve stimulation of receptors (beta-adrenic) on the juxtaglomerular cells. Renin is needed to form Angiotensin I and Angiotensin II which stimulate the secretion of aldosterone by the adrenal cortex.

2. PROXIMAL CONVOLUTED TUBULE (PCT)

The proximal tubule can be anatomically divided into two segments: the *proximal convoluted tubule* and the proximal *straight tubule*. The proximal convoluted tubule can be divided further into S_1 and S_2 segments based on the histological appearance of its cells. Following this naming convention, the proximal straight tubule is commonly called the S_3 segment. The proximal convoluted tubule has one layer of cuboidal cells in the lumen. This is the only place in the nephron that contains cuboidal cells. These cells are covered with millions of microvilli. The microvilli serve to increase surface area for reabsorption.

Fluid in the filtrate entering the proximal convoluted tubule is reabsorbed into the peritubular capillaries, including approximately two-thirds of the filtered salt and water and all filtered organic solutes (primarily glucose and amino acids). This is driven by sodium transport from the lumen into the blood by the Na^+/K^+ ATPase in the basolateral membrane of the epithelial cells. Much of the mass movement of water and solutes occurs in between the cells through the tight junctions, which in this case are not selective.

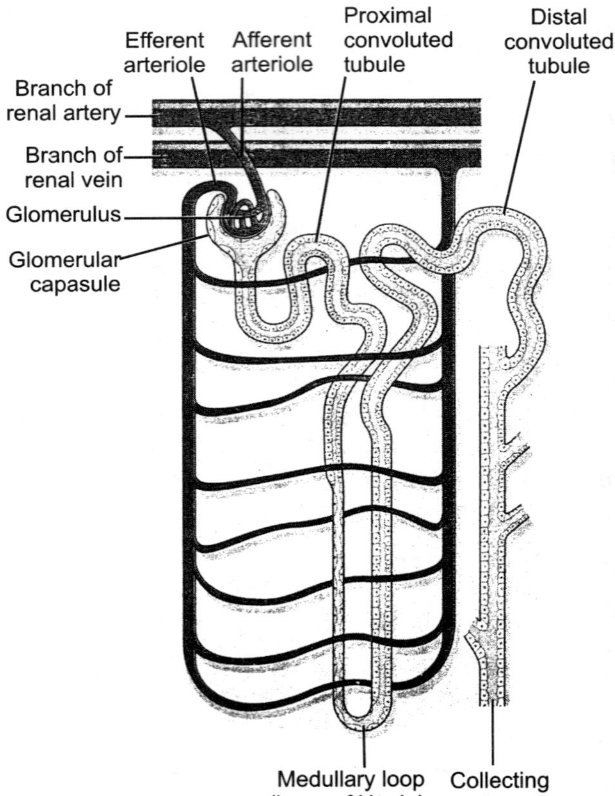

Fig. 10.4 *A nephron and associated blood vessel.*

The solutes are absorbed isotonically, in that the osmotic potential of the fluid leaving the proximal tubule is the same as that of the initial glomerular filtrate. However, glucose, amino acids, inorganic phosphate, and some other solutes are reabsorbed via secondary active transport through cotransport channels driven by the sodium gradient out of the nephron.

3. LOOP OF THE NEPHRON OR LOOP OF HENLE

The loop of Henle (sometimes known as the nephron loop) is a U-shaped tube that consists of a descending limb and ascending limb. It begins in the cortex, receiving filtrate from the proximal convoluted tubule, extends into the medulla, and then returns to the cortex to empty into the distal convoluted tubule. Its primary role is to concentrate the salt in the interstitium, the tissue surrounding the loop.

(a) Descending Limb

Its descending limb is permeable to water but completely impermeable to salt, and thus only indirectly contributes to the concentration of the interstitium. As the filtrate descends deeper into the hypertonic interstitium of the renal medulla, water flows freely out of the descending limb by osmosis until the tonicity of the filtrate and interstitium equilibrate. Longer descending limbs allow more time for water to flow out of the filtrate, so longer limbs make the filtrate more hypertonic than shorter limbs.

(b) Ascending Limb

Unlike the descending limb, the ascending limb of Henle's loop is impermeable to water, a critical feature of the countercurrent exchange mechanism employed by the loop. The ascending limb actively pumps sodium out of the filtrate, generating the hypertonic interstitium that drives countercurrent exchange. In passing through the ascending limb, the filtrate grows hypotonic since it has lost much of its sodium content. This hypotonic filtrate is passed to the distal convoluted tubule in the renal cortex.

4. DISTAL CONVOLUTED TUBULE (DCT)

The distal convoluted tubule is similar to the proximal convoluted tubule in structure and function. Cells lining the tubule have numerous mitochondria, enabling active transport to take place by the energy supplied by ATP. Much of the ion transport taking place in the distal convoluted tubule is regulated by the endocrine system. In the presence of parathyroid hormone, the distal convoluted tubule reabsorbs more calcium and excretes more phosphate. When aldosterone is present, more sodium is reabsorbed and more potassium excreted. Atrial natriuretic peptide causes the distal convoluted tubule to excrete more sodium. In addition, the tubule also secretes hydrogen and ammonium to regulate pH. After travelling the length of the distal convoluted tubule, only 3% of water remains, and the remaining salt content is negligible. 97.9% of the water in the glomerular filtrate enters the convoluted tubules and collecting ducts by osmosis.

5. COLLECTING DUCTS

Each distal convoluted tubule delivers its filtrate to a system of collecting ducts, the first segment of which is the connecting tubule. The collecting duct system begins in the renal cortex and extends deep into the medulla. As the urine travels down the collecting duct system, it passes by the medullary interstitium which has a high sodium concentration as a result of the loop of Henle's countercurrent multiplier system. Though the collecting duct is normally impermeable to water, it becomes permeable in the presence of antidiuretic hormone (ADH). As much as three-fourths of the water from urine can be reabsorbed as it leaves the collecting duct by osmosis. Thus, the levels of ADH determine whether urine will be concentrated or dilute. Dehydration results in an increase in ADH, while water sufficiency results in low ADH allowing for diluted urine. Lower portions of the collecting duct are also permeable to urea, allowing some of it to enter the medulla of the kidney, thus maintaining its high ion concentration (which is very important for the nephron).

Urine leaves the medullary collecting ducts through the renal papilla, emptying into the renal calyces, the renal pelvis, and finally into the bladder via the ureter. Because it has a different embryonic origin than the rest of the nephron (the collecting duct is from endoderm whereas the nephron is from mesoderm), the collecting duct is usually not considered a part of the nephron proper.

URINARY BLADDER

The urinary bladder is a hollow, muscular and distendible or elastic organ that sits on the pelvic floor (superior to the prostate in males). On its anterior border lies the pubic symphysis and, on its posterior border, the vagina (in females) and rectum (in males). The urinary bladder can hold approximately 17 to 18 ounces (500 to 530 ml) of urine, however the desire to micturate is usually experienced when it contains about 150 to 200 ml. When the bladder fills with urine (about half/full), stretch receptors send nerve impulses to the spinal cord, which then sends a reflex nerve impulse back to the sphincter (muscular valve) at the neck of the bladder, causing it to relax and allow the flow of urine into the urethra. The internal urethral sphincter is involuntary. The ureters enter the bladder diagonally from its dorsolateral floor in an area called the trigone. The trigone is a triangular shaped area on the postero-inferior wall of the bladder. The urethra exits at the lowest point of the triangle of the trigone. The urine in the bladder also helps regulate body temperature. If the bladder becomes completely void of fluid, it causes the patient to chill.

URETHRA

The male urethra laid open on its anterior (upper) surface. (Region visible, but muscle not labelled.) The urethra is a muscular tube that connects the bladder with the outside of the body. The function of the urethra is to remove urine from the body. It measures about 1.5 inches (3.8 cm) in a woman but up to 8 inches (20 cm) in a man. Because the urethra is so much shorter in a woman it makes it much easier for a woman to get harmful bacteria in her bladder, this is commonly called a bladder infection or a UTI. The most common bacteria of a UTI is *E. coli* from the large intestines that have been excreted in faecal matter. In the human male, the urethra is about 8 inches (20 cm) long and opens at the end of the penis. The length of a male's urethra, and the fact it contains a number of bends, makes catheterisation more difficult.

In the human female, the urethra is about 1-2 inches long and opens in the vulva between the clitoris and the vaginal opening. Men have a longer urethra than women. This means that women tend to be more susceptible to infections of the bladder (cystitis) and the urinary tract. Human males have much stronger sphincter muscles than females, meaning that they can retain a large amount of urine for twice as long, as much as 800 mL, i.e., "hold it".

RENAL HORMONES

1. *Vitamin D*: Becomes metabolically active in the kidney. Patients with renal disease have symptoms of disturbed calcium and phosphate balance.
2. *Erythropoietin*: Released by the kidneys in response to decreased tissue oxygen levels (hypoxia).
3. *Natriuretic Hormone*: Released from cardiocyte granules located in the right atria of the heart in response to increased atrial stretch. It inhibits ADH secretions which can contribute to the loss of sodium and water.

FORMATION OF URINE

Urine is formed in three steps: Filtration, Reabsorption, and Secretion.

1. FILTRATION

Blood enters the afferent arteriole and flows into the glomerulus. Blood in the glomerulus has both filterable blood components and non-filterable blood components. Filterable blood components move toward the inside of the glomerulus while non-filterable blood components bypass the filtration process by exiting through the efferent arteriole. Filterable blood components now take on plasma-like form called glomerular filtrate. A few of the filterable blood components are water, nitrogenous waste, nutrients and salts (ions). Non-filterable blood components include formed elements such as blood cells and platelets along with plasma proteins. The glomerular filtrate is not of the same consistency as urine, as much of it is reabsorbed into the blood as the filtrate passes through the tubules of the nephron.

2. REABSORPTION

Within the peritubular capillary network, molecules and ions are reabsorbed back into the blood. Sodium chloride reabsorbed into the system increases the osmolarity of blood in comparison to the glomerular filtrate. This reabsorption process allows water (H_2O) to pass from the glomerular filtrate back into the circulatory system.

Glucose and various amino acids also are reabsorbed into the circulatory system. These nutrients have carrier molecules that claim the glomerular molecule and release it back into the circulatory system. If all of the carrier molecules are used up, excess glucose or amino acids are set free into the urine. A complication of diabetes is the inability of the body to reabsorb glucose. If too much glucose appears in the glomerular filtrate it increases the osmolarity of the filtrate, causing water to be released into the urine rather than reabsorbed by the circulatory system. Frequent urination and unexplained thirst are warning signs of diabetes, due to water not being reabsorbed.

Glomerular filtrate has now been separated into two forms: reabsorbed filtrate and non-reabsorbed filtrate. Non-reabsorbed filtrate is now known as tubular fluid as it passes through the collecting duct to be processed into urine.

3. SECRETION

Some substances are removed from blood through the peritubular capillary network into the distal convoluted tubule or collecting duct. These substances are hydrogen ions, creatinine, and drugs. Urine is a collection of substances that have not been reabsorbed during glomerular filtration or tubular secretion.

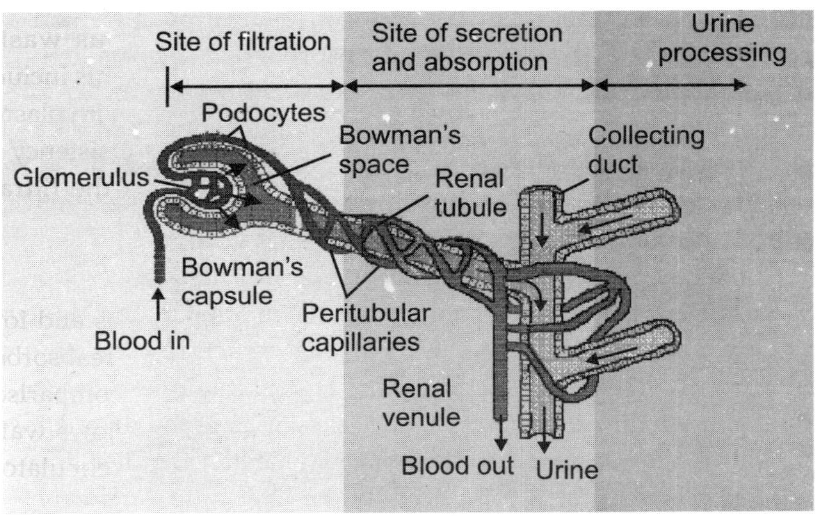

Fig. 10.5 *Filtration of the blood in the fine structure of the kidneys.*

MAINTAINING WATER-SALT BALANCE

It is the job of the kidneys to maintain the water-salt balance of the blood. They also maintain blood volume as well as blood pressure. Simple examples of ways that this balance can be changed include ingestion of water, dehydration, blood loss and salt ingestion.

1. REABSORPTION OF WATER

Direct control of water excretion in the kidneys is exercised by the anti-diuretic hormone (ADH), released by the posterior lobe of the pituitary gland. ADH causes the insertion of water channels into the membranes of cells lining the collecting ducts, allowing water reabsorption to occur. Without ADH, little water is reabsorbed in the collecting ducts and dilute urine is excreted. There are several factors that influence the secretion of ADH. The first of these happen when the blood plasma gets too concentrated. When this occurs, special receptors in the hypothalamus release ADH. When blood pressure falls, stretch receptors in the aorta and carotid arteries stimulate ADH secretion to increase volume of the blood.

2. REABSORPTION OF SALT

The kidneys also regulate the salt balance in the blood by controlling the excretion and the reabsorption of various ions. As noted above, ADH plays a role in increasing water reabsorption in the kidneys, thus helping to dilute bodily fluids. The kidneys also have a regulated mechanism for reabsorbing sodium in the distal nephron. This mechanism is controlled by aldosterone, a steroid hormone produced by the adrenal cortex. Aldosterone promotes the excretion of potassium ions and the reabsorption of sodium ions. The release of aldosterone is initiated by the kidneys. The juxtaglomerular apparatus is a renal structure consisting of the macula densa, mesangial cells, and juxtaglomerular cells. Juxtaglomerular cells (JG cells, also known as granular cells) are the site of renin secretion. Renin is an enzyme that angiotensinogen (a large plasma protein produced by the liver) into Angiotensin I and eventually into Angiotensin II which stimulates the adrenal cortex to produce aldosterone. The reabsorption of sodium ions is followed by the reapsorption of water. This causes blood pressure as well as blood volume to increase.

Atrial natriuretic hormone (ANH) is released by the atria of the heart when cardiac cells are streatched due to increased blood volume. ANH inhibits the secretion of renin by the juxta-glomerular apparatus and the secretion of the aldosterone by the adrenal cortex. This promotes the excretion of sodium. When sodium is excreted so is water. This causes blood pressure and volume to decrease.

MICTURITION

Micturition is the process of disposing urine from the urinary bladder through the urethra to the outside of the body. In healthy adults, the process of urination is under voluntary control; in infants and individuals with neurological injury, urination may occur as an involuntary reflex. *Micturition disorders* include neurogenic disorders controlling urination, urinary incontinence from several causes, and behavioural disorders.

DISORDERS OF EXCRETORY OR URINARY SYSTEM

HYPERNATREMIA

An increase in plasma sodium levels above normal is hypernatremia. Sodium is the primary solute in the extracellular fluid. Sodium levels have a major role in osmolarity regulation. For excitable cells the electrochemical gradient for sodium across the plasma membrane is critical for life. Water retention and an increased blood pressure usually are signs of hypernatremia. If the plasma sodium levels are below normal it is called hyponatremia. Signs of this are low plasma volume and hypotension.

DIURETICS

A diuretic (colloquially called a water pill) is any drug that elevates the rate of bodily urine excretion (diuresis). Diuretics also decrease the extracellular fluid (ECF) volume, and are primarily used to produce a negative extracellular fluid balance. Caffeine, cranberry juice and alcohol are all weak diuretics. In medicine, diuretics are used to treat heart failure, liver cirrhosis, hypertension and certain kidney diseases. Diuretics alleviate the symptoms of these diseases by causing sodium and water loss through the urine. As urine is produced by the kidney, sodium and water – which cause edema related to the disease – move into the blood to replace the volume lost as urine, thereby reducing the pathological edema. Some diuretics, such as acetazolamide, help to make the urine more alkaline and are helpful in increasing excretion of substances such as aspirin in cases of overdose or poisoning. The antihypertensive actions of some diuretics (thiazides and loop diuretics in particular) are independent of their diuretic effect, that is, the reduction in blood pressure is not due to decreased blood volume resulting from increased urine production, but occurs through other mechanisms and at lower doses than that required to produce diuresis. Indapamide was specifically designed with this is mind, and has a larger therapeutic window for hypertension (without pronounced diuresis) than most other diuretics. Chemically, diuretics are a diverse group of compounds that either stimulate or inhibit various hormones that naturally occur in the body to regulate urine production by the kidneys. Alcohol produces diuresis through modulation of the vasopressin system.

DIABETES INSIPIDUS

This is caused by the deficiency of or decrease of ADH. The person with (DI) has the inability to concentrate their urine in water restriction, in turn they will void up 3 to 20 litres/day. There are two forms of (DI): neurogenic, and nephrogenic. In nephrogenic (DI) the kidneys do not respond to ADH. Usually the nephrogenic (DI) is characterized by the impairment of the urine concentrating capability of the kidney along with concentration of water. The cause may be a genetic trait, electrolyte disorder, or side effect of drugs such as, lithium. In the neurogenic (DI), it is usually caused by head injury near the hypophysisal tract.

URINARY TRACT INFECTIONS (UTI'S)

The second most common type of bacterial infections seen by health care providers is UTI's. Out of all the bacterias that colonize and cause urinary tract infections the big gun is *Escherichia coli*. In the hospital indwelling catheters and straight catheterizing predispose the opportunity for urinary tract infections. In females there are three stages in life that predispose urinary tract infections, that is menarche, manipulation between intercourse, and menopause.

However, a small percentage of men and children will get urinary tract infections. In men it is usually due to the prostate gland growth which usually occurs in older age men. In children it can occur 3% to 5% in girls and 1% in boys, uncircumcised boys it is more common than circumcised ones to have a urinary tract infection, in girls it may be the result of onset of toilet training, some predispositions for getting urinary tract infection include family history and urinary tract anomalies. In neonates urinary tract infections is most common when bacteremia is present.

DIALYSIS AND KIDNEY TRANSPLANT

Generally, humans can live normally with just one kidney. Only when the amount of functioning kidney tissue is greatly diminished will renal failure develop. If renal function is impaired, various forms of medications are used, while others are contraindicated. Provided that treatment is begun early, it may be possible to reverse chronic kidney failure due to diabetes or high blood pressure. If creatinine clearance (a measure of renal function) has fallen very low ("end-stage renal failure"), or if the renal dysfunction leads to severe symptoms, dialysis is commenced. Dialysis is a medical procedure, performed in various different forms, where the blood is filtered outside of the body.

Kidney transplantation is the only cure for end stage renal failure; dialysis, is a supportive treatment; a form of "buying time" to bridge the inevitable wait for a suitable organ.

The first successful kidney transplant was announced on March 4, 1954 at *Peter Bent Brigham Hospital in Boston*. The surgery was performed by *Dr. Joseph E. Murray*, who was awarded the Nobel Prize in Medicine in 1990 for this feat.

There are two types of kidney transplants: living donor transplant and a cadaveric (dead donor) transplant. When a kidney from a living donor, usually a blood relative, is transplanted into the patient's body, the donor's blood group and tissue type must be judged compatible with the patient's, and extensive medical tests are done to determine the health of the donor. Before a cadaveric donor's organs can be transplanted, a series of medical tests have to be done to determine if the organs are healthy. Also, in some countries, the family of the donor must give its consent for the organ donation. In both cases, the recipient of the new organ needs to take drugs to suppress their immune system to help prevent their body from rejecting the new kidney.

STUDY QUESTIONS

1. Explain the structure of the kidney. Also explain the different kinds of nephron.
2. Discuss the functions of urinary system.
3. Explain the formation of urine.
4. Discuss the various disorders of excretory system.
5. Write short note on Micturition.

■■■

11

CHAPTER

THE NERVOUS SYSTEM

INTRODUCTION

The nervous system monitors and controls almost every organ system through a series of positive and negative feedback loops. The nervous system consists of the *brain* and *spinal cord* and *peripheral nerves*.

The Central Nervous System (CNS) includes the *brain* and *spinal cord*. The Peripheral Nervous System (PNS) connects the CNS to other parts of the body, and is composed of *nerves* (bundles of neurons). The *nerves* involved are cranial nerves and spinal nerves.

FUNCTIONS OF NERVOUS SYSTEM

The nervous system has three main functions: *sensory input, integration and output;* and *endocrine output.*

1. SENSORY INPUT

Receptors are parts of the nervous system that sense changes in the internal or external environments. Sensory input can be in many forms, including pressure, taste, sound, light, blood pH, or hormone levels, that are converted to a signal and sent to the brain or spinal cord.

2. INTEGRATION AND OUTPUT

In the sensory centers of the brain or in the spinal cord, the barrage of input is integrated and a response is generated. The response, a motor output, is a signal transmitted to organs that can convert the signal into some form of action, such as movement, changes in heart rate, release of hormones, etc.

3. ENDOCRINE OUTPUT

The nervous system coordinates rapid responses to external stimuli. The endocrine system controls slower, longer lasting responses to internal stimuli. Activity of both systems is integrated.

STRUCTURE OF NEURONS

The neuron is the functional unit of the nervous system. Humans have about 100 billion neurons in their brain alone. While variable in size and shape, all neurons have three parts:

Dendrites receive information from another cell and transmit the message to the cell body.

The *cell body* contains the nucleus, mitochondria and other organelles typical of eukaryotic cells.

The *axon* conducts messages away from the cell body.

Some axons are wrapped in a myelin sheath formed from the plasma membranes of specialized glial cells known as *Schwann cells.* Schwann cells serve as supportive, nutritive, and service facilities for neurons. The gap between Schwann cells is known as the *node of Ranvier,* and serves as points along the neuron for generating a signal. Signals jumping from node to node travel hundreds of times faster than signals travelling along the surface of the axon. This allows your brain to communicate with your toes in a few thousandths of a second.

There are *three* types of neurons in the body: *sensory neurons, interneurons,* and *motor neurons*. Neurons are sometimes called *nerve cells.* In vertebrates, neurons are found in the brain, the spinal cord and in the nerves and ganglia of the peripheral nervous system.The *main role* of neuron is to *process and transmit information.* Neurons have excitable membranes, which allow them to generate and propagate electrical impulses. Sensory neuron takes nerve impulses or messages right from the sensory receptor and delivers it to the central nervous system. A sensory receptor is a structure that can find any kind of change in its surroundings or environment.

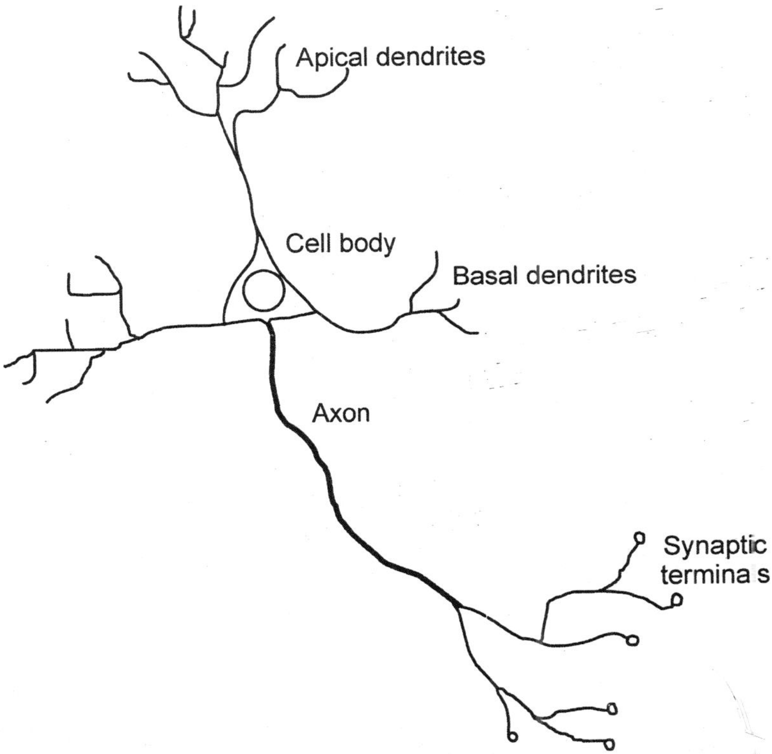

Fig. 11.1 *The structure of neuron.*

MYELIN SHEATH

Schwann cells contain a lipid substance called myelin in their plasma membranes. When Schwann cells wrap around axons, a myelin sheath forms. There are gaps that have no myelin sheath around them; these gaps are called nodes of Ranvier. Myelin sheaths make excellent insulators. Axons that are longer have a myelin sheath, while shorter axons do not. The disease multiple sclerosis is an autoimmune disease where the body attacks the myelin sheath of the central nervous system.

FUNCTIONS

Sensory afferent neurons convey information from tissues and organs into the central nervous system. Efferent neurons transmit signals from the central nervous system to the effector cells and are sometimes called motor neurons. Interneurons connect neurons within specific regions of the central nervous system. Afferent and efferent can also refer generally to neurons which, respectively, bring information to or send information from brain region.

The neurons of the brain release inhibitory neuro-transmitters far more than excitatory neurotransmitters, which helps explain why we are not aware of all memories and all sensory stimuli simultaneously. The majority of information stored in the brain is inhibited most of the time.

TRANSMISSION OF IMPULSE

The plasma membrane of neurons, like all other cells, has an unequal distribution of ions and electrical charges between the two sides of the membrane. The outside of the membrane has a positive charge, inside has a negative charge. This charge difference is a resting potential and is measured in millivolts. Passage of ions across the cell membrane passes the electrical charge along the cell. The voltage potential is –65 mV (millivolts) of a cell at rest (*resting potential*). Resting potential results from differences between sodium and potassium positively charged ions and negatively charged ions in the cytoplasm. Sodium ions are more concentrated outside the membrane, while potassium ions are more concentrated inside the membrane. This imbalance is maintained by the active transport of ions to reset the membrane known as the *sodium-potassium pump*. The sodium-potassium pump maintains this unequal concentration by actively transporting ions against their concentration gradients.

Changed polarity of the membrane, the *action potential*, results in propagation of the nerve impulse along the membrane. An action potential is a temporary reversal of the electrical potential along the membrane for a few milliseconds. Sodium gates and potassium gates open in the membrane to allow their respective ions to cross. Sodium and potassium ions reverse positions by passing through membrane protein channel gates that can be opened or closed to control ion passage. Sodium crosses first. At the height of the membrane potential reversal, potassium channels open to allow potassium ions to pass to the outside of the membrane. Potassium crosses second, resulting in changed ionic distributions, which must be reset by the continuously running sodium-potassium pump. Eventually enough potassium ions pass to the outside to restore the membrane charges to those of the original resting potential. The cell begins then to pump the ions back to their original sides of the membrane.

The action potential begins at one spot on the membrane, but spreads to adjacent areas of the membrane, propagating the message along length of the cell membrane. After passage of the action potential, there is a brief period, the refractory period, during which the membrane cannot be stimulated. This prevents the message from being transmitted backward along the membrane.

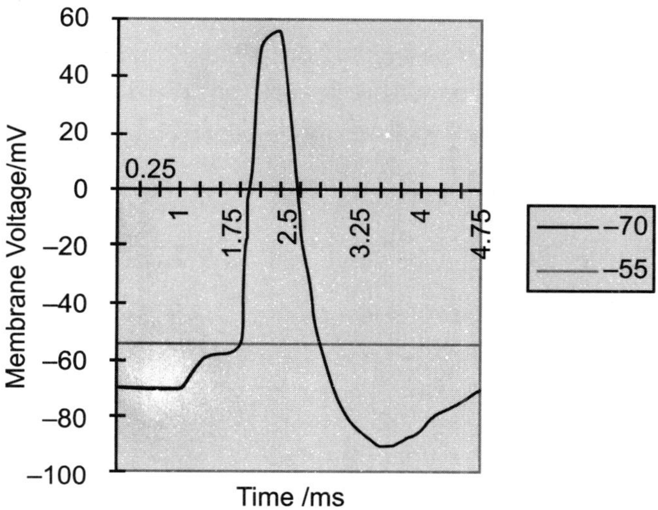

Fig. 11.2 *Transmission of impulses.*

Steps in an Action Potential

At rest the outside of the membrane is more positive than the inside. Sodium moves inside the cell causing an action potential, the influx of positive sodium ions makes the inside of the membrane more positive than the outside.

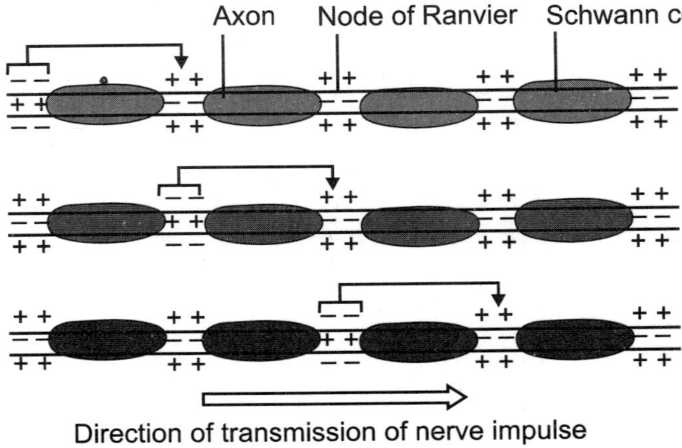

Fig. 11.3 *Saltatory conduction of an impulse in a myelinated nerve fiber.*

Potassium ions flow out of the cell, restoring the resting potential net charges.

Sodium ions are pumped out of the cell and potassium ions are pumped into the cell, restoring the original distribution of ions.

SYNAPSES AND NEUROTRANSMITTERS

The junction between a nerve cell and another cell is called a *synapse*. Messages travel within the neuron as an electrical action potential. The space between two cells is known as the *synaptic cleft*. To cross the synaptic cleft requires the actions of *neuro-transmitters*. Neurotransmitters are stored in small synaptic vesicles clustered at the tip of the axon.

Arrival of the action potential causes some of the vesicles to move to the end of the axon and discharge their contents into the synaptic cleft. Released neurotransmitters diffuse across the cleft, and bind to receptors on the other cell's membrane, causing ion channels on that cell to open. Some neurotransmitters cause an action potential, others are inhibitory.

Neurotransmitters tend to be small molecules, some are even hormones. The time for neurotransmitter action is between 0.5 and 1 millisecond.

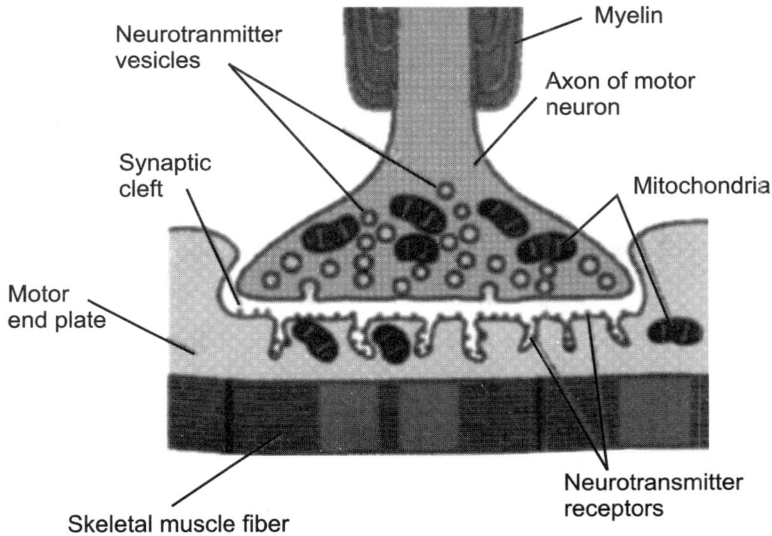

Fig. 11.4 *A synapse.*

Neurotransmitters are either destroyed by specific enzymes in the synaptic cleft, diffuse out of the cleft, or are reabsorbed by the cell. More than 30 organic molecules are thought to act as neurotransmitters. The neurotransmitters cross the cleft, binding to receptor molecules on the next cell, prompting transmission of the message along that cell's membrane.

Acetylcholine is an example of a neurotransmitter, as is norepinephrine, although each acts in different responses. Once in the cleft, neurotransmitters are active for only a short time. Enzymes in the cleft inactivate the neurotransmitters. Inactivated neurotransmitters are taken back into the axon and recycled.

Diseases that affect the function of signal transmission can have serious consequences. Parkinson's disease has a deficiency of the neurotransmitter dopamine. Progressive death of brain cells increases this deficit, causing tremours, rigidity and unstable posture.

L-dopa is a chemical related to dopamine that eases some of the symptoms (by acting as a substitute neurotransmitter) but cannot reverse the progression of the disease.

The bacterium Clostridium tetani produces a toxin that prevents the release of GABA. GABA is important in control of skeletal muscles. Without this control chemical, regulation of muscle contraction is lost; it can be fatal when it effects the muscles used in breathing.

Clostridium botulinum produces a toxin found in improperly canned foods. This toxin causes the progressive relaxation of muscles, and can be fatal. A wide range of drugs also operate in the synapses: cocaine, LSD, caffeine, and insecticides.

INFORMATION TRANSMISSION

Messages travel through the SNS in a bidirectional flow. Efferent messages can trigger changes in different parts of the body simultaneously. For example, the sympathetic nervous system can accelerate heart rate; widen bronchial passages; decrease motility (movement) of the large intestine; constrict blood vessels; increase peristalsis in the esophagus; cause pupil dilation, piloerection (goose bumps) and perspiration (sweating); and raise blood pressure. Afferent messages carry sensations such as heat, cold, or pain.

The first synapse (in the sympathetic chain) is mediated by nicotinic receptors physiologically activated by acetylcholine, and the target synapse is mediated by adrenergic receptors physiologically activated by either noradrenaline or adrenaline. An exception is with sweat glands which receive sympathetic innervation but have muscarinic acetylcholine receptors which are normally characteristic of PNS. Another exception is with certain deep muscle blood vessels, which have acetylcholine receptors and which dilate (rather than constrict) with an increase in sympathetic tone. The sympathetic system cell bodies are located on the spinal cord excluding the cranial and sacral regions. The preganglonic neurons exit from the vertebral column and synapse with the postganglonic nerons in the sympathetic trunk.

The parasympathetic nervous system is one of three divisions of the autonomic nervous system. Sometimes called the rest and digest system, the parasympathetic system conserves energy as it slows the heart rate, increases intestinal and gland activity, and relaxes sphincter muscles in the gastrointestinal tract.

THE NERVOUS SYSTEM

The nervous system is comprised of two major parts, or subdivisions, the *central nervous system* (CNS) and the *peripheral nervous system* (PNS).

The *central nervous system* includes the brain and spinal cord. The brain is the body's "control center". The CNS has various centers located within it that carry out the sensory, motor and integration of data. These centers can be subdivided to lower centers (including the spinal cord and brain stem) and higher centers communicating with the brain via effectors.

1. PERIPHERAL NERVOUS SYSTEM

The Peripheral Nervous System (PNS) contains only nerves and connects the brain and spinal cord (CNS) to the rest of the body. The axons and dendrites are surrounded by a white *myelin sheath*. Cell bodies are in the central nervous system (CNS) or ganglia. *Ganglia* are collections of nerve cell bodies. Cranial nerves in the PNS take impulses to and from the brain (CNS). Spinal nerves take impulses to and away from the spinal cord. There are two major subdivisions of the PNS motor pathways: the *somatic nervous system* and the *autonomic nervous system*.

Two main functional parts of the Peripheral Nervous System (PNS) are:

(i) *Sensory* (afferent) pathways that provide input from the body into the CNS.

(ii) *Motor* (efferent) pathways that carry signals to muscles and glands (effectors).

Most sensory input carried in the PNS remains below the level of conscious awareness. Input that does reach the conscious level contributes to perception of our external environment.

SPINAL NERVE

The peripheral nerves contain the axons of neurons that are running to and from the CNS. Many of the axons are myelinated, but others are not. These axons are bundled together to form a nerve. There are levels of axonal bundling. The *epineurium* is the connective tissue that wraps around the entire nerve. Axons within the nerve are bundled into large *fascicles* held together by *perineurium*. And connective tissue that runs along individual myelinated axons or groups of unmyelinated axons is called *endoneurium*.

There are 31 pairs of spinal nerves. These nerves are mixed, having both a sensory and a motor aspect. Their motor fibers begin on the ventral part of the spinal cord at the anterior horns of the gray matter. The roots of their sensory fibers are located on the dorsal side of the spinal cord in the posterior root ganglia. When the motor and sensory fibers exit the spinal column through the intervertebral foramina and pass through the meninges, they join together to form the spinal nerves.

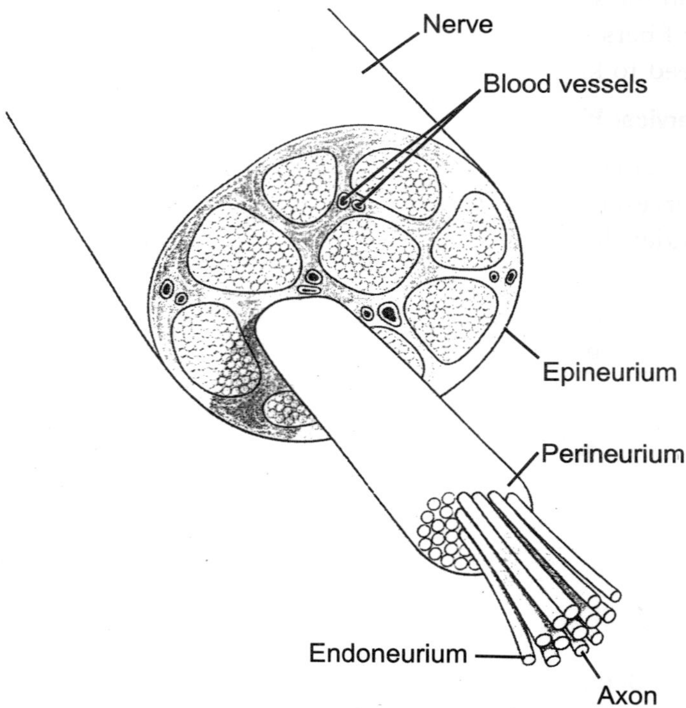

Fig. 11.5 *Transverse section of a peripheral nerve showing the protective coverings.*

Spinal nerves receive only contralateral innervation from first order neurons.

Eight pairs of spinal nerves are located in the uppermost, cervical region of the cord:

- 12 pairs are found in the thoracic region.
- 5 pairs are in the lumbar area.
- 5 pairs are in the sacral area.
- 1 pair is found in the most inferior, coccygeal region.

Spinal nerves join together in *plexuses*. A plexus is an interconnection of fibers which form new combinations as the "named" or peripheral nerves. There are four voluntary plexuses (there are some autonomic plexuses which will be mentioned later): they are the cervical plexus, the brachial plexus, the lumbar plexus, and the sacral plexus. Each plexus gives rise to new combinations of fibers as the peripheral nerves. The nerves and plexuses you need to know are:

Cervical Plexus

This is formed by the anterior rami of the first four cervical nerves. It lies opposite the 1st, 2nd, 3rd, and 4th cervical vertebrae under the protection of the sternocleiodomastoid muscle.

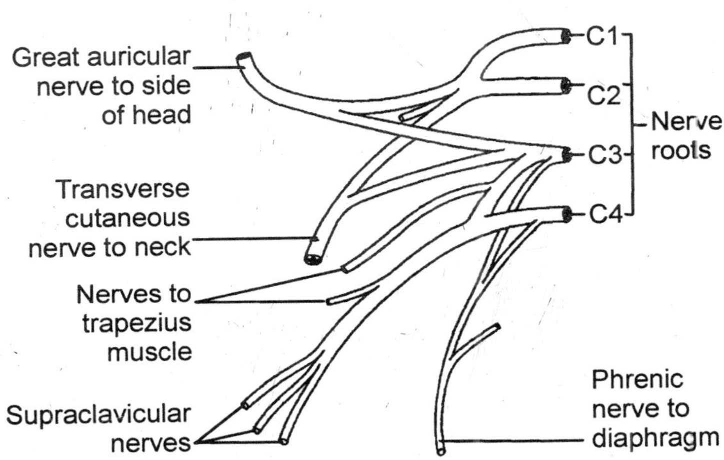

Fig. 11.6 *Cervial plexus (Anterior view).*

Brachial Plexus

- *Axillary nerve* – innervates the deltoid muscle and shoulder, along with the posterior aspect of the upper arm.
- *Musculocutaneous nerve* – innervates anterior skin of upper arm and elbow flexors.
- *Radial nerve* – innervates dorsal aspect of the arm and extensors of the elbow, wrist, and fingers, abduction of thumb.
- *Median nerve* – innervates the middle elbow, wrist and finger flexors, adducts the thumb.
- *Ulnar nerve* – innervates the medial aspect wrist and finger flexors.

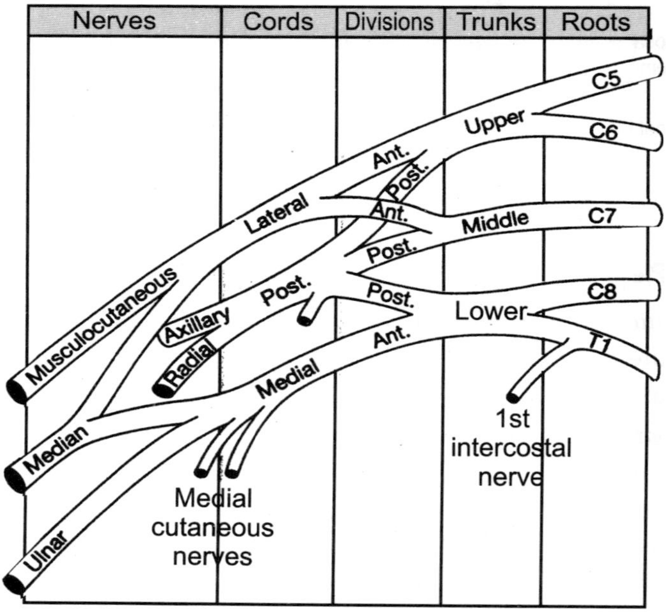

Fig. 11.7 *Brachial plexus. Anterior view. ant= anterior, post= posterior.*

Lumbar Plexus

- *Genitofemoral*: To the external genitalia.
- *Obturator*: To the adductor muscles.
- *femoral*: Innervates the skin and muscles of upper thigh, including the quadriceps.

- Iliohypogastric nerve.
- Ilioinguinal nerve.
- Lateral cutaneous nerve of thigh.
- Lumbosacral trunk.

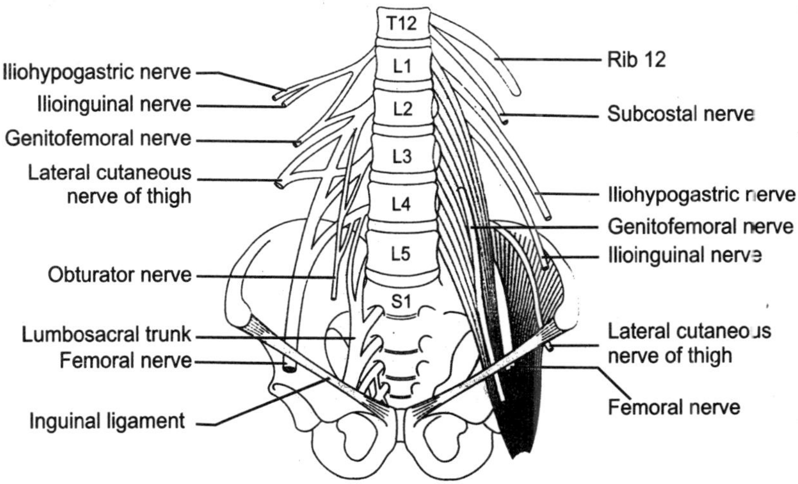

Fig. 11.8 *Lumber plexus.*

Sacral Plexus

- *Gluteal nerve* (superior and inferior): Superior innervates the gluteus medius and minimus, inferior innervates the gluteus maximus.
- *Sciatic nerve:* The body's largest nerve, consisting of two major branches, the tibial and common peroneal. Together they innervate most, all of leg including the flexors of the knee, part of adductor magnus, muscles for plantar flexion, dorsiflexion, and other movements of the foot and toes.
- *Tibia nerve* descends through the popliteal fossa to the posterior aspect of the leg where it supplies muscles and skin.
- The *common peroneal nerve* descends obliquely along the lateral aspect of the popliteal fossa, which is round the neck of the fibula in front of the leg where it divides into the deep peroneal and *supraficial peroneal nerves.*

- *The pudendal nerve*: The peroneal branch supplies the external and sphincter, the external urethral sphincter and adjacent skin.

Coccygeal Plexus

- The coccygeal plexus is a very small plexus fromed by part of the fourth and fifth sacral and the coccygeal nerves. The nerves from this plexus supply the skin around the coccyx andanal area.

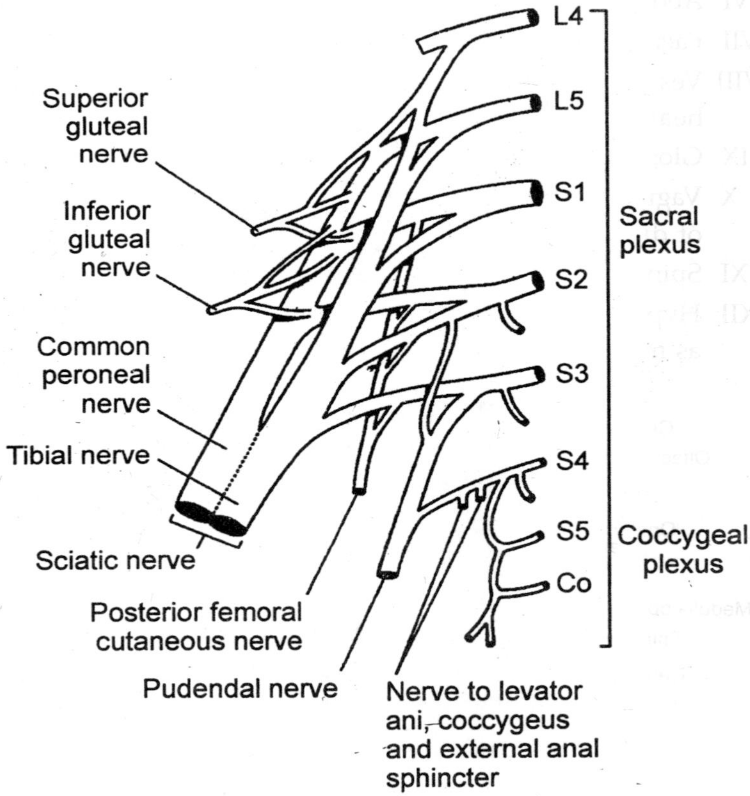

Fig. 11.9 *Sacral and coccygeal plexuses.*

CRANIAL AND SPINAL NERVES

The peripheral nervous system includes 12 cranial nerves, 31 pairs of spinal nerves. It can be subdivided into the somatic and autonomic systems. It is a way of communication from the central nervous system to the rest of the body by nerve impulses that regulate the functions of the human body. The twelve cranial nerves are:

I Olfactory nerve for smell.
II Optic nerve for vision.
III Oculomotor for looking around.
IV Trochlear for moving eye.
V Trigeminal for feeling touch on face.
VI Abducens to move eye muscles.
VII Facial to smile, wink, and help us taste.
VIII Vestibulocochlear to help with balance, equilibrium, and hearing.
IX Glossopharyngeal for swallowing and gagging.
X Vagus for swallowing, talking, and parasympathetic actions of digestion.
XI Spinal accessory for shrugging shoulders.
XII Hypoglossal for tongue more divided into different regions as muscles.

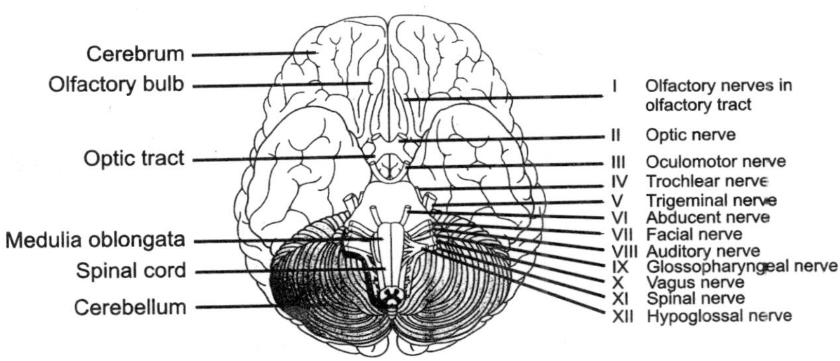

Fig. 11.10 *The inferior surface of the brain showing the cranial nerves.*

The 10 out of the 12 cranial nerves originate from the brainstem, and mainly control the functions of the anatomic structures of the head with some exceptions. CN X receives visceral sensory information from the thorax and abdomen, and CN XI is responsible for innervating the sternocleidomastoid and trapezius muscles, neither of which is exclusively in the head.

The Autonomic Nervous System

The autonomic nervous system is a part of the *peripheral nervous system* that functions to regulate the basic visceral (organ) processes needed for the maintenance of normal bodily functions. It operates independently of voluntary control, although certain events, such as emotional stress, fear, sexual excitement, and alterations in the sleep-wakefulness cycle, change the level of autonomic activity.

The autonomic system is usually defined as a *motor system* that innervates three major types of tissue: cardiac muscle, smooth muscle, and glands. However, this definition needs to be expanded to encompass the fact that it also relays visceral sensory information into the central nervous system and processes it in such a way as to make alterations in the activity of specific autonomic motor outflows, such as those that control the heart, blood vessels, and other visceral organs. It also causes the release of certain hormones involved in energy metabolism (e.g., *insulin, glucagon, epinephrine*) or cardiovascular functions (e.g., *renin, vasopressin*). These integrated responses maintain the normal internal environment of the body in an equilibrium state called *homeostasis*.

Rami Communicantes

The rami of the autonomic nervous system are the axons of *pre-ganglionic* and *ganglionic fibers*. Most of the axons of pre-ganglionic fibers are myelinated. Their cell bodies are found in the gray matter of the brain stem and spinal cord. Their axons synapse with neurons within the two ganglionic chains.

Pre-ganglionic cells of the autonomic nervous system are neurons located in some of the cranial nerves of the brain stem and in some of the spinal nerves that project to the ganglionic chains of the autonomic nervous system. The autonomic nervous system is closely connected with the central and peripheral nervous systems.

Ganglionic cells originate within the ganglia. They project to post-ganglionic neurons.

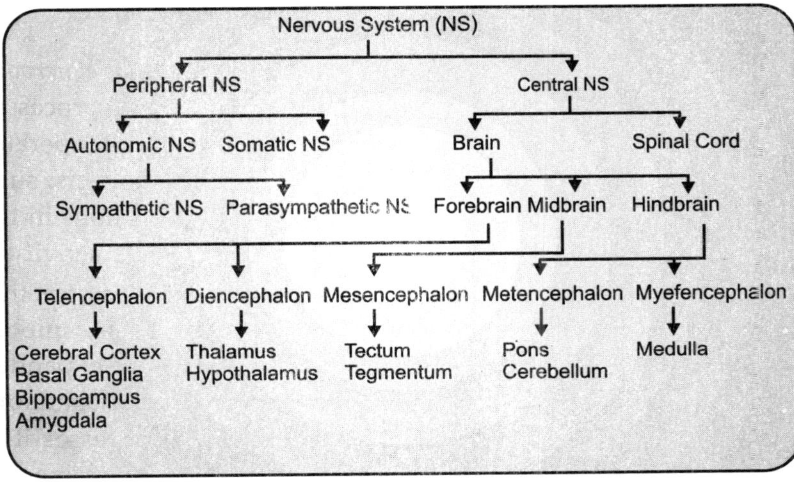

Post-ganglionic cells are neurons that are located in the target organs and muscles of the autonomic nervous system.

It can be said that the motor pathways of the autonomic nervous system are made up of its pre-ganglionic and ganglionic cells.

The fibers of the ganglionic chain of the parasympathetic system are not as well-defined as those of the sympathetic chain. All ***pre-ganglionic neurons*** of the sympathetic system synapse with the sympathetic chain. This is not true of the parasympathetic pre-ganglionic cells, however. Some of them synapse with the chain, but others go directly to end organs or muscles.

Division of Autonomic Nervous System

The autonomic nervous system has two components, the sympathetic system and the parasympathetic system. These two aspects have antagonistic functions.

(a) Sympathetic System

The preganglionic motor neurons of the sympathetic system arise in the spinal cord. They pass into sympathetic ganglia which are organized into two chains that run parallel to and on either side of the spinal cord.

The *preganglionic neuron* may do one of *three* things in the sympathetic ganglion:

(i) *Synapse* with postganglionic neurons which then re-enter the spinal nerve and ultimately pass out to the sweat glands and the walls of blood vessels near the surface of the body.

(ii) Pass up or down the sympathetic chain and finally synapse with postganglionic neurons in a higher or lower ganglion.

(iii) Leave the ganglion by way of a cord leading to special ganglia (e.g., the solar plexus) in the viscera. Here it may synapse with postganglionic sympathetic neurons running to the smooth muscular walls of the viscera. However, some of these preganglionic neurons pass right on through this second ganglion and into the adrenal medulla. Here they synapse with the highly-modified postganglionic cells that make up the secretory portion of the adrenal medulla.

The neurotransmitter of the preganglionic sympathetic neurons is ***acetylcholine*** (ACh). It stimulates action potentials in the postganglionic neurons. The neurotransmitter released by the postganglionic neurons is *noradrenaline* (also called norepinephrine).

The action of noradrenaline on a particular gland or muscle is excitatory is some cases, inhibitory in others. (At excitatory terminals, ATP may be released along with noradrenaline.) The release of noradrenaline

- stimulates heartbeat,
- raises blood pressure,
- dilates the pupils,
- dilates the trachea and bronchi,
- stimulates the conversion of liver glycogen into glucose,
- shunts blood away from the skin and viscera to the skeletal muscles, brain, and heart,
- inhibits peristalsis in the gastrointestinal (GI) tract,
- inhibits contraction of the bladder and rectum, and
- at least in rats and mice, increases the number of AMPA receptors in the hippocampus and thus increases long-term potentiation (LTP).

In short, stimulation of the sympathetic branch of the autonomic nervous system prepares the body for emergencies: for "fight or flight" (and, perhaps, enhances the memory of the event that triggered the response).

Activation of the sympathetic system is quite general because a single preganglionic neuron usually synapses with many postganglionic neurons; the release of adrenaline from the adrenal medulla into the blood ensures that all the cells of the body will be exposed to sympathetic stimulation even if no postganglionic neurons reach them directly.

(b) Parasympathetic System

The main nerves of the parasympathetic system are the tenth cranial nerves, the *vagus nerves*. They originate in the *medulla oblongata*. Other *preganglionic* parasympathetic neurons also extend from the brain as well as from the lower tip of the spinal cord.

Each preganglionic parasympathetic neuron synapses with just a few *postganglionic* neurons, which are located near— or in — the effector organ, a muscle or gland. *Acetylcholine* (ACh) is the neurotransmitter at all the pre and many of the post-ganglionic neurons of the parasympathetic system. However, some of the postganglionic neurons release nitric oxide (NO) as their neurotransmitter. Parasympathetic stimulation causes

- slowing down of the heartbeat,
- lowering of blood pressure,
- constriction of the pupils,
- increased blood flow to the skin and viscera, and
- peristalsis of the GI tract,

In short, the parasympathetic system returns the body functions to normal after they have been altered by sympathetic stimulation. In times of danger, the sympathetic system prepares the body for violent activity. The parasympathetic system reverses these changes when the danger is over.

The vagus nerves also help keep inflammation under control. Inflammation stimulates nearby sensory neurons of the vagus. When these nerve impulses reach the medulla oblongata, they are relayed back along motor fibers to the inflamed area. The acetylcholine from the motor neurons suppresses the release of inflammatory cytokines, e.g., tumor necrosis factor (TNF), from macrophages in the inflamed tissue.

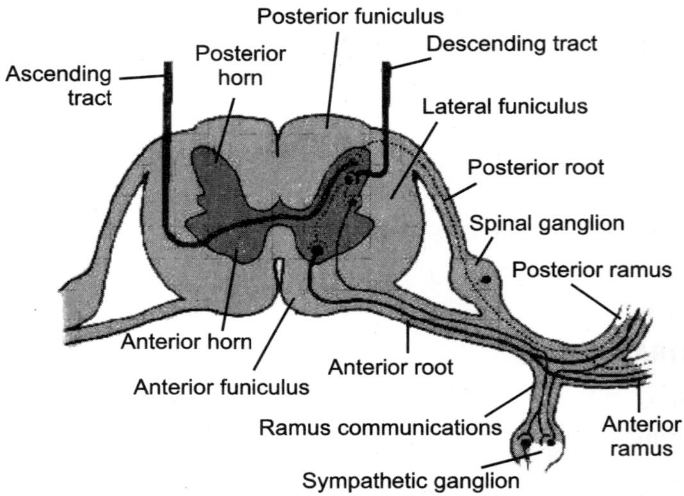

Fig. 11.11. *Spinal cord.*

2. SOMATIC NERVOUS SYSTEM

The Somatic Nervous System (SNS) includes all nerves controlling the muscular system and external sensory receptors. External sense organs (including skin) are receptors. Muscle fibers and gland cells are effectors. The reflex arc is an automatic, involuntary reaction to a stimulus. When the doctor taps your knee with the rubber hammer, she/he is testing your reflex (or knee-jerk). The reaction to the stimulus is involuntary, with the CNS being informed but not consciously controlling the response. Examples of reflex arcs include balance, the blinking reflex, and the stretch reflex.

Sensory input from the PNS is processed by the CNS and responses are sent by the PNS from the CNS to the organs of the body.

Motor neurons of the somatic system are distinct from those of the autonomic system. Inhibitory signals, cannot be sent through the motor neurons of the somatic system.

In the SNS and other components of the peripheral nervous system, these synapses are made at sites called ganglia. The cell that sends its fiber is called a *preganglionic cell,* while the cell whose fiber leaves the ganglion is called a postganglionic cell. As mentioned previously, the preganglionic cells of the SNS are located between the first thoracic segment and the second or third lumbar segments of the spinal cord. Postganglionic cells have their cell bodies in the ganglia and send their axons to target organs or glands.

The ganglia include not just the sympathetic trunks but also the superior cervical ganglion (which sends sympathetic nerve fibers to the head), and the celiac and mesenteric ganglia (which send sympathetic fibers to the gut).

3. CENTRAL NERVOUS SYSTEM

The Central Nervous System (CNS) is composed of the *brain* and *spinal cord*. The CNS is surrounded by bone-skull and vertebrae. Fluid and tissue also insulate the brain and spinal cord.

NEUROGLIA

Neuroglia or glial cell are non-neuronal cells that provide support and nutrition, maintain homeostasis, form myelin, and participate in signal transmission in the nervous system. In the human brain, glia are estimated to outnumber neurons by about 10 to 1.

Glial cells provide support and protection for neurons, the other main type of cell in the nervous system. They are thus known as the "glue" of the nervous system. The four main functions of glial cells are to surround neurons and hold them in place, to supply nutrients and oxygen to neurons, to insulate one neuron from another, and to destroy pathogens and remove dead neurons.

Types of Glial Cells

Microglia

Microglia are specialized macrophages capable of phagocytosis that protect neurons of the central nervous system. They are derived from hemopoietic precursors rather than ectodermal tissue;

they are commonly categorized as such because of their supportive role to neurons.

These cells comprise approximately 15% of the total cells of the central nervous system. They are found in all regions of the brain and spinal cord. Microglial cells are small relative to macroglial cells, with changing shapes and oblong nuclei. They are mobile within the brain and multiply when the brain is damaged. In the healthy central nervous system, microglia processes constantly sample all aspects of their environment (neurons, macroglia and blood vessels).

Macroglia

Astrocytes

The most abundant type of macroglial cell, astrocytes (also called astroglia) have numerous projections that anchor neurons to their blood supply. They regulate the external chemical environment of neurons by removing excess ions, notably potassium, and recycling neurotransmitters released during synaptic transmission. The current theory suggests that astrocytes may be the predominant "building blocks" of the blood-brain barrier. Astrocytes may regulate vasoconstriction and vasodilation by producing substances such as arachidonic acid, whose metabolites are vasoactive.

Astrocytes signal each other using calcium. The gap junctions (also known as electrical synapses) between astrocytes allow the messenger molecule IP3 to diffuse from one astrocyte to another. IP3 activates calcium channels on cellular organelles, releasing calcium into the cytoplasm. This calcium may stimulate the production of more IP3. The net effect is a calcium wave that propagates from cell to cell. Extracellular release of ATP, and consequent activation of purinergic receptors on other astrocytes, may also mediate calcium waves in some cases.

There are generally two types of astrocytes, *protoplasmic* and *fibrous*, similar in function but distinct in morphology and distribution. Protoplasmic astrocytes have short, thick, highly branched processes and are typically found in gray matter. Fibrous astrocytes have long, thin, less branched processes and are more commonly found in white matter.

Oligodendrocytes

Oligodendrocytes are cells that coat axons in the central nervous system (CNS) with their cell membrane forming a specialized membrane differenciation called myelin, producing the so-called myelin sheath. The myelin sheath provides insulation to the axon that allows electrical signals to propagate more efficiently.

Ependymal cells

Ependymal cells, also named ependymocytes, line the cavities of the CNS and make up the walls of the ventricles. These cells create and secrete cerebrospinal fluid (CSF) and beat their cilia to help circulate that CSF.

Radial glia

Radial glia cells arise from neuroepithelial cells after the onset of neurogenesis. Their differentiation abilities are more restricted than those of neuroepithelial cells. In the developing nervous system, radial glia function both as neuronal progenitors and as a scaffold upon which newborn neurons migrate. In the mature brain, the cerebellum and retina retain characteristic radial glial cells. In the cerebellum, these are Bergmann glia, which regulate synaptic plasticity. In the retina, the radial Müller cell is the principal glial cell, and participates in a bidirectional communication with neurons.

Schwann cells

Similar in function to oligodendrocytes, Schwann cells provide myelination to axons in the peripheral nervous system (PNS). They also have phagocytotic activity and clear cellular debris that allows for regrowth of PNS neurons.

MENINGES

The meninges (singular meninx) is the system of membranes which envelops the central nervous system. The meninges consist of three layers: the pia mater, arachnoid mater, and the dura mater. The primary function of the meninges and of the cerebrospinal fluid is to protect the central nervous system.

PIA MATER

The pia or pia mater is a very delicate membrane. It is attached to (nearest) the brain or the spinal cord. As such it follows all the minor contours of the brain (gyri and sulci). The pia mater is the meningeal envelope which firmly adheres to the surface of the brain and spinal cord. It is a very thin membrane composed of fibrous tissue covered on its outer surface by a sheet of flat cells thought to be impermeable to fluid. The pia mater is pierced by blood vessels which travel to the brain and spinal cord, and its capillaries are responsible for nourishing the brain.

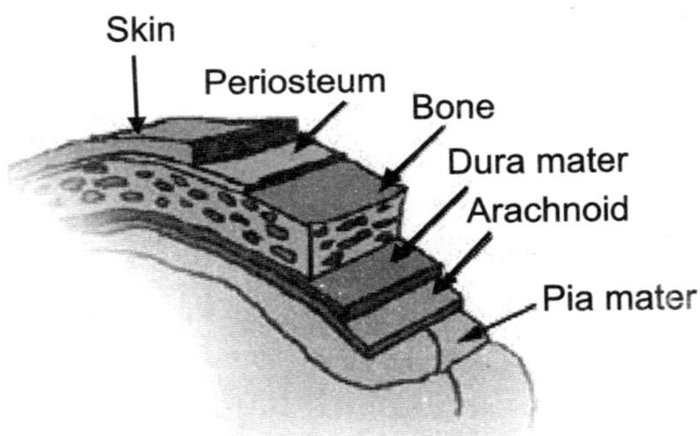

Fig. 11.12 *Meninges.*

ARACHNOID MATER

The middle element of the meninges is the arachnoid mater, so named because of its spider web-like appearance. It provides a cushioning effect for the central nervous system. The arachnoid mater exists as a thin, transparent membrane. It is composed of fibrous tissue and, like the pia mater, is covered by flat cells also thought to be impermeable to fluid. The arachnoid does not follow the convolutions of the surface of the brain and so looks like a loosely fitting sac. In the region of the brain, particularly, a large number of fine filaments called arachnoid trabeculae pass from the arachnoid through the subarachnoid space to blend with the tissue of the pia mater. The arachnoid and pia mater are sometimes together called the *leptomeninges*.

DURA MATER

The dura mater (also rarely called meninx fibrosa, or pachymeninx) is a thick, durable membrane, closest to the skull. It contains larger blood vessels which split into the capilliaries in the pia mater. It is composed of dense fibrous tissue, and its inner surface is covered by flattened cells like those present on the surfaces of the pia mater and arachnoid. The dura mater is a sac which envelops the arachnoid and has been modified to serve several functions. The dura mater surrounds and supports the large venous channels (dural sinuses) carrying blood from the brain toward the heart.

SUBARACHNOID SPACES

The subarachnoid space is the space which normally exists between the arachnoid and the pia mater, which is filled with cerebrospinal fluid.

Normally, the dura mater is attached to the skull, or to the bones of the vertebral canal in the spinal cord. The arachnoid is attached to the dura mater, and the pia mater is attached to the central nervous system tissue. When the dura mater and the arachnoid separate through injury or illness, the space between them is the subdural space.

CEREBROSPINAL FLUID (CSF)

Cerebrospinal fluid (CSF), liquor cerebrospinalis, is a clear bodily fluid that occupies the subarachnoid space and the ventricular system around and inside the brain. Essentially, the brain "floats" in it.

More specifically the CSF occupies the space between the arachnoid mater (the middle layer of the brain cover, meninges) and the pia mater (the layer of the meninges closest to the brain). Moreover it constitutes the content of all intra-cerebral (inside the brain, cerebrum) ventricles, cisterns and sulci (singular sulcus), as well as the central canal of the spinal cord.

It is produced in the brain by modified ependymal cells in the choroid plexus. It circulates from the choroid plexus through the interventricular foramina (foramen of Monro) into the third ventricle, and then through the mesencephalic duct (cerebral aqueduct) into the fourth ventricle, where it exits through two lateral apertures (foramina of Luschka) and one median aperture (foramen of Magendie). It then flows through the cerebromedullary cistern down the spinal cord and over the cerebral hemispheres.

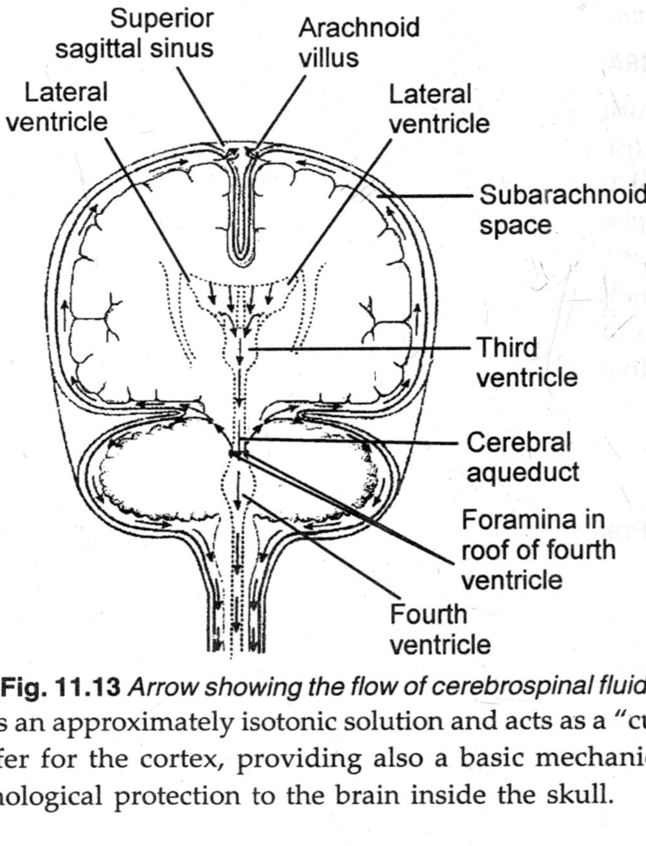

Fig. 11.13 *Arrow showing the flow of cerebrospinal fluid.*

It is an approximately isotonic solution and acts as a "cushion" or buffer for the cortex, providing also a basic mechanical and immunological protection to the brain inside the skull.

BRAIN

The human brain controls the central nervous system (CNS), by way of the cranial nerves and spinal cord, the peripheral nervous system (PNS) and regulates virtually all human activity. Involuntary, or "lower", actions, such as heart rate, respiration, and digestion, are unconsciously governed by the brain, specifically through the autonomic nervous system. Complex, or "higher", mental activity, such as thought, reason, and abstraction, is consciously controlled.

During embryonic development, the brain first forms as a tube, the anterior end of which enlarges into three hollow swellings that form the brain, and the posterior of which develops into the spinal cord. Sub-division and increasing specialization of the *forebrain, midbrain,* and *hindbrain.*

FOREBRAIN OR CEREBRUM OR TELENCEPHALON

During vertebrate embryonic development, the *prosencephalon,* the most anterior of three vesicles that form from the embryonic neural tube, is further subdivided into the *telencephalon* and *diencephalon*. The telencephalon then forms two lateral telencephalic vesicles which develop into the *left* and *right cerebral hemispheres.*

The cerebrum, or forebrain is the most anterior part of dorsal region of the vertebrate central nervous system. The cerebrum is also divided into symmetric left and right cerebral hemispheres.

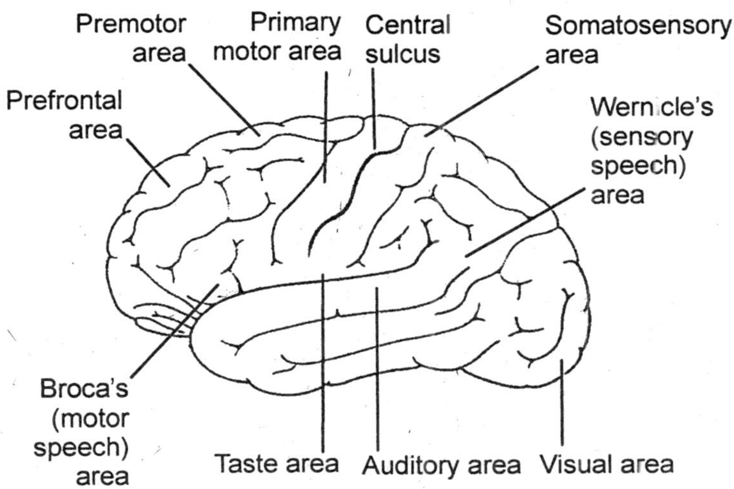

Fig. 11.14 *The cerebrum showing the main functional areas.*

The cerebrum is composed of the following sub-regions:

- Cerebral cortex, or cortices of the cerebral hemispheres.

- Basal ganglia, or basal nuclei (also often called the striatum).
- Olfactory bulb.

In humans, the cerebrum surrounds older parts of the brain. Limbic, olfactory, and motor systems project fibers from the cerebrum to the brainstem and spinal cord. The cerebrum directs the conscious or volitional motor functions of the body. These functions originate within the primary motor cortex and other frontal lobe motor areas where actions are planned. Upper motor neurons in the primary motor cortex send their axons to the brainstem and spinal cord to synapse on the lower motor neurons, which innervate the muscles. Damage to motor areas of cortex can lead to certain types of motor neuron disease. This kind of damage results in loss of muscular power and precision rather than total paralysis.

Cerebral Cortex

The cerebral cortex is a structure within the brain that plays a key role in memory, attention, perceptual awareness, thought, language, and consciousness. The cerebral cortex develops from the most anterior part of the neural plate, a specialized part of the embryonic ectoderm. The neural plate folds and closes to form the neural tube.

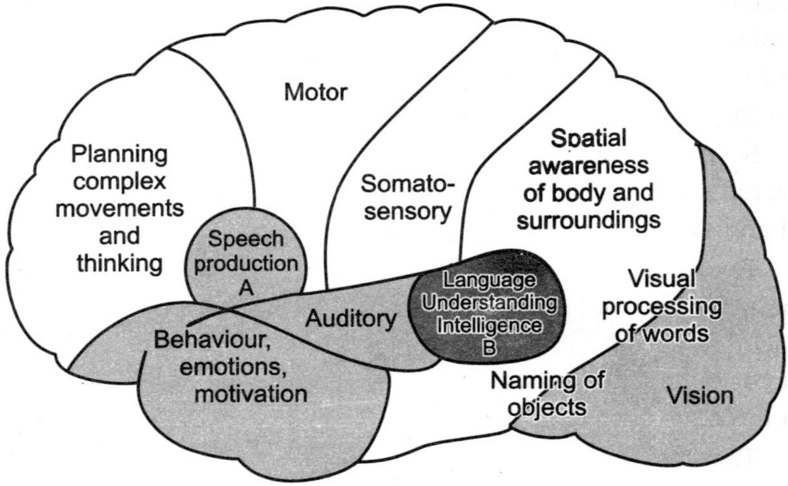

Fig. 11.15 *The cerebral cortex showing the mental functional areas.*

The most anterior (frontal) part of the neural tube, the telencephalon, gives rise to the cerebral hemispheres and cortex. The cerebral cortex is connected to various subcortical structures such as the *thalamus* and the *basal ganglia,* sending information to them along efferent connections and receiving information from them via afferent connections. Most sensory information is routed to the cerebral cortex via the thalamus. Olfactory information, however, passes through the olfactory bulb to the olfactory cortex (piriform cortex). The vast majority of connections are from one area of the cortex to another rather than to subcortical areas.

THE MIDBRAIN (MESENCEPHALON)

The mesencephalon is the most superior part of the brainstem. It is divided into an anterior and a posterior section by the ***Aqueduct of Sylvius*** which connects the third and fourth ventricles. Motor tracts, including the fibers of the pyramidal system, pass downward on the midbrain's anterior surface. Sensory axons, including those of the spinothalamic tract also ascend, along the front of the midbrain behind the motor tracts.

The ***corpora quadrigemina,*** which is located on the posterior surface of the midbrain, is composed of two *superior colliculi* and two *inferior colliculi.* The superior colliculi are part of the visual system, relaying input from the optic tract to the lateral geniculate bodies of the thalamus. The inferior colliculi are part of the auditory pathway and send information to the medial geniculate bodies of the thalamus.

Several important nuclei are located in the midbrain, including the red nuclei, the substantia nigra, and the nuclei of cranial nerves III and IV.

The red nuclei connect the midbrain to the cerebellum and to the inner ear. It is also an important part of the extra pyramidal tract. The cerebellum compares input from muscles and joints with motor output from the cortex and relays subsequent adjustments to the cortex through the red nucleus and thalamus.

The substantia nigra is a group of dark-coloured, dopaminergic cells.

CN III is the oculomotor nerve.

CN IV is the trochlear nerve.

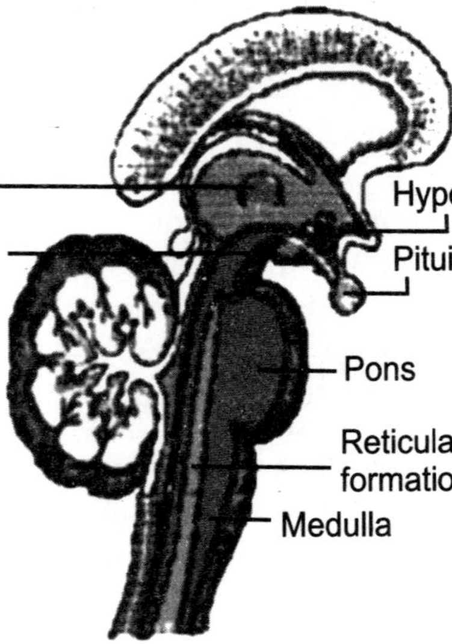

Fig. 11.16 *Midbrain.*

Both of these cranial nerves provide innervation for motor movements of the eyes.

The cerebral peduncles (cruz cerebri) are two very large bundles of axons which are a continuation of the efferent projections within the internal capsule. It includes cortico bulbar (cortex to brain stem) and cortico spinal (cortex to spinal cord) axons.

The Pons

The pons, which is also part of the brain stem, is inferior to the midbrain and superior to the medulla. Its posterior border is separated from the cerebellum by the *Aqueduct of Sylvius,* and more inferiorly, by the fourth ventricle. Motor and sensory tracts traverse the anterior surface of the pons. The sensory fibers are located behind the motor fibres.

The nuclei of cranial nerves V and VI are located in the pons. CN V, or the trigeminal, sends motor messages to the jaw and receives sensory messages from the teeth, tongue, and parts of the face. CN VI, or the abducens, provides motor innervation to the eye.

The motor nucleus of cranial nerve VII, the facial nerve, is located on the border of the pons and medulla. The upper part of the nerve innervates the muscles of facial expression including the eye lids, forehead and the lips. The lower part innervates the voluntary muscles of the face below the eyelids. Cortico bulbar (pyramidal) fibres provide contralateral and ipsa innervation (bilateral) to the muscles of the upper face but only contralateral (unilateral) innervation to the lower face. Additionally, facial paralysis due to a pyramidal lesion will not permit voluntary control of the muscles but these paralyzed muscles will respond to emotional expression. This is due to extrapyramidal involuntary control.

The Medulla Oblongata

The medulla is the most inferior part of the brainstem. The cell bodies of the following cranial nerves are located there:

- CN IX, the glossopharyngeal nerve.
- CN X, the vagus nerve.
- CN XI, the spinal accessory nerve.
- CN XII, the hypoglossal nerve.

Because the nuclei of the vagus nerve are found in the medulla, it is considered to be a center for circulation and respiration. It is also quite important to swallowing. It controls muscles of the pharynx, larynx and velum for swallowing.

The Reticular Formation

The reticular formation is a set of interconnected nuclei that are located throughout the brain stem. Its dorsal tegmental nuclei are in the midbrain while its central tegmental nuclei are in the pons and its central and inferior nuclei are found in the medulla. The reticular formation has two components:

The *ascending reticular formation* is also called the reticular activating system. It is responsible for the sleep-wake cycle, thus mediating various levels of alertness. This part of the reticular system projects to the mid-line group of the thalamus, which also plays a role in wakefulness. From there, information is sent to the cortex.

The *descending reticular formation* is involved in posture and equilibrium as well as autonomic nervous system activity. It receives information from the hypothalamus. The descending reticular formation also plays a role in motor movement.

Interneurons of the reticular formation receive some of the cortico-bulbar fibers from the motor cortex. It is those fibers that innervate the three cranial nerves involved in eye movement. Other cortico-bulbar fibers innervate cranial nerves directly. The descending reticular nuclei in the brain are involved in reflexive behaviour such as coughing, chewing, swallowing and vomiting.

The *medulla oblongata* is closest to the spinal cord, and is involved with the regulation of heartbeat, breathing, vasoconstriction (blood pressure), and reflex centers for vomiting, coughing, sneezing, swallowing, and hiccuping. The hypothalamus regulates homeostasis. It has regulatory areas for thirst, hunger, body temperature, water balance, and blood pressure, and links the Nervous System to the Endocrine System. The midbrain and pons are also part of the unconscious brain. The thalamus serves as a central relay point for incoming nervous messages.

CEREBELLUM

The cerebellum is the third part of the hindbrain. It functions for muscle coordination and maintains normal muscle tone and posture.

The conscious brain includes the *cerebral hemispheres,* which are separated by the corpus callosum. In reptiles, birds, and mammals, the cerebrum coordinates sensory data and motor functions. The cerebrum governs intelligence and reasoning, learning and memory. While the cause of memory is not yet definitely known, studies on slugs indicate learning is accompanied by a synapse decrease. Within the cell, learning involves change in gene regulation and increased ability to secrete transmitters.

The *cortex* in each hemisphere of the cerebrum is between 1 and 4 mm thick. Folds divide the cortex into ***four lobes: occipital, temporal, parietal,*** and ***frontal***. No region of the brain functions alone, although major functions of various parts of the lobes have been determined.

The *occipital lobe* (back of the head) receives and processes visual information. The *temporal lobe* receives auditory signals, processing language and the meaning of words. The *parietal lobe* is associated with the sensory cortex and processes information about touch, taste, pressure, pain, and heat and cold. The *frontal lobe* conducts three functions:

(i) Motor activity and integration of muscle activity.
(ii) Speech.
(iii) Thought processes.

Most people who have been studied have their language and speech areas on the left hemisphere of their brain. Language comprehension is found in Wernicke's area. Speaking ability is in Broca's area. Damage to Broca's area causes speech impairment but not impairment of language comprehension. Lesions in

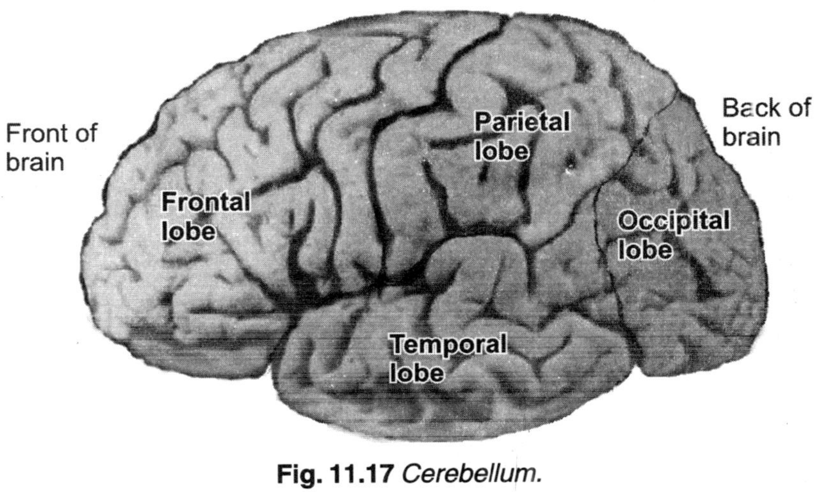

Fig. 11.17 *Cerebellum.*

Wernicke's area impairs ability to comprehend written and spoken words but not speech. The remaining parts of the cortex are associated with higher thought processes, planning, memory, personality and other human activities.

THE SPINAL CORD

The spinal cord runs along the dorsal side of the body and links the brain to the rest of the body. Vertebrates have their spinal cords encased in a series of (usually) bony vertebrae that comprise the vertebral column. The human spinal cord extends from the medulla oblongata and continues through the conus medullaris near the first or second lumbar vertebrae, terminating in a fibrous extension known as the filum terminale. It is about 45 cm long in men and 42 cm long in women, ovoid-shaped, and is enlarged in the cervical and lumbar regions. In cross-section, the peripheral region of the cord contains neuronal white matter tracts containing sensory and motor neurons. Internal to this peripheral region is the gray, butterfly shaped central region made up of nerve cell bodies. This central region surrounds the central canal, which is an anatomic extension of the spaces in the brain known as the ventricles and, like the ventricles, contains cerebrospinal fluid.

The three meninges that cover the spinal cord — the outer *dura mater*, the *arachnoid mater*, and the innermost *pia mater* — are continuous with that in the brainstem and cerebral hemispheres. Similarly, *cerebrospinal fluid* is found in the *subarachnoid space*. The cord is stabilized within the dura mater by the connecting denticulate ligaments which extend from the enveloping pia mater laterally between the dorsal and ventral roots. The dural sac ends at the vertebral level of the second sacral vertebra.

The human spinal cord is divided into 31 different segments, with motor nerve roots exiting in the ventral aspects and sensory nerve roots entering in the dorsal aspects. The ventral and dorsal roots later join to form paired spinal nerves, one on each side of the spinal cord.

There are 31 spinal cord nerve segments in a human spinal cord:

(i) 8 cervical segments (cervical nerves exit spinal column above C1 and below C1-C7).

(ii) 12 thoracic segments (thoracic nerves exit spinal column below T1-T12).

(iii) 5 lumbar segments (lumbar nerves exit spinal column below L1-L5).

(iv) 5 sacral segments (sacral nerves exit spinal column below S1-S5).

(v) 1 coccygeal segment (coccygeal nerves exit spinal column at coccyx)

Because the vertebral column grows longer than the spinal cord, spinal cord segments become higher than the corresponding vertebra, especially in the lower spinal cord segments in adults. In a faetus, the vertebral levels originally correspond with the spinal cord segments. In the adult, the cord ends around the L1/L2 vertebral level at the conus medullaris, with all of the spinal cord segments located superiorly to this.

REFLEX ACTION

A reflex action is an automatic neuromuscular action elicited by a defined stimulus. A reflex is a biological control system linking stimulus to response and mediated by a reflex arc.

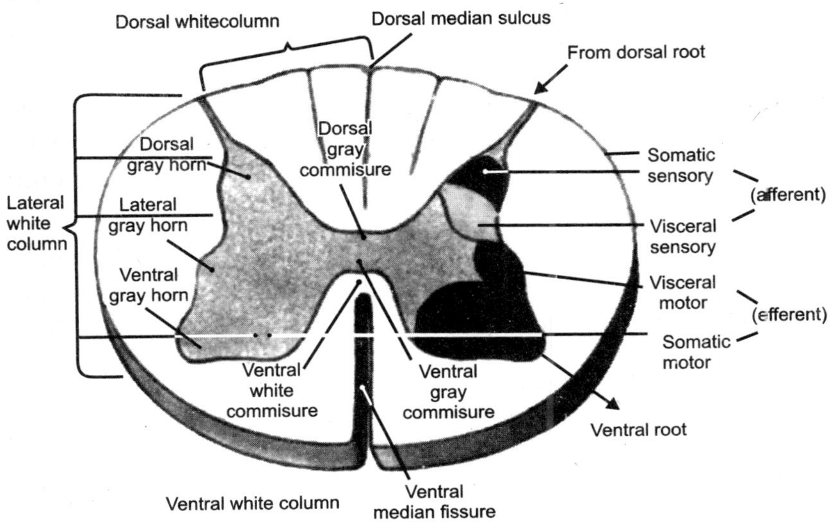

Fig. 11.18 *A simple reflex action.*

The spinal cord is the medium by which motor and sensory impressions are conducted to and from the brain. It receives impressions from all parts of the body by means of the sensory nerves, and conveys them to the brain, where they produce sensation. It conducts the command of the brain to the voluntary muscles by the motor nerves, and thus causes movement. In all this the brain is the power, and the cord the conductor; but, as well as this, the cord has a special function — that of reflex action. If the connection of the cord with the brain is severed, and the skin supplied by afferent nerves below the injured part is irritated, movement will be produced in the part supplied by *efferent nerves* from the same part of the cord. This is *reflex action*.

The irritation of an *afferent nerve* connected with the spinal cord sends an impulse to a nerve centre (*gray matter*) in the cord, and without communication with the brain this nerve centre has the power of sending back an impulse by an efferent nerve (or nerves), producing contraction of the muscle or muscles in which the efferent fibres terminate. A person paralysed from spinal injury will thus draw up his legs and kick out when the soles of his feet are tickled. Both in the brain and cord active power is confined to the gray matter. The brain itself gives rise to reflex actions—actions which take place without the will or consciousness of the individual, such as instinctive shrinking from a threatened blow, or blinking from a flash of light.

Reflexes are tested as part of a neurological examination to assess damage to or functioning of the central and peripheral nervous system. Reflexes may be trained, such as during repetition of motor actions during sport practice, or the linking of stimuli with autonomic reactions during classical conditioning.

FUNCTIONS OF THE CNS

The Central Nervous System (CNS) represents the largest part of the nervous system, including the brain and the spinal cord. The CNS is conceived as a system devoted to information processing, where an appropriate motor output is computed as a response to a sensory input. Many threads of research suggest that motor activity exists well before the maturation of the sensory systems, and senses only influence behaviour without dictating it. This has brought the conception of the CNS as an autonomous system. The central nervous system is the control center for the body. It regulates organ function, higher thought, and movement of the body. The central nervous system consists of the brain and spinal cord.

THALAMUS

Lesions or stimulation of the medial, dorsal, and anterior nuclei of the thalamus are associated with changes in emotional reactivity. However, the importance of these nuclei on the regulation of emotional behaviour is not due to the thalamus itself, but to the connections of these nuclei with other limbic system structures. The medial dorsal nucleus makes connections with cortical zones of the prefrontal area and with the hypothalamus. The anterior nuclei connect with the mamillary bodies and through them, via fornix, with the hippocampus and the cingulated gyrus, thus taking part in what is known as the Papez's circuit.

RECEPTORS

The parasympathetic nervous system uses only acetylcholine (ACh) as its neurotransmitter. The ACh acts on two types of receptors: the *muscarinic* and *nicotinic cholinergic* receptors. Most transmissions occur in two stages—when stimulated, the preganglionic nerve releases ACh at the ganglion, which acts on nicotinic receptors of the postganglionic nerve. The postganglionic nerve then releases ACh to stimulate the muscarinic receptors of the target organ.

The three main types of muscarinic receptors that are well characterised are:

(i) The M1 muscarinic receptors are located in the neural system.

(ii) The M2 muscarinic receptors are located in the heart, and act to bring the heart back to normal after the actions of the sympathetic nervous system: slowing down the heart rate, reducing contractile forces of the atrial cardiac muscle, and reducing conduction velocity of the atrioventricular node (AV node). Note, they have no effect on the contractile forces of the ventricular muscle.

(iii) The M3 muscarinic receptors are located at many places in the body, such as the smooth muscles of the blood vessels, as well as the lungs, which means that they cause vasoconstriction and bronchoconstriction. They are also in the smooth muscles of the gastrointestinal tract (GIT), which help in increasing intestinal motility and dilating sphincters. The M3 receptors are also located in many glands that help to stimulate secretion in salivary glands and other glands of the body.

ELECTROENCEPHALOGRAM (EEG)

An electroencephalogram (EEG) is a test that measures and records the electrical activity of your brain. Special sensors (electrodes) are attached to your head and hooked by wires to a computer. The computer records your brain's electrical activity on the screen or on paper as wavy lines. Certain conditions, such as seizures, can be seen by the changes in the normal pattern of the brain's electrical activity.

An electroencephalogram (EEG) may be done in a hospital or in a doctor's office by an EEG technologist. The EEG record is read by a doctor who is specially trained to diagnose and treat disorders affecting the nervous system (neurologist).

EEG (electroencephalographic) *biofeedback,* now more commonly known as *neurofeedback,* is a specialized form of biofeedback that aims to retrain brain waves.

BRAIN WAVES

Our brains generate electrical activity (brain waves) all the time. The waves that one can measure at any one time depend on the state the brain. The state of the brain varies from being drowsy and sleepy, to being fully awake and focused. As we engage in different activities, the electrical activity of the brain also changes. In biofeedback, we are interested in three different brain waves:

(i) *Theta,*
(ii) *Alpha,* and
(iii) *Beta.*

These waves, which we see as tracings across the computer screen, differ from each other in two respects. Firstly, they differ in *size* or *amplitude*.

(i) *High: Small amplitude*: The waves also differ in the number of cycles per second (hertz abbreviated as Hz). They can be *slow waves*, or *fast waves*.

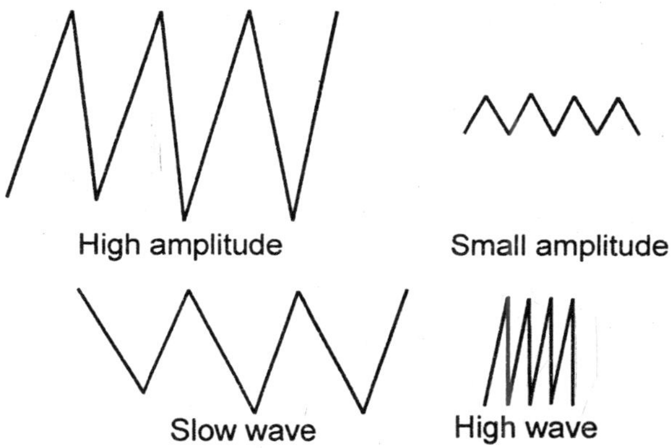

1. Theta Waves

Theta waves are slow high amplitude waves. There are only 4–7 cycles (Hz) per second, hence they are described as slow. They are present during sleep. Brain waves that are slower than 3 Hz are called Delta waves and they are found in coma.

Theta waves are abnormal in awake adults. They are implicated in anxiety, and in neurological conditions such as epilepsy, traumatic brain injury, and Attention Deficit Disorders (ADD/ADHD).

In neurofeedback, we treat epilepsy, traumatic brain injury (slowed information processing associated with inattention and memory problems), and ADD/ADHD, by retraining patients to inhibit theta waves, whilst they increase beta waves. In insomnia that is associated with tension and anxiety, some patients benefit from training to increase theta waves.

2. Alpha Waves

Alpha waves have moderate amplitude and medium speed (8-12 Hz). They are associated with closing of one's eyes. Alpha waves are associated with calmness and relaxation. Interestingly, when we pray, or when we meditate, we tend to close their eyes. Perhaps we are unwittingly trying to get ourselves into alpha states. People in alpha states are awake but relaxed.

In neurofeedback, we use alpha training and sometimes alpha/theta training for the treatment of depression, anxiety, post-traumatic stress disorder (PTSD), general stress, and addictions (alcohol, cigarettes, and other drugs). Healthy individuals may use alpha training to enhance their relaxation skills.

3. Beta Waves

Beta waves are fast low amplitude waves, cycling at 12-40 Hz. These waves are associated with arousal, problem solving, attention and concentration, and other intellectual processes. Beta waves are classified into low beta, also known as *Sensory-Motor Rhythm* [SMR (approx. 12-15 Hz)] Beta (16-20 Hz), and High Beta (22-40 Hz). Low beta is associated with the organization of brain processes, whilst the high beta is more associated with arousal, and is implicated in anxiety states.

In neurofeedback, retraining of beta waves is used in the treatment of epilepsy, ADD/ADHD, learning disorders, depression, migraines, traumatic brain injury, and premenstrual syndrome. In insomnia, patients who are relaxed but are still sleepless benefit from training to increase the SMR.

Other tests that may also be done include:

1. Video EEG

Video EEG records seizures on videotape and on computer, so that the doctor can see what happens just before, during, and right after a seizure. This test can be very helpful in finding the specific area of the brain that the seizures may be coming from. It is also helpful in diagnosing psychogenic seizures, which may look like real seizures but do not affect the electrical activity in the brain. Video EEG may be used:

- *Short-term monitoring* is done on an outpatient basis and may last up to 6 hours.
- *Long-term monitoring* is done in the hospital and may last 3 to 7 days.

2. Brain Mapping

Brain mapping is a fairly new method that is very similar to EEG. With electrodes placed on the person's scalp to transmit the brain's electrical activity, a computer makes a colour-coded map of signals from the brain. It is sometimes done to find a specific problem area in the brain that has already shown up on a regular EEG. Doctors are still not certain how brain mapping could be best used.

3. Ambulatory EEG Monitoring

In ambulatory EEG monitoring, the person is able to move around, and the test allows for long periods of time in recording of electrical activity in the brain. Fewer electrodes are attached to the person, and the person carries a small, portable recording unit. The recording may last for a full day or more, and the person is allowed to leave the hospital. Ambulatory EEG monitoring is not as accurate as a regular EEG.

In the past, EEGs played a bigger roll than they do now in the diagnosis of brain injury due to strokes and in the diagnosis and identification of brain tumors. Computer-assisted techniques such as CT-scans (an X-ray image of the body, also called a CAT scan); MRIs (magnetic resonance imaging, which uses radio waves and magnetic fields to produce and image); and PET scans (positron emission tomography, which uses a radioactive tracer that is injected into the body to help form a picture), have taken over most of the tasks of diagnosing these conditions, since they tend to be more sensitive and specific in the diagnosis of strokes and tumors and are simpler to do and easier to interpret than EEGs.

STUDY QUESTIONS

1. What is neuron? Describe the structure of neuron.
2. Explain the different parts of peripheral nervous system.
3. What is spinal cord?
4. Write short notes on:
   (a) Brain
   (b) Cranial Nerve
   (c) Sacral Nerve
   (d) Autonomic Nervous System.

12

CHAPTER

SENSE ORGANS

WHAT ARE SENSES?

Sense is a faculty by which outside stimuli are perceived. We experience reality through our senses. A sense is a faculty by which outside stimuli are perceived. Many neurologists disagree about how many senses there actually are due to a broad interpretation of the definition of a sense. Our senses are split into two different groups. Our exteroceptors detect stimulation from the outsides of our body. For example, smell, taste, and equilibrium. The interoceptors receive stimulation from the inside of our bodies. For instance, blood pressure dropping, changes in the gluclose and Ph levels. Children are generally taught that there are five senses (sight, hearing, touch, smell, and taste). However, it is generally agreed that there are at least seven different senses in humans, and a minimum of two more observed in other organisms. Sense can also differ from one person to the next. Take taste for an example: what may taste great to one person will taste awful to someone else. This all has to do with how the brain interprets the stimuli that are received.

CHEMORECEPTORS

The senses of gustation (taste) and olfaction (smell) fall under the category of chemoreception. Specialized cells act as receptors for certain chemical compounds. As these compounds react with the receptors, an impulse is sent to the brain and is registered as a certain taste or smell. Gustation and olfaction are chemical senses because the receptors they contain are sensitive to the molecules in the food we eat, along with the air we breath.

GUSTATORY SYSTEM

In humans, the sense of taste is transduced by taste buds and is conveyed via three of the twelve cranial nerves. Cranial nerve VII, the facial nerve, carries taste sensations from the anterior two-thirds of the tongue (excluding the circumvallate papillae, see lingual papilla) and soft palate. Cranial nerve IX the glossopharyngeal nerve carries taste sensations from the posterior one-third of the tongue (including the circumvallate papillae). Also a branch of the vagus nerve carries some taste sensations from the back of the oral cavity (i.e., pharynx and epiglottis). Information from these cranial nerves is processed by the gustatory system. Though there are small differences in sensation, which can be measured with highly specific instruments, all taste buds can respond to all types of taste. Sensitivity to all tastes is distributed across the whole tongue and indeed to other regions of the mouth where there are taste buds (epiglottis, soft palate).

PAPILLA

Papilla are specialized epithelial cells. There are four types of papillae: *filiform* (thread-shape), *fungiform* (mushroom-shape), *foliate* (leaf-shape), and *circumvallate* (ringed-circle). All papillae except the filiform have taste buds on their surface. Some act directly by ion channels, others act indirectly.

Filiform papillae: These are thin, longer papillae that do not contain taste buds but are the most numerous. These papillae are mechanical and not involved in gustation.

Fungiform papillae: As the name suggests, are slightly mushroom shaped if looked at in section. These are present mostly at the apex (tip) of the tongue.

Foliate papillae: These are ridges and grooves towards the posterior part of the tongue.

Circumvallate papillae: There are only about 3-14 of these papillae on most people and they are present at the back of the oral part of the tongue. They are arranged in a circular-shaped row just in front of the sulcus terminalis of the tongue.

TANGORECEPTORS

The receptors for taste, called taste buds, are situated chiefly in the tongue, but they are also located in the roof of the mouth and near the pharynx. They are able to detect four basic tastes: salty, sweet, bitter, and sour. The tongue also can detect a sensation called "umami" from taste receptors sensitive to amino acids. Generally, the taste buds close to the tip of the tongue are sensitive to sweet tastes, whereas those in the back of the tongue are sensitive to bitter tastes. The taste buds on top and on the side of the tongue are sensitive to salty and sour tastes. At the base of each taste bud there is a nerve that sends the sensations to the brain. The sense of taste functions in coordination with the sense of smell. The number of taste buds varies substantially from individual to individual, but greater numbers increase sensitivity. Women, in general, have a greater number of taste buds than men. As in the case of colour blindness, some people are insensitive to some tastes.

On some of the filiform papillæ the epithelial prolongations stand erect, in one they are spread out, and in three they are folded in. Each taste bud is flask-like in shape, its broad base resting on the corium, and its neck opening by an orifice, the gustatory pore, between the cells of the epithelium. The bud is formed by two kinds of cells: *supporting cells* and *gustatory cells.*

The ***supporting cells*** are mostly arranged like the staves of a cask, and form an outer envelope for the bud. Some, however, are found in the interior of the bud between the gustatory cells. The gustatory cells occupy the central portion of the bud; they are spindle-shaped, and each possesses a large spherical nucleus near the middle of the cell. The peripheral end of the cell terminates at the gustatory pore in a fine hair-like filament, the gustatory hair.

Fig. 12.1 *Tongue.*

The central process passes toward the deep extremity of the bud, and there ends in single or bifurcated varicosities. The nerve fibrils after losing their medullary sheaths enter the taste bud, and end in fine extremities between the gustatory cells; other nerve fibrils ramify between the supporting cells and terminate in fine extremities; these, however, are believed to be nerves of ordinary sensation and not gustatory.

TYPES OF TASTE

Salt

Arguably the simplest receptor found in the mouth is the salt (NaCl) receptor. An ion channel in the taste cell wall allows Na^+ ions to enter the cell. This on its own depolarizes the cell, and opens voltage-regulated Ca^{2+} gates, flooding the cell with ions and leading to neurotransmitter release. This sodium channel is known as EnAC and is composed of three subunits. EnAC can be blocked by the drug amiloride in many mammals, especially rats. The sensitivity of the salt taste to amiloride in humans, however, is much less pronounced, leading to conjecture that there may be additional receptor proteins besides EnAC that may not have been discovered yet.

Sour

Sour taste signals the presence of acidic compounds (H^+ ions in solution). There are three different receptor proteins at work in sour taste. The first is a simple ion channel which allows hydrogen ions to flow directly into the cell. The protein for this is EnAC, the same protein involved in the distinction of salt taste (this implies a relationship between salt and sour receptors and could explain why salty taste is reduced when a sour taste is present). There are also H^+ gated channels present. The first is a K^+ channel, which ordinarily allows K^+ ions to escape from the cell. H^+ ions block these, trapping the potassium ions inside the cell (this receptor is classified as MDEG1 of the EnAC/Deg Family). A third protein opens to Na^+ ions when a hydrogen ion attaches to it, allowing the sodium ions to flow down the concentration gradient into the cell. The influx of ions leads to the opening of a voltage regulated Ca^{2+} gate. These receptors work together and lead to depolarization of the cell and neurotransmitter release.

Bitter

There are many classes of bitter compounds which can be chemically very different. It is interesting that the human body has evolved a very sophisticated sense for bitter substances: we can distinguish between the many radically different compounds which produce a generally "bitter" response. This may be because the sense of bitter taste is so important to survival, as ingesting a bitter compound may lead to injury or death. Bitter compounds act through structures in the taste cell walls called G-protein coupled receptors (GPCR's). Recently, a new group of GPCR's was discovered, known as the T2R's, which is thought to only respond to bitter stimuli. When the bitter compound activates the GPCR, it in turn releases gustducin, the G-protein it was coupled to.

Gustducin is made of three subunits. When it is activated by the GPCR, its subunits break apart and activate phosphodiesterase, a nearby enzyme. It then converts a precursor within the cell into a secondary messenger, which closes potassium ion channels. This secondary messenger can stimulate the endoplasmic reticulum to release Ca^{2+}, which contributes to depolarization. This leads to a build-up of potassium ions in the cell, depolarization, and neurotransmitter release. It is also possible for some bitter tastants to interact directly with the G-protein, because of a structural similarity to the relevant GPCR.

Sweet

Like bitter tastes, sweet taste transduction involves GPCR's. The specific mechanism depends on the specific molecule. "Natural" sweeteners such as saccharides activate the GPCR, which releases gustducin. The gustducin then activates the molecule adenylate cyclase, which is already inside the cell. This molecule increases concentration of the molecule cAMP, or adenosine 3', 5'-cyclic monophosphate. This protein will either directly or indirectly close potassium ion channels, leading to depolarization and neurotransmitter release. Synthetic sweeteners such as saccharin activate different GPCR's, initiating a similar process of protein transitions, starting with the protein phospholipase A, which ultimately leads to the blocking of potassium ion channels.

Umami

Umami is a Japanese word meaning "savory" or "meaty". It is thought that umami receptors act much the same way as bitter and sweet receptors (they involve GPCR's), but not much is known about their specific function. We do know that umami detects glutamates that are common in meats, cheese and other protein-heavy foods. Umami receptors react to foods treated with monosodium glutamate (MSG). This explains why eating foods that have MSG in them often give a sense of fullness. It is thought that the amino acid L-glutamate bonds to a type of GPCR known as a *metabotropic glutamate receptor* (mGluR4). This causes the G-protein complex to activate a secondary receptor, which ultimately leads to neurotransmitter release. The intermediate steps are not known.

DISORDERS OF THE TONGUE

Loss of Taste

You may lose your sense of taste if the facial nerve is damaged. Then there is also Sjogren's syndrome where the saliva production is reduced. In most cases the loss of taste is typically a symptom of anosmia – a loss of the sense of smell.

Sore Tongue

It is usually caused by some form of trauma, such as biting your tongue, or eating piping-hot or highly acidic food or drink. If your top and bottom teeth do not fit neatly together, tongue trauma is more likely. Some people may experience a sore tongue from grinding their teeth (bruxism). Disorders such as diabetes, anemia, some types of vitamin deficiency and certain skin diseases can include a sore tongue among the range of symptoms.

Benign Migratory Glossitis

This condition is characterized by irregular and inflammed patches on the tongue surface that often have white borders. The tongue may be generally swollen, red and sore. Another name for this condition is geographic tongue. The cause of benign migratory glossitis is unknown.

OLFACTORY SYSTEM

Olfaction is the sense of smell. In humans the sence of smell is received in nasopharynx. Airborne molecules go into solution on moist epithelial surface of nasal passage. An olfactory receptors neuron sends an impulse via Cranial nerve I the olfactory nerve. Although 80-90% of what we think is "taste" actually is due to smell. This is why when we have a head cold or stuffed up nose we have a harder time tasting our foods.

Humans have 347 functional odor receptor genes; the other genes have nonsense mutations. This number was determined by analyzing the genome in the Human Genome Project; the number may vary among ethnic groups, and does vary among individuals. For example, not all people can smell androstenone, a component of male sweat.

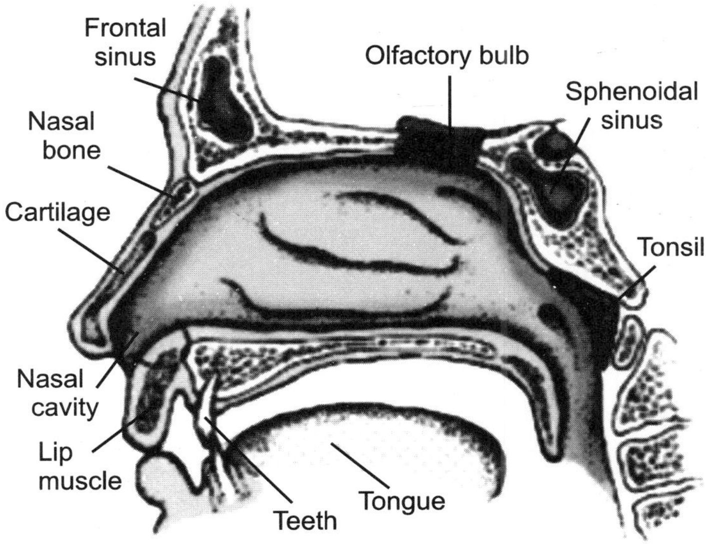

Fig. 12.2 *Olfactory receptor.*

Each olfactory receptor neuron in the nose expresses only one functional odor receptor. Odor receptor nerve cells may function like a key-lock system; if the odor molecules can fit into the lock the nerve cell will respond. According to shape theory, each receptor detects a feature of the odor molecule. Weak-shape theory, known as odotope theory, suggests that different receptors detect only small pieces of molecules, and these minimal inputs are combined to create a larger olfactory perception (similar to the way visual perception is built up of smaller, information-poor sensations, combined and refined to create a detailed overall perception). An alternative theory, the vibration theory proposed by Luca Turin, posits that odor receptors detect the frequencies of vibrations of odor molecules in the infrared range by electron tunneling. However, the behavioural predictions of this theory have been found lacking.

An olfactory receptor neuron, also called an olfactory sensory neuron, is the primary transduction cell in the olfactory system. Humans have about 40 million olfactory receptor neurons. In vertebrates, olfactory receptor neurons reside on the olfactory epithelium in the nasal cavity. These cells are bipolar neurons with a dendrite facing the interior space of the nasal cavity and an axon that travels along the olfactory nerve to the olfactory bulb.

Many tiny hair-like cilia protrude from the olfactory receptor cell's dendrite and into the mucus covering the surface of the olfactory epithelium. These cilia contain olfactory receptors, a type of G protein-coupled receptor. Each olfactory receptor cell contains only one type of olfactory receptor, but many separate olfactory receptor cells contain the same type of olfactory receptor. The axons of olfactory receptor cells of the same type converge to form glomeruli in the olfactory bulb.

Olfactory receptors can bind to a variety of odor molecules. The activated olfactory receptor in turn activates the intracellular G-protein GOLF, and adenylate cyclase and production of cyclic AMP opens ion channels in the cell membrane, resulting in an influx of sodium and calcium ions into the cell. This influx of positive ions causes the neuron to depolarize, generating an action potential.

Individual olfactory receptor neurons are replaced approximately every 40 days by neural stem cells residing in the olfactory epithelium. The regeneration of olfactory receptor cells, as one of the only few instances of adult neurogenesis in the central nervous system, has raised considerable interest in dissecting the pathways for neural development and differentiation in adult organisms.

OLFACTION AND GUSTATION

Olfaction, taste and trigeminal receptors together contribute to flavor. It should be emphasized that there are no more than 5 distinctive tastes: salty, sour, sweet, bitter, and umami. The 10,000 different scents which humans usually recognize as 'tastes' are often lost or severely diminished with the loss of olfaction. This is the reason why food has little flavor when your nose is blocked, as from a cold.

The key nutrition players in our taste is the olfactory function, 80-90% of what we consider taste is dependent on our senses of smell. With aging our olfactory function declines. In the elderly careful monitoring of appetite is necessary due to the alterations in the olfactory function. Nutritionist suggest giving a dual approach of supplementation of the trace minerals zinc and iron to enhance the smell and taste senses.

DISORDERS OF OLFACTION

ANOSMIA

Anosmia is the lack of olfaction, or a loss of the sense of smell. It can be either temporary or permanent. A related term, hyposmia refers to a decrease in the ability to smell. Some people may be anosmic for one particular odor. This is called "specific anosmia" and may be genetically based. Anosmia can have a number of detrimental effects. Patients with anosmia may find food less appetizing. Loss of smell can also be dangerous because it hinders the detection of gas leaks, fire, body odor, and spoiled food. The common view of anosmia as trivial can make it more difficult for a patient to receive the same types of medical aid as someone who has lost other senses, such as hearing or sight. A temporary loss of smell can be caused by a stuffy nose or infection. In contrast, a permanent loss of smell may be caused by death of olfactory receptor neurons in the nose, or by brain injury in which there is damage to the olfactory nerve or damage to brain areas that process smell. The lack of the sense of smell at birth, usually due to genetic factors, is referred as congenital anosmia. Anosmia may be an early sign of degenerative brain diseases such as Parkinson's disease and Alzheimer's disease. Another specific cause of permanent loss could be from damage to olfactory receptor neurons due to use of nasal sprays. To avoid loss of smell from nasal sprays, use them for only a short amount of time. Nasal sprays that are used to treat allergy related congestion are the only nasal sprays that are safe to use for extended periods of time.

PHANTOSMIA

Phantosmia is the phenomenon of smelling odors that are not really present (as known as Phantom odors). The most common odors are unpleasant smells such as rotting flesh, vomit, feces, smoke etc. Phantosmia often results from damage to the nervous tissue in the olfactory system. The damage can be caused by viral infection, trauma, surgery, and possibly exposure to toxins or drugs. It can also be induced by epilepsy affecting the olfactory cortex. It is also thought the condition can have psychiatric origins.

PHOTORECEPTORS

A photoreceptor, or photoreceptor cell, is a specialized type of neuron found in the eye's retina that is capable of phototransduction. More specifically, the photoreceptor sends signals to other neurons by a change in its membrane potential when it absorbs photons. Eventually, this information will be used by the visual system to form a complete representation of the visual world. There are two types of photoreceptors: rods are responsible for scotopic, or night vision, whereas cones are responsible for photopic, or daytime vision as well as colour perception.

The eye is the organ of vision. It has a complex structure consisting of a transparent lens that focuses light on the retina. The retina is covered with two basic types of light-sensitive cells-rods and cones. The cone cells are sensitive to colour and are located in the part of the retina called the *fovea,* where the light is focused by the lens. The rod cells are not sensitive to colour, but have greater sensitivity to light than the cone cells. These cells are located around the fovea and are responsible for peripheral vision and night vision. The eye is connected to the brain through the optic nerve. The point of this connection is called the "blind spot" because it is insensitive to light. Experiments have shown that the back of the brain maps the visual input from the eyes.

The brain combines the input of our two eyes into a single three-dimensional image. In addition, even though the image on the retina is upside-down because of the focusing action of the lens, the brain compensates and provides the right-side-up perception. Experiments have been done with subjects fitted with prisms that invert the images. The subjects go through an initial period of great confusion, but subsequently they perceive the images as right side up.

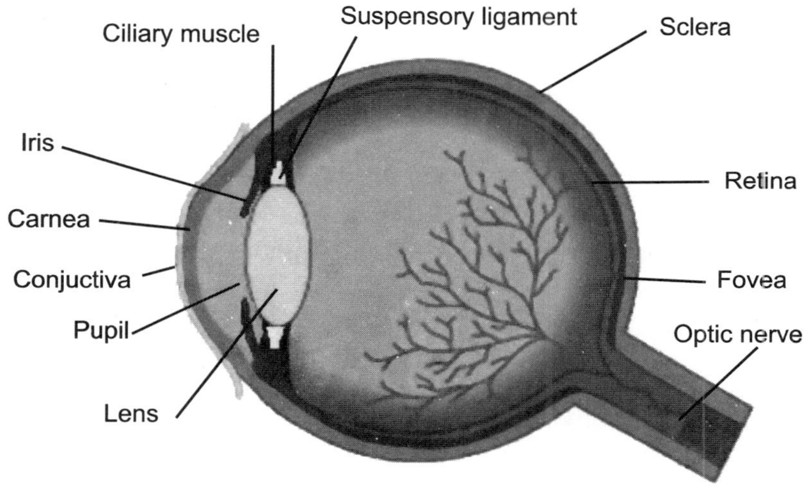

Fig. 12.3 *The eye.*

The range of perception of the eye is phenomenal. In the dark, a substance produced by the rod cells increases the sensitivity of the eye, so that it is possible to detect very dim light. In strong light, the iris contracts reducing the size of the aperture that admits light into the eye and a protective obscure substance reduces the exposure of the light-sensitive cells. The spectrum of light to which the eye is sensitive varies from the red to the violet. Lower electromagnetic frequencies in the infrared are sensed as heat, but cannot be seen. Higher frequencies in the ultraviolet and beyond cannot be seen either, but can be sensed as tingling of the skin or eyes depending on the frequency. The human eye is not sensitive to the polarization of light, i.e., light that oscillates on a specific plane. Bees, on the other hand, are sensitive to polarized light, and have a visual range that extends into the ultraviolet. Some kinds of snakes have special infrared sensors that enable them to hunt in absolute darkness using only the heat emitted by their prey. Birds have a higher density of light-sensing cells than humans do in their retinas, and therefore, higher visual acuity.

Colour blindness or "Daltonism" is a common abnormality in human vision that makes it impossible to differentiate colours accurately. One type of colour blindness results in the inability to distinguish red from green. This can be a real handicap for certain types of occupations. To a colourblind person, a person with normal colour vision would appear to have extrasensory perception. However, we want to reserve the term "extrasensory perception" for perception that is beyond the range of the normal.

THE SENSES OF HEARING

The ear is the sense organ that detects sound and plays a major role in the sense of balance and body position. It is also a device used for collecting and funneling sound waves recieved by the ear. The sensory receptors for both hearing and equilibrium are found in the inner ear, consisting of hair cells that have stereocilia (long mircovilli). The stereocillia are extremely sensitive to mechanical stimulations, which are known as mechanoreceptors.

Anatomy of the Ear

The ear has three divisions: the outer ear, middle ear, and the inner ear.

The *outer ear* is the most external portion of the ear. The outer ear includes the pinna (also called auricle), the ear canal, and the very most superficial layer of the ear drum (also called the tympanic membrane). Although the word "ear" may properly refer to the pinna (the flesh covered cartilage appendage on either side of the head), this portion of the ear is not vital for hearing. The complicated design of the human outer ear does help capture sound, but the most important functional aspect of the human outer ear is the ear canal itself. This outer ear canal skin is applied to cartilage; the thinner skin of the deep canal lies on the bone of the skull. If the ear canal is not open, hearing will be dampened. Ear wax (medical name – cerumen) is produced by glands in the skin of the outer portion of the ear canal. Only the thicker cerumen-producing ear canal skin has hairs. The outer ear ends at the most superficial layer of the tympanic membrane. The tympanic membrane is commonly called the ear drum.

The *middle ear* includes most of the ear drum (tympanic membrane) and the three ear bones ossicles: malleus (or hammer), incus (or anvil), and stapes (or stirrup). The opening of the Eustachian tube is also within the middle ear. The malleus has a long process (the handle) that is attached to the mobile portion of the ear drum. The incus is the bridge between the malleus and stapes. The stapes is the smallest named bone in the human body. The stapes transfers the vibrations of the incus to the oval window, a portion of the inner ear to which it is connected. It is the final bone in the chain to transfer vibrations from the eardrum to the inner ear. The arrangement of these three bones is a sort of Rube Goldberg device: movement of the tympanic membrane causes movement of the first bone, which causes movement of the second, which causes movement of the third. When this third bone pushes down, it causes movement of fluid within the cochlea (a portion of the inner ear). This particular fluid only moves when the stapes

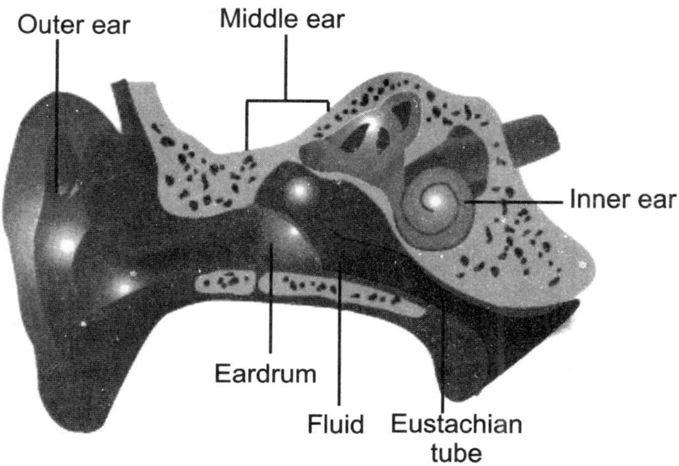

Fig.12.4 *The ear.*

footplate is depressed into the inner ear. Unlike the open ear canal, however, the air of the middle ear is not in direct contact with the atmosphere outside the body. The Eustachian tube connects from the chamber of the middle ear to the back of the pharynx. The middle ear in humans is very much like a specialized paranasal sinus, called the tympanic cavity, it, like the paranasal sinuses, is a hollow mucosa lined cavity in the skull that is ventilated through the nose. The mastoid portion of the temporal bone, which can be felt as a bump in the skull behind the pinna, also contains air, which ventilates through the middle ear.

The *inner ear* includes both the organ of hearing (the cochlea) and a sense organ that is attuned to the effects of both gravity and motion labyrinth or vestibular apparatus. The balance portion of the inner ear consists of three semi-circular canals and the vestibule. The inner ear is encased in the hardest bone of the body. Within this ivory hard bone, there are fluid-filled hollows. Within the cochlea are three fluid filled spaces: the tympanic canal, the vestibular canal, and the middle canal. The eighth cranial nerve comes from the brain stem to enter the inner ear. When sound strikes the ear drum, the movement is transferred to the footplate of the stapes, which presses into one of the fluid-filled ducts of the cochlea. The hair cells in the organ of Corti are tuned to certain sound frequencies, being responsive to high frequencies near the oval window and to low frequencies near the apex of the cochlea.

The fluid inside this duct is moved, flowing against the receptor cells of the organ of Corti, which fire. These stimulate the Spiral Ganglion, which sends information through the auditory portion of the eighth cranial nerve to the brain.

PROCESS OF HEARING

Detection of sound motion is associated with the right posterior superior temporal gyrus. The superior temporal gyrus contains several important structures of the brain, including: marking the location of the primary auditory cortex, the cortical region responsible for the sensation of sound. Sections 41 and 42 are called the primary auditory area of the cerebrum, and processes the basic characteristics of sound such as pitch and rhythm. The auditory association area is located within the temporal lobe of the brain, in an area called the Wernicke's area, or area 22. This area, near the lateral cerebral sulcus, is an important region for the processing of acoustic energy so that it can be distinguished as speech, music, or noise. It also interprets words that are heard into an associated thought pattern of understanding. The gnostic area of the cerebrum, (areas 5, 7, 39, and 40) helps to integrate all incoming sense patterns so that a common thought can be formed (correlated) using all arriving sensory information.

HEARING UNDER WATER

Hearing threshold and the ability to localize sound sources are reduced underwater. In which the speed of sound is faster than in air. Underwater, hearing is by bone conduction and localization of sound appears to depend on differences in amplitude detected by bone conduction.

LOCALIZATION OF SOUND BY HUMANS

Humans are normally able to hear a variety of sound frequencies, from about 20 Hz to 20 kHz. Our ability to estimate just where the sound is coming from, sound localization, is dependent on both hearing ability of each of the two ears, and the exact quality of the sound. Since each ear lies on an opposite side of the head, a sound will reach the closest ear first, and its amplitide will be loudest in that ear. Much of the brain's ability to localize sound depends on interaural (between ears) intensity differences and interaural temporal or phase differences.

DISORDERS OF SENSE ORGANS

ANOSMIA

The medical term describing the total absence of the sense of smell, i.e., the inability to detect or recognize any vapor. Anosmia occurs more frequently than a total loss of taste. Anosmia has been reported to occur in about 2% of the people with smell problems, based upon results obtained in a large group of patients with various taste and smell dysfunctions.

AGNOSIA

A general term for a loss of ability to recognize objects, people, sounds, shapes, or smells, that is, the inability to attach appropriate meaning to objective sense-data. It usually is used when the primary sense organ involved is not impaired.

DYSOSMIA

Distortion or perversion of the sense of smell. It may occur with hyposmia or it may occur alone. Dysosmia is a general term, including cacosmia, phantosmia and heterosmia. Dysosmia occurs in about 5 million people in the U.S., based upon a recent survey on the sense of smell.

HYPOSMIA

The most common type of smell loss experienced by humans, it may occur following an influenza like illness, a blow to the head, nasal allergies or from unknown causes. A recent survey of the sense of smell determined that 15 million people in the U.S. have had this type of smell loss. Hyposmia has been classified into two major types:

KALLMANN'S SYNDROME

Disorder that can include several characteristics such as absence of the sense of smell and decreased functional activity of the gonads (organs that produce sex cells), affecting growth and sexual development.

PAROSMIA

Any disease or perversion of the sense of smell, especially the subjective perception of odors that do not exist.

PHANTOSMIA

A smell that occurs in the nose without the presence of an external stimulation vapor.

STUDY QUESTIONS

1. Explain the different types of sense organs.
2. Describe the accessory structures of the eye.
3. Explain the various types of receptors.
4. Write short notes on:
   (a) Glaucoma
   (b) Myopia
   (c) Astigmatism
   (d) Diabetic.

13 CHAPTER THE ENDOCRINE SYSTEM

INTRODUCTION

The endocrine system is a network of glands that plays a vital role in a wide variety of bodily functions. The glands of this system produce and secrete hormones that control the following functions:

(i) Growth and development.
(ii) Internal balance of bodily systems (homeostasis).
(iii) Metabolism.
(iv) Regulation of mood and energy levels.
(v) Responses to surroundings, stress and injury.
(vi) Sexual function and reproduction.
(vii) Tissue function.

The endocrine system specializes in processes of the body that occur gradually, whereas the nervous system generally directs faster processes, such as breathing and body movements. However, in many cases the endocrine system and nervous system work together to guide some body processes.

Glands and *hormones* are the primary features of the endocrine system. *Glands* are collections of cells that produce and secrete substances called *hormones* that act as chemical messengers in the body. Glands that do not make hormones, such as sweat glands, salivary glands and the prostate gland, are not part of the endocrine system. Hormones move information and instructions from one group of cells to another.

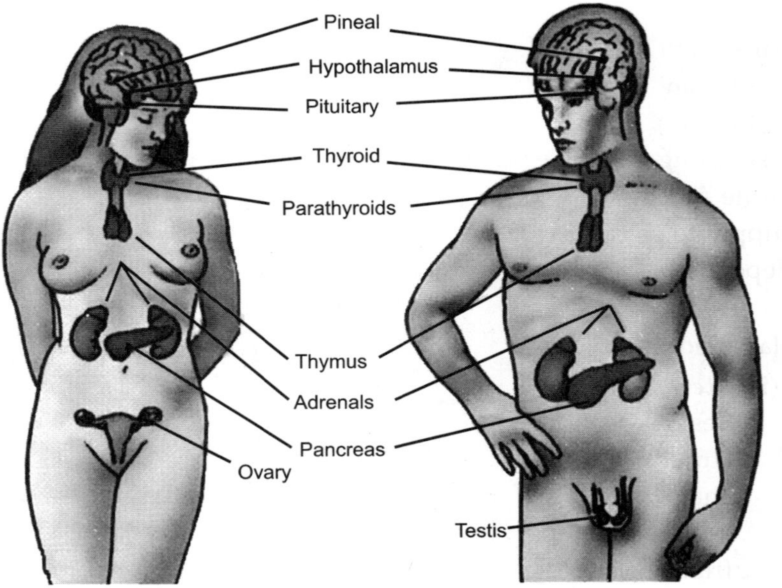

Fig. 13.1 *Endocrine system.*

Pheromones are also communication chemicals, but are used to send signals to other members of the same species. Queen bees, ants, and naked mole rats exert control of their respective colonies via pheromones. One common use for pheromones is as attractants in mating. Pheromones are widely studied in insects and are the basis for some kinds of Japanese beetle and gypsy moth traps. While pheromones have not been so widely studied in humans, some interesting studies have been done in recent years on pheromonal control of menstrual cycles in women. It has been found that pheromones in male sweat and/or sweat from another "dominant" female will both influence/regulate the cycles of women when smeared on their upper lip, just below the nose. Also, there is evidence that continued reception of a given man's pheromone(s) by a woman in the weeks just after ovulation/ fertilization can significantly increase the chances of successful implantation of the new baby in her uterus. Pheromones are also used for things like territorial markers (urine) and alarm signals.

Each hormone's shape is specific and can be recognized by the corresponding target cells. The binding sites on the target cells are called hormone receptors. Many hormones come in antagonistic pairs that have opposite effects on the target organs. For example, insulin and glucagon have opposite effects on the liver's control of blood sugar level. Insulin lowers the blood sugar level by instructing the liver to take glucose out of circulation and store it, while glucagon instructs the liver to release some of its stored supply to raise the blood sugar level. Much hormonal regulation depends on feedback loops to maintain balance and homeostasis.

There are *three* general classes (groups) of *hormones*. These are classified by chemical structure, not function.

(i) *Steroid hormones* are lipids derived from cholesterol. Testosterone is the male sex hormone. Estradiol, similar in structure to testosterone, is responsible for many female sex characteristics. Steroid hormones are secreted by the gonads, adrenal cortex, and placenta. Steroid hormones are derived from cholesterol by a biochemical reaction series. Defects along this series often lead to hormonal imbalances with serious consequences. Once synthesized, steroid hormones pass into the bloodstream; they are not stored by cells, and the rate of synthesis controls them.

(ii) *Amino acid derivatives* (like *epinephrine*): Amines are derived from the amino acid tyrosine and are secreted from the thyroid and the adrenal medulla. Solubility of the various hormone classes varies. Amine hormones (notably epinephrine) are stored as granules in the cytoplasm until needed.

(iii) *Peptide hormones* (like *insulin*): Peptides are short chains of amino acids; most hormones are peptides. They are secreted by the pituitary, parathyroid, heart, stomach, liver, and kidneys. Peptide hormones are synthesized as precursor molecules and processed by the endoplasmic reticulum and Golgi where they are stored in secretory granules. When needed, the granules are dumped into the bloodstream.

Different hormones can often be made from the same precursor molecule by cleaving it with a different enzyme.

ENDOCRINE SYSTEMS AND FEEDBACK CYCLES

The endocrine system uses cycles and negative feedback to regulate physiological functions. Negative feedback regulates the secretion of almost every hormone. Cycles of secretion maintain physiological and homeostatic control. These cycles can range from hours to months in duration.

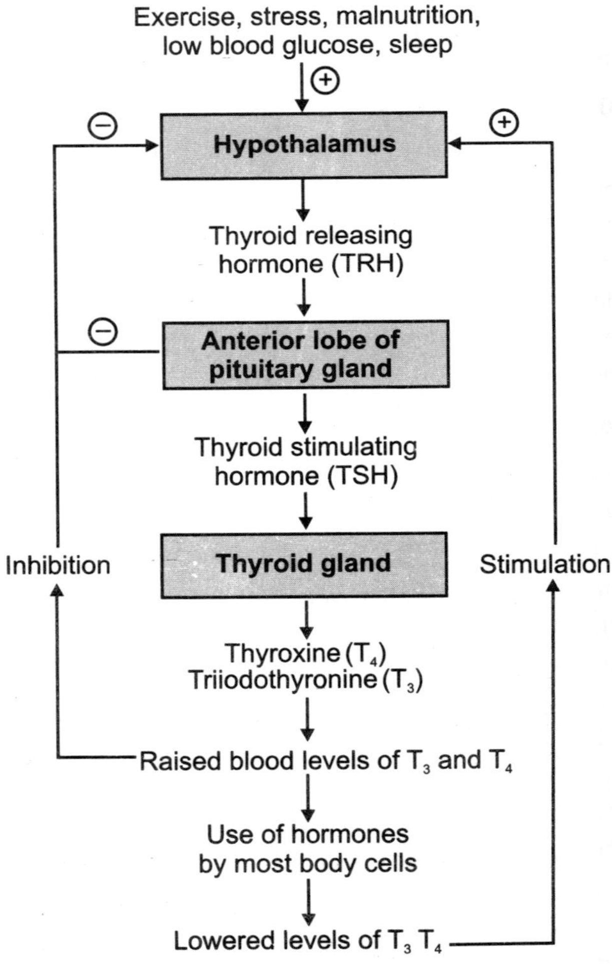

Fig. 13.2 *Negative feedback in the thyroxine release reflex.*

MECHANISMS OF HORMONE ACTION

The endocrine system acts by releasing hormones that in turn trigger actions in specific target cells. Receptors on target cell membranes bind only to one type of hormone. More than fifty human hormones have been identified; all act by binding to receptor molecules. The binding hormone changes the shape of the receptor causing the response to the hormone. There are two mechanisms of hormone action on all target cells.

MAJOR HUMAN ENDOCRINE GLANDS

The major human endocrine glands include:

THE HYPOTHALAMUS AND PITUITARY GLAND

The pituitary gland is no larger than a pea, located at the base of the brain. The pituitary gland is sometimes called the "*master gland*" of the endocrine system, because it controls the functions of the other endocrine glands. The gland is attached to the hypothalamus (a part of the brain that affects the pituitary gland) by nerve fibers. The pituitary gland itself consists of *three* lobes. Each lobe of the pituitary gland produces certain hormones.

(i) Anterior Lobe

They secrete a number of hormones, especially several which are important to the female menstural cycle, pregnancy, birth, and lactation (milk production). These include:

(a) *Growth Hormone* (*GH*): GH is a peptide anterior pituitary hormone essential for growth. GH-releasing hormone stimulates release of GH. GH-inhibiting hormone suppresses the release of GH. The hypothalamus maintains homeostatic levels of GH. Cells under the action of GH increase in size (hypertrophy) and number (hyperplasia). GH also causes increase in bone length and thickness by deposition of cartilage at the ends of bones. During adolescence, sex hormones cause replacement of cartilage by bone, halting further bone growth even though GH is still present. Too little or two much GH can cause dwarfism or gigantism, respectively.

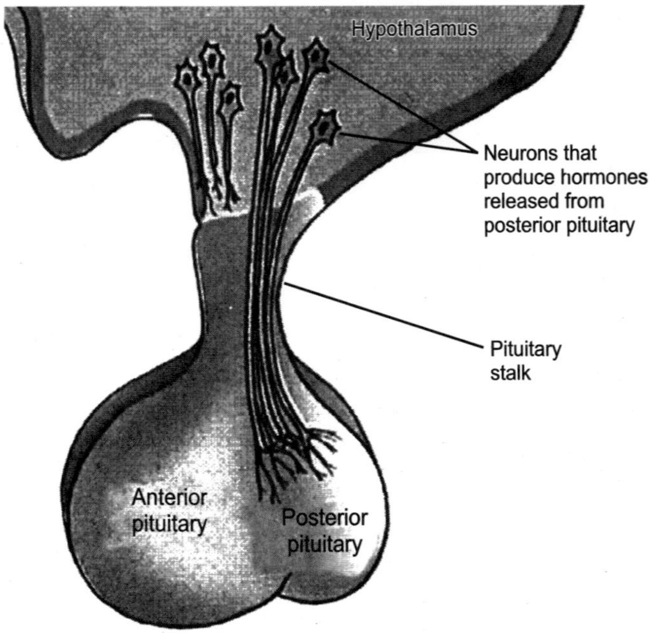

Fig. 13.3 *Hypothalamus and pituitary gland.*

(b) *Prolactin*: To stimulate milk production after giving birth.

(c) *ACTH Adrenocorticotropic Hormone (ACTH)*: To stimulate the adrenal glands.

(d) *Thyroid-Stimulating Hormone* (*TSH*): To stimulate the thyroid gland.

(e) *Follicle-Stimulating Hormone* (*TSH*): To stimulate the ovaries and testes

(f) *Luteinizing Hormone* (*TSH*): To stimulate the ovaries or testes

(ii) Intermediate Lobe

Melanocyte-stimulating hormone to control skin pigmentation.

(iii) Posterior Lobe

One non-sex hormone secreted by the posterior pituitary is:

(a) *Antidiuretic Hormone* (*ADG*): To increase absorption of water into the blood by the kidneys. *Diuretics* are chemicals which interfere with the production of or action of ADH so the kidneys secrete more water. Thus, diuretics are often prescribed for people with high blood pressure, in an attempt to decrease blood volume.

(b) Another group of non-sex hormones that many people have heard of is the *endorphins,* which belong to the category of chemicals known as *opiates* and serve to deaden our pain receptors. Endorphins, which are chemically related to morphine, are produced in response to pain. The natural response to rub an injured area, such as a pinched finger, helps to release endorphins in that area. People who exercise a lot and push their bodies "until it hurts" thereby stimulate the production of endorphins. It is thought that some people who constantly over-exercise and push themselves too much may actually be addicted to their own endorphins which that severe exercise regime releases.

(c) *Oxytocin:* To contract the uterus during childbirth and stimulate milk production.

THE THYROID GLAND

The thyroid gland is located in the front of the neck, below the larynx (voice box). The small, two-inch gland consists of two lobes, one on each side of the windpipe, connected by tissue called the *isthmus*. The thyroid tissue is made up of two types of cells: *follicular cells* and *parafollicular cells*. Most of the thyroid tissue consists of the follicular cells, which secrete iodine-containing hormones called *thyroxine* (T4) and *tri-iodothyronine* (T3). The parafollicular cells secrete the hormone calcitonin. The thyroid needs iodine to produce the hormones.

Functions of the Thyroid Gland

(i) The thyroid plays an important role in regulating the body's metabolism, temperature, weight and calcium balance.

(ii) The thyroid hormones contain *iodine,* which the thyroid needs in order to manufacture these hormones.

(iii) The T4 and T3 hormones stimulate every tissue in the body to produce proteins and increase the amount of oxygen used by cells. The harder the cells work, the harder the organs work. The *calcitonin hormone* works together with the parathyroid hormone to regulate calcium levels in the body.

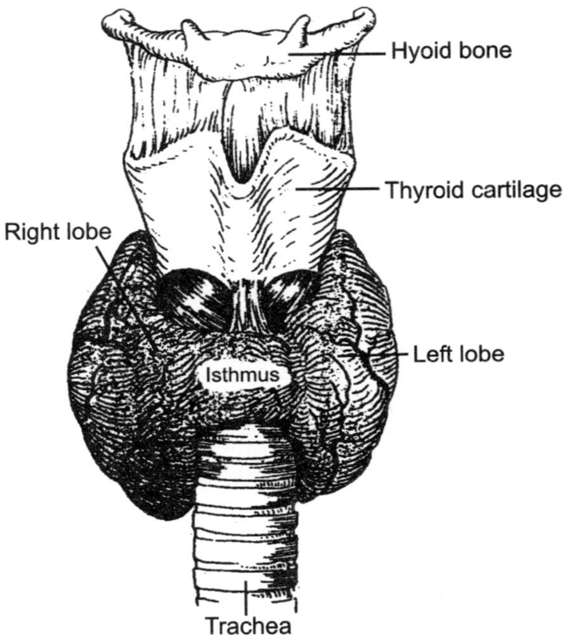

Fig. 13.4 *Thyroid gland.*

(iv) Levels of hormones secreted by the thyroid are controlled by the pituitary gland's thyroid-stimulating hormone, which in turn is controlled by the hypothalamus.

If a person lacks iodine in his/her diet, the thyroid cannot make the hormones, causing a deficiency. In response to the body's feedback loops calling for more thyroid hormones, the thyroid gland then enlarges to attempt to compensate. (The body's plan here is if it's bigger it can make more, but that does not help if there is not enough iodine). This disorder is called *goiter*. Dietary sources of iodine include any "ocean foods" because ocean-dwelling organisms tend to accumulate iodine from the seawater, and would include foods like ocean fish (tuna) and seaweeds like kelp. Because of this, people who live near the ocean do not have as much of a problem with goiter as people who live inland and do not have access to these foods.

THE PANCREASE

The *pancreas* is an elongated, tapered organ located across the back of the abdomen, behind the stomach. The right side of the organ (called the head) is the widest part of the organ and lies in the curve of the duodenum, the first division of the small intestine. The tapered left side extends slightly upward (called the body of the pancreas) and ends near the spleen (called the tail). The pancreas is made up of two types of tissue:

(i) *Exocrine Tissue:* The exocrine tissue secretes digestive enzymes. These enzymes are secreted into a network of ducts that join the main pancreatic duct, which runs the length of the pancreas.

(ii) *Endocrine Tissue:* The endocrine tissue, which consists of the islets of Langerhans, secretes hormones into the bloodstream.

Functions of the Pancrease

The pancrease has digestive and hormonal functions:

(i) The enzymes secreted by the exocrine tissue in the pancreas help breakdown carbohydrates, fats, proteins, and acids in the duodenum. These enzymes travel down the pancreatic duct into the bile duct in an inactive form. When they enter the duodenum, they are activated. The exocrine tissue also secretes a bicarbonate to neutralize stomach acid in the duodenum (the first section of the small intestine).

(ii) The hormones secreted by the endocrine tissue in the pancrease are insulin and glucagon (which regulate the level of glucose in the blood) and somatostatin (which prevents the release of the other two hormones).

(iii) The *islet cells* secrete glucagon, which tells the liver to take carbohydrate out of storage to raise a low blood sugar level. The islet cells secrete insulin to tell the liver to take excess glucose out of circulation to lower a blood sugar level that's too high. If a person's body does not make enough insulin (and/or there is a reduced response of the target cells in the liver), the blood sugar rises, perhaps out of control, and we say that the person has diabetes mellitus.

THE ADRENAL GLANDS

Adrenal glands, which are also called *suprarenal glands,* are small, triangular glands located on top of both kidneys. An adrenal gland is made of two parts: the outer region is called the *adrenal cortex* and the inner region is called the *adrenal medulla.* Both parts of the adrenal glands – the adrenal cortex and the adrenal medulla — perform very separate functions.

Functions of Adrenal Cortex

The adrenal cortex, the outer portion of the adrenal gland, is essential to life by secreting hormones that have an effect on the body's metabolism, on chemicals in the blood, and on certain body characteristics. The adrenal cortex secretes corticosteroids and other hormones directly into the bloodstream. The hormones produced by the adrenal cortex include:

(i) *Corticosteroid hormones*

(a) *Hydrocortisone hormone:* This hormone, also known as *cortisol,* controls the body's use of fats, proteins, and carbohydrates.

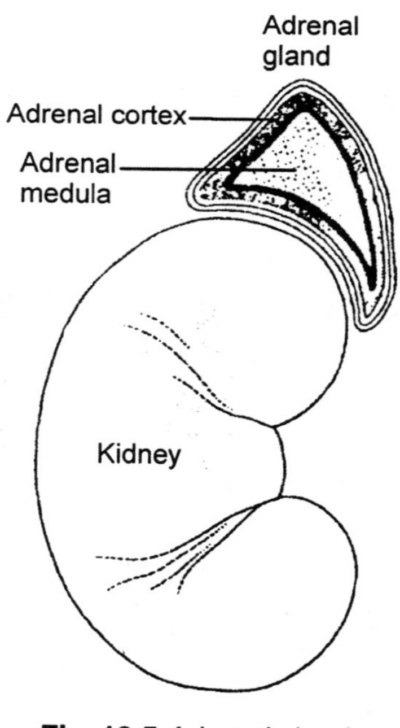

Fig. 13.5 *Adrenal glands.*

(b) *Corticosterone:* This hormone, together with hydro-cortisone hormones, suppresses inflammatory reactions in the body and also affects the immune system.

(ii) *Aldosterone hormone*

This hormone inhibits the level of sodium excreted into the urine, maintaining blood volume and blood pressure.

(iii) *Androgenic steroids (androgen hormones)*

These hormones have minimal effect on the development of male characteristics.

Functions of Adrenal Medulla

The adrenal medulla, the inner part of the adrenal gland, is not essential to life, but helps a person in coping with physical and emotional stress. The adrenal medulla secretes the following hormones:

(i) *Epinephrine* (also called *adrenaline*): This hormone increases the heart rate and force of heart contractions, facilitates blood flow to the muscles and brain, causes relaxation of smooth muscles, helps with conversion of glycogen to glucose in the liver, and other activities.

(ii) *Norepinephrine* (also called *noradrenaline*): This hormone has little effect on smooth muscle, metabolic processes, and cardiac output, but has strong vasoconstrictive effects, thus increasing blood pressure.

THE GONADS OR SEX HORMONES

In addition to producing gametes, the female ovaries and male testes (singular = testis) also secrete hormones. Therefore, these hormones are called sex hormones. The secretion of sex hormones by the gonads is controlled by pituitary gland hormones such as FSH and LH. While both sexes make some of each of the hormones, typically male testes secrete primarily androgens including testosterone. Female ovaries make estrogen and progesterone in varying amounts depending on where in her cycle a woman is. In a pregnant woman, the baby's placenta also secretes hormones to maintain the pregnancy.

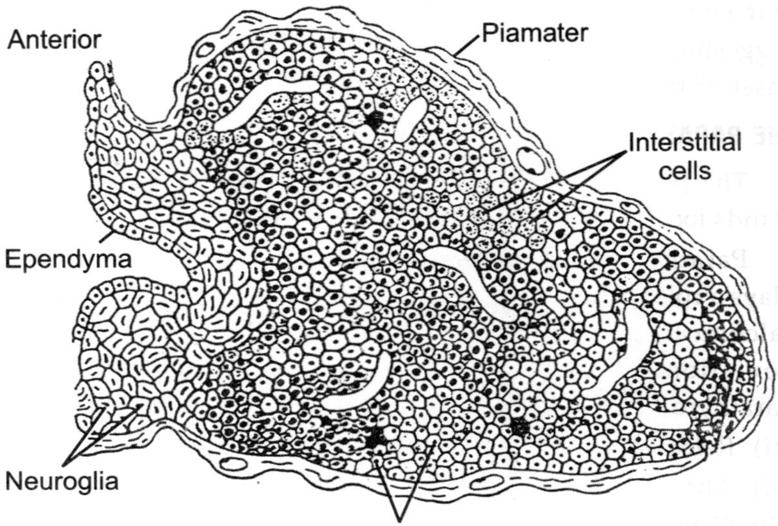

Fig. 13.6 *Pineal gland.*

THE PINEAL GLAND

This gland is located near the center of the brain in humans, and is stimulated by nerves from the eyes. In some other animals, the pineal gland is closer to the skin and directly stimulated by light (some lizards even have a third eye). The pineal gland secreted melatonin at night when it's dark, thus secretes more in winter when the nights are longer. Melatonin promotes sleep (makes you feel sleepy). It also affects reproductive functions by depressing the activity of the gonads. Additionally, it affects thyroid and adrenal cortex functions. In some animals, melatonin affects skin pigmentation. Because melatonin production is affected by the amount of light to which a person is exposed, this is tied to circadian rhythm (having an activity cycle of about 24 hours), annual cycles, and biological clock functions. SAD or seasonal affective disorder (syndrome) is a disorder in which too much melatonin is produced, especially during the long nights of winter, causing profound depression, oversleeping, weight gain, tiredness, and sadness. Treatment consists of exposure to bright lights for several hours each day to inhibit melatonin production. It has also been found that melatonin levels drop 75% suddenly just before puberty, suggesting the involvement of melatonin in the regulation of the onset of puberty.

THE PARATHYROID GLANDS

The parathyroid glands are two pairs of small, oval-shaped glands located adjacent to the two thyroid gland lobes in the neck.

Parathyroid glands produce parathyroid hormone, which plays a role in the regulation of calcium levels in the blood. Precise calcium levels are important in the human body, since small deviations can cause muscle and nerve impairment. The parathyroid hormone stimulates the following functions:

(i) Release of calcium by bones into the bloodstream.

(ii) Absorption of food by the intestines.

(iii) Conservation of calcium by the kidneys.

PLACENTAL HORMONES

In addition to its role in transporting molecules between mother and fetus, the placenta is a major endocine organ. It turns out that the placenta synthesizes a huge and diverse number of hormones and cytokines that have major influences on ovarian, uterine, mammary and fetal physiology, not to mention other endocrine systems of the mother.

Steroid Hormones

Sex steroids are the best known examples of placental hormones. Two major groups are produced by all mammals:

Progestins: Progestins are molecules that bind to the progesterone receptor. Progesterone itself is often called the hormone of pregnancy because of the critical role it plays in supporting the endometrium and hence on survival of the conceptus. Progestins, including progesterone, have two major roles during pregnancy.

Support of the endometrium to provide an environment conducive to fetal survival. If the endometrium is deprived of progestins, the pregnancy will inevitably be terminated.

Suppression of contractility in uterine smooth muscle, which, if unchecked, would clearly be a disaster. This is often called the "progesterone block" on the myometrium. Toward the end of gestation, this myometrial-quieting effect is antagonized by rising levels of estrogens, thereby facilitating parturition.

Progesterone and other progestins also potently inhibit secretion of the pituitary gonadotropins luteinizing hormone and follicle stimulating hormone. This effect almost always prevents ovulation from occuring during pregnancy.

Estrogens: The placenta produces several distinct estrogens. In women, the major estrogen produced by the placenta is estriol, and the equine placenta synthesizes a unique group of estrogens not seen in other animals. Depending on the species, placental estrogens are derived from either fetal androgens, placental progestins, or other steroid precursors.

With few exceptions, the concentration of estrogens in maternal blood rises to maximal toward the end of gestation. Two of the principle effects of placental estrogens are:

(a) Stimulate growth of the myometrium and antagonize the myometrial-suppressing activity of progesterone. In many species, the high levels of estrogen in late gestation induces myometrial oxytocin receptors, thereby preparing the uterus for parturition.

(b) Stimulate mammary gland development. Estrogens are one in a battery of hormones necessary for both ductal and alveolar growth in the mammary gland. Like progestins, estrogens suppress gonadotropin secretion from the pituitary gland. In species like humans and horses, where placental estrogens are synthesized from androgens produced by the fetus, maternal estrogen levels are often a useful indicator of fetal well being.

Protein Hormones

Several protein and peptide hormones are synthesized in placentae of various species. They have effects on the mother's endocrine system, fetal metabolism and preparation of the mother for postpartum support of her offspring.

Chorionic gonadotropins: As the name implies, these hormones have the effect of stimulating the gonads, similar to the pituitary gonadotropins. The only species known to produce a placental gonadotropin are primates and equids.

The human hormone is called *human chorionic gonadotropin* or simply **HCG**. This hormone is produced by fetal trophoblast cells. It binds to the luteinizing hormone receptor on cells of the corpus luteum, which prevents luteal regression. Thus, HCG serves as the signal for maternal recognition of pregnancy.

Equine chorionic gonadotropin is also produced by fetal trophoblast cells. It is actually the same molecule as equine luteinizing hormone.

Placental lactogens: These hormones are molecular relatives of prolactin and growth hormone. These hormones have been identified in primates, ruminants and rodents, but not in other species.

The functions of placental lactogens are not well understood. They are thought to modulate fetal and maternal metabolism, perhaps mobilizing energy substrates for fetal use. In some species they have been shown to stimulate function of the corpus luteum, and to participate in development of the mammary gland prior to parturition.

Relaxin: Relaxin is a hormone thought to act synergistically with progesterone to maintain pregancy. It also causes relaxation of pelvic ligaments at the end of gestation and may therefore aid in parturation. In some of the species in which relaxin is known to be produced, it is produced by the placenta, while in others, the major source is the corpus luteum. In some species, relaxin is produced by both the corpus luteum and placenta.

ENDOCRINE DISORDERS

Endocrine disorders involve either too much or too little hormone secretion. Disorders may result from a problem in the gland itself, or because the hypothalamic-pituitary axis provides too much or too little stimulation. Depending on the type of cell they originate in, tumors can produce excess hormones or squeeze out normal glandular tissue, decreasing hormone production.

Doctors usually measure levels of hormones in the blood to tell how an endocrine gland is functioning. Sometimes blood levels alone do not give enough information about endocrine gland function, so doctors measure hormone levels after giving a stimulus (such as a sugar-containing drink, a drug, or a hormone that can trigger hormone release) or after having the patient take an action (such as fasting).

HYPERPARATHYROIDISM

Primary hyperparathyroidism is a disorder of the parathyroid glands. Most people with this disorder have one or more enlarged, overactive parathyroid glands that secrete too much parathyroid hormone. In secondary hyper-parathyroidism, a problem such as kidney failure makes the body resistant to the action of parathyroid hormone.

ACROMEGALY

Acromegaly is caused by excessive secretion of growth hormone resulting from a non-cancerous tumor on the pituitary gland, which is located at the base of the brain. A life-threatening disorder, its mortality rate is two to four times higher than that of the general population-comparable to that of more prevalent diseases, such as diabetes and Parkinson's disease. On average, individuals with acromegaly die up to 10 years earlier than healthy individuals.

GALACTORRHEA

Galactorrhea is a condition that occurs when a woman's breast makes milk (or a milky discharge) even though she is not breast feeding a baby. The milk may come from one or both breasts. It may leak with no stimulation or it may leak only when the breasts are touched.

HYPOPITUITARISM

Hypopituitarism is an underactive pituitary gland that results in deficiency of one or more pituitary hormones. Hypo-pituitarism, an uncommon disorder, can be caused by a number of factors, including a pituitary tumor or an insufficient blood supply to the pituitary gland.

PROLACTINOMA

A prolactinoma is a benign tumor of the pituitary gland that produces a hormone called prolactin. It is the most common type of pituitary tumor. Symptoms of prolactinoma are caused by too much prolactin in the blood (hyperprolactinemia) or by pressure of the tumor on surrounding tissues. Prolactin stimulates the breast to produce milk during pregnancy. After delivery of the baby, a mother's prolactin levels fall unless she breast feeds her infant. Each time the baby nurses, prolactin levels rise to maintain milk production.

SHEEHAN'S SYNDROME

Sheehan's syndrome, also referred to as postpartum hypopituitarism, is a delayed effect of intrapartum or postpartum hemorrhage — life-threatening blood loss during or after childbirth.

Severe blood loss deprives body tissues and organs of oxygen, causing areas of tissue death. In Sheehan's syndrome, this damage affects the pituitary gland — a small, bean-shaped gland at the base of your brain. The result, which may not be apparent for months or even years, is permanent underproduction of pituitary hormones.

Pituitary hormones regulate the rest of the endocrine system, signaling other glands to increase or decrease production of the hormones that control metabolism, fertility, wound healing and many other vital processes. When the regulatory hormones from the pituitary are in short supply, the signs and symptoms may affect almost any part of your body — although they may develop so gradually that they escape notice. Hypopituitarism may seem to cause no symptoms at all. At the other extreme, though, Sheehan's syndrome and other forms of hypopituitarism can cause an adrenal crisis — a sudden, potentially fatal undersupply of the hormone cortisol.

STUDY QUESTIONS

Write short notes on the following:

(a) Growth hormone

(b) Adrenal Glands

(c) Thyroid Gland

(d) Gonads or Sex Hormones

(e) Progestron

(f) Pinal Gland

(h) Sheehan's Syndrome.

■■■

14

CHAPTER

THE REPRODUCTIVE SYSTEM

INTRODUCTION

Most organ systems of the body function almost continuously to maintain the well-being of the individual. The reproductive system, however, appears to "slumber" until puberty. The primary sex organs, or gonads, are the *testes* in males and the *ovaries* in females. The gonads produce sex cells, or gametes, and secrete sex hormones. The remaining reproductive system structures are *accessory reproductive organs*. Although male and female *reproductive systems* are quite different, their joint purpose is to produce offspring. Male reproductive organs are adapted for producing sperm cells and transporting them to a location where fertilization can occur. The female reproductive organs perform similar functions for eggs and, following fertilization, support and maintain the offspring.

The major function of the reproductive system is to ensure survival of the species. Other systems in the body, such as the endocrine and urinary systems, work continuously to maintain homeostasis for survival of the individual. An individual may live a long, healthy, and happy life without producing offspring, but if the species is to continue, at least some individuals must produce offspring.

MALE REPRODUCTIVE SYSTEM

The male reproductive system, like that of the female, consists of those organs whose function is to produce a new individual, i.e., to accomplish reproduction. This system consists of:

TESTES

The male gonads, testes, or testicles, begin their development high in the abdominal cavity, near the kidneys. Each testis is an oval structure about 5 cm long and 3 cm in diameter. A tough, white fibrous connective tissue capsule, the tunica albuginea, surrounds each testis and extends inward to form septa that partition the organ into lobules. There are about 250 lobules in each testis. Each lobule contains 1 to 4 highly coiled *seminiferous tubules* that converge to form a single straight tubule, which leads into the rete testis. Short *efferent ducts* exit the testes. Interstitial cells (*cells of Leydig*), which produce male sex hormones, are located between the seminiferous tubules within a lobule.

SCROTUM

During the last two months before birth, or shortly after birth, testes descend through the inguinal canal into the *scrotum*, a pouch that extends below the abdomen, posterior to the penis. Although this location of the testes, outside the abdominal cavity, may seem to make them vulnerable to injury, it provides a temperature about 3°C below normal body temperature. This lower temperature is necessary for the production of viable sperm. The scrotum consists of skin and subcutaneous tissue. A vertical partition, of subcutaneous tissue in the center divides it into two parts, each containing one testis. Smooth muscle fibers, called the *dartos muscle*, in the subcutaneous tissue contract to give the scrotum its wrinkled appearance. When these fibers are relaxed, the scrotum is smooth. Another muscle, the *cremaster muscle*, consists of skeletal muscle fibers and controls the position of the scrotum and testes. When it is cold or a man is sexually aroused, this muscle contracts to pull the testes closer to the body for warmth.

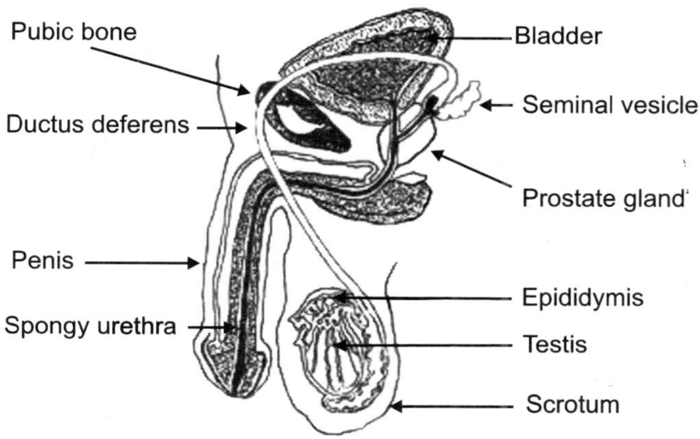

Fig.14.1 *Male reproductive system.*

SPERMATOGENESIS

Sperm are produced by spermatogenesis within the *seminiferous tubules*.

A transverse section of a seminiferous tubule shows that it is packed with cells in various stages of development. Interspersed with these cells, there are large cells that extend from the periphery of the tubule to the lumen. These large cells are the supporting, or sustentacular cells (*Sertoli's cells* or *nurse cell*), which support and nourish the other cells. Early in embryonic development, primordial germ cells enter the testes and differentiate into spermatogonia, immature cells that remain dormant until puberty.

Spermatogonia are diploid cells, each with 46 chromosomes (23 pairs) located around the periphery of the seminiferous tubules. At puberty, hormones stimulate these cells to begin dividing by mitosis. Some of the daughter cells produced by mitosis remain at the periphery as spermatogonia.

Others are pushed toward the lumen, undergo some changes, and become *primary spermatocytes*. Because they are produced by *mitosis*, primary spermatocytes, like spermatogonia, are diploid and have 46 chromosomes. Each primary spermatocytes goes through the first meiotic division, meiosis I, to produce two *secondary spermatocytes*, each with 23 chromosomes (haploid). Just prior to, this division, the genetic material is replicated, so that each chromosome consists of two strands, called *chromatids,* that are joined by a centromere. During meiosis I, one chromosome, consisting of two chromatids, goes to each secondary spermatocyte. In the *second meiotic division,* meiosis II, each secondary spermatocyte divides to produce two spermatids. There is no replication of genetic material in this division, but the centromere divides so that a single-stranded chromatid goes to each cell. As a result of the two meiotic divisions, each primary spermatocyte produces *four spermatids*. During spermatogenesis there are two

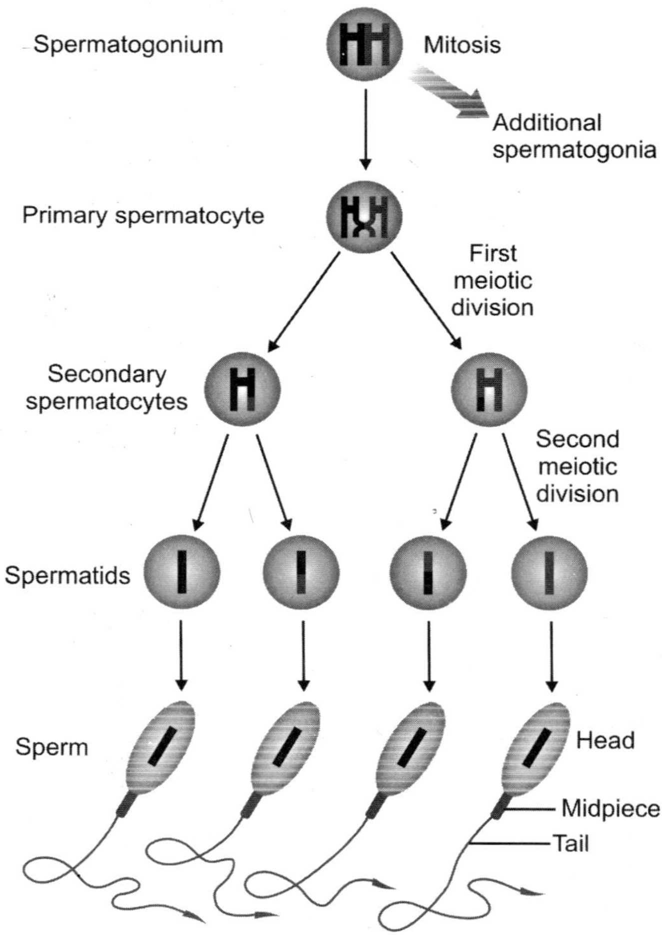

Fig. 14.2 *Spermatogenesis.*

cellular divisions, but only one replication of DNA so that each spermatid has 23 chromosomes (haploid), one from each pair in the original primary spermatocyte. Each successive stage in spermatogenesis is pushed toward the center of the tubule, so that the more immature cells are at the periphery and the more differentiated cells are nearer the center.

Spermatogenesis (and oogenesis in the female) differs from mitosis because the resulting cells have only half the number of chromosomes as the original cell. When the sperm cell nucleus unites with an egg cell nucleus, the full number of chromosomes is restored. If sperm and egg cells were produced by mitosis, then each successive generation would have twice the number of chromosomes as the preceding one.

The final step in the development of sperm is called *spermiogenesis*. In this process, the spermatids formed from spermatogenesis become mature spermatozoa, or *sperm*.

Sperm

The mature sperm cell has a head, midpiece, and tail. The head, also called the nuclear region, contains the 23 chromosomes surrounded by a nuclear membrane. The tip of the head is covered by an *acrosome,* which contains enzymes that help the sperm penetrate the female gamete. The midpiece, metabolic region, contains mitochondria that provide adenosine triphosphate (ATP). The *tail,* locomotor region, uses a typical *flagellum* for locomotion. The sperm are released into the lumen of the seminiferous tubule and leave the testes. They then enter the epididymis where they undergo their final maturation and become capable of fertilizing a female gamete.

Sperm production begins at puberty and continues throughout the life of a male. The entire process, beginning with a primary spermatocyte, takes about 74 days. After ejaculation, the sperm can live for about 48 hours in the female reproductive tract.

Sperm cells pass through a series of ducts to reach the outside of the body. After they leave the testes, the sperm passes through the epididymis, ductus deferens, ejaculatory duct, and urethra.

EPIDIDYMIS

Sperm leave the testes through a series of efferent ducts that enter the epididymis. Each epididymis is a long (about 6 meters) tube that is tightly coiled to form a comma-shaped organ located along the superior and posterior margins of the testes. When the sperm leave the testes, they are immature and incapable of fertilizing ova. They complete their maturation process and become fertile as they move through the epididymis. Mature sperm are stored in the lower portion, or tail, of the epididymis.

DUCTUS DEFERENS OR VAS DEFERENS

The ductus deferens, also called *vas deferens,* is a fibromuscular tube that is continuous (or contiguous) with the epididymis. It begins at the bottom (tail) of the epididymis then turns sharply upward along the posterior margin of the testes. The ductus deferens enters the abdominopelvic cavity through the inguinal canal and passes along the lateral pelvic wall. It crosses over the ureter and posterior portion of the urinary bladder, and then descends along the posterior wall of the bladder toward the prostate gland. Just before it reaches the prostate gland, each ductus deferens enlarges to form an ampulla. Sperm are stored in the proximal portion of the ductus deferens, near the epididymis, and peristaltic movements propel the sperm through the tube.

The proximal portion of the ductus deferens is a component of the spermatic cord, which contains vascular and neural structures that supply the testes. The spermatic cord contains the ductus deferens, testicular artery and veins, lymph vessels, testicular nerve, cremaster muscle that elevates the testes for warmth and at times of sexual stimulation, and a connective tissue covering.

EJACULATORY DUCT

Each ductus deferens, at the ampulla, joins the duct from the adjacent seminal vesicle (one of the accessory glands) to form a short ejaculatory duct. Each ejaculatory duct passes through the prostate gland and empties into the urethra.

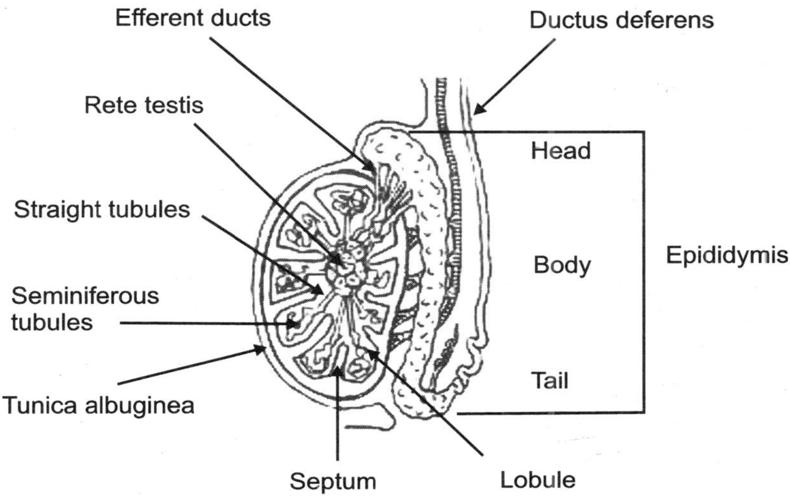

Fig.14.3 *Sagittal section of a testis and epididymis.*

URETHRA

The urethra extends from the urinary bladder to the external urethral orifice at the tip of the penis. It is a passageway for sperm and fluids from the reproductive system and urine from the urinary system. While reproductive fluids are passing through the urethra, sphincters contract tightly to keep urine from entering the urethra.

The male urethra is divided into three regions. The prostatic urethra is the proximal portion that passes through the prostate gland. It receives the ejaculatory duct, which contains sperm and secretions from the seminal vesicles, and numerous ducts from the prostate glands. The next portion, the membranous urethra, is a short region that passes through the pelvic floor. The longest portion is the penile urethra (also called spongy urethra or cavernous urethra), which extends the length of the penis and opens to the outside at the external urethral orifice. The ducts from the bulbourethral glands open into the penile urethra.

ACCESSORY GLANDS

The accessory glands of the male reproductive system are the seminal vesicles, prostate gland, and the bulbourethral glands. These glands secrete fluids that enter the urethra.

Seminal Vesicles

The paired seminal vesicles are saccular glands posterior to the urinary bladder. Each gland has a short duct that joins with the ductus deferens at the ampulla to form an ejaculatory duct, which then empties into the urethra. The fluid from the seminal vesicles is viscous and contains fructose, which provides an energy source for the sperm; prostaglandins, which contribute to the mobility and viability of the sperm; and proteins that cause slight coagulation reactions in the semen after ejaculation.

Prostate Gland

The prostate gland is a firm, dense structure that is located just inferior to the urinary bladder. It is about the size of a walnut and encircles the urethra as it leaves the urinary bladder. Numerous short ducts from the substance of the prostate gland empty into the prostatic urethra. The secretions of the prostate are thin, milky coloured, and alkaline. They function to enhance the motility of the sperm.

Bulbourethral Glands

The paired bulbourethral (Cowper's) glands are small, about the size of a pea, and located near the base of the penis. A short duct from each gland enters the proximal end of the penile urethra. In response to sexual stimulation, the bulbourethral glands secrete an alkaline mucus-like fluid. This fluid neutralizes the acidity of the urine residue in the urethra, helps to neutralize the acidity of the vagina, and provides some lubrication for the tip of the penis during intercourse.

Seminal Fluid

Seminal fluid, or semen, is a slightly alkaline mixture of sperm cells and secretions from the accessory glands. Secretions from the seminal vesicles make up about 60 percent of the volume of the semen, with most of the remainder coming from the prostate gland. The sperm and secretions from the bulbourethral gland contribute only a small volume.

Volume of Semen

The volume of semen in a single ejaculation may vary from 1.5 to 6.0 ml. There are usually between 50 to 150 million sperm per milliliter of semen. Sperm counts below 10 to 20 million per milliliter usually present fertility problems. Although only one sperm actually penetrates and fertilizes the ovum, it takes several million sperm in an ejaculation to ensure that fertilization will take place.

PENIS

The penis, the male copulatory organ, is a cylindrical pendant organ located anterior to the scrotum and functions to transfer sperm to the vagina. The penis consists of three columns of erectile tissue that are wrapped in connective tissue and covered with skin. The two dorsal columns are the *corpora cavernosa*. The single, midline ventral column surrounds the urethra and is called the *corpus spongiosum*. The penis has a root, body (shaft), and glans penis. The root of the penis attaches it to the pubic arch and the body is the visible, pendant portion. The corpus spongiosum expands at the distal end to form the glans penis. The urethra, which extends throughout the length of the corpus spongiosum, opens through the external urethral orifice at the tip of the glans penis. A loose fold of skin, called the *prepuce*, or foreskin, covers the *glans penis*.

MALE SEXUAL RESPONSE

The male sexual response includes erection and orgasm accompanied by ejaculation of semen. Orgasm is followed by a variable time period during which it is not possible to achieve another erection.

Three hormones are the principle regulators of the male reproductive system. Follicle-stimulating hormone (FSH) stimulates spermatogenesis; luteinizing hormone (LH) stimulates the production of testosterone; and testosterone stimulates the development of male secondary sex characteristics and spermatogenesis.

FEMALE REPRODUCTIVE SYSTEM

The organs of the female reproductive system produce and sustain the female sex cells (egg cells or ova), transport these cells to a site where they may be fertilized by sperm, provide a favourable environment for the developing fetus, move the fetus to the outside at the end of the development period, and produce the female sex hormones. The female reproductive system includes the ovaries, fallopian tubes, uterus, vagina, accessory glands, and external genital organs.

OVARIES

The primary female reproductive organs, or gonads, are the two ovaries. Each ovary is a solid, ovoid structure about the size and shape of an almond, about 3.5 cm in length, 2 cm wide, and 1 cm thick. The ovaries are located in shallow depressions, called ovarian fossae, one on each side of the uterus, in the lateral walls of the pelvic cavity. They are held loosely in place by peritoneal ligaments.

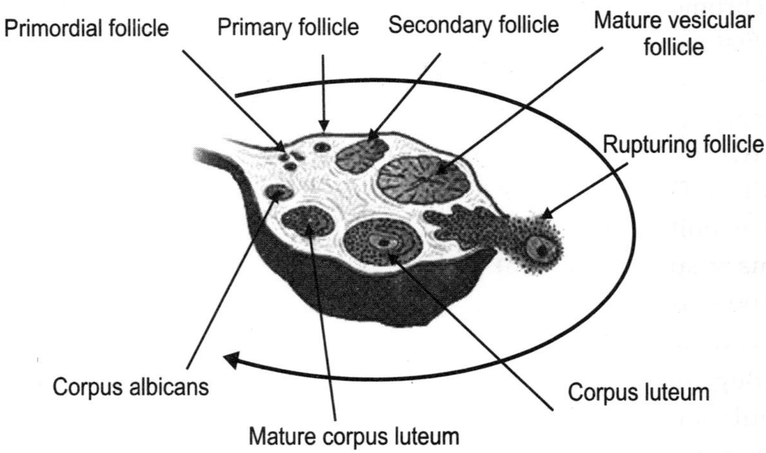

Fig. 14.4 *Structure of ovary.*

Structure

The ovaries are covered on the outside by a layer of simple cuboidal epithelium called germinal (ovarian) epithelium. This is actually the visceral peritoneum that envelops the ovaries.

Underneath this layer there is a dense connective tissue capsule, the tunica albuginea. The substance of the ovaries is distinctly divided into an outer cortex and an inner medulla. The cortex appears more dense and granular due to the presence of numerous ovarian follicles in various stages of development. Each of the follicles contains an oocyte, a female germ cell. The medulla is loose connective tissue with abundant blood vessels, lymphatic vessels, and nerve fibers.

Oogenesis

Female sex cells, or gametes, develop in the ovaries by a form of meiosis called oogenesis. The sequence of events in oogenesis is similar to the sequence in spermatogenesis, but the timing and final result are different. Early in fetal development, primitive germ cells in the ovaries differentiate into oogonia. These divide rapidly to form thousands of cells, still called *oogonia,* which have a full complement of 46 (23 pairs) chromosomes. Oogonia then enter a growth phase, enlarge, and become *primary oocytes.* The diploid (46 chromosomes) primary oocytes replicate their DNA and begin the *first meiotic division,* but the process stops in prophase and the cells remain in this suspended state until puberty. Many of the primary oocytes degenerate before birth, but even with this decline, the two ovaries together contain approximately 7,00,000 oocytes at birth. This is the lifetime supply, and no more will develop. This is quite different than the male in which spermatogonia and primary spermatocytes continue to be produced throughout the reproductive lifetime. By puberty the number of primary oocytes has further declined to about 4,00,000.

Beginning at puberty, under the influence of follicle-stimulating hormone, several primary oocytes start to grow again each month. One of the primary oocytes seems to outgrow the others and it resumes meiosis I. The other cells degenerate. The large cell undergoes an unequal division, so that nearly all the cytoplasm, organelles, and half the chromosomes go to one cell, which becomes a secondary oocyte. The remaining half of the chromosomes go to a smaller cell called the first polar body. The *secondary oocyte* begins the second meiotic division, but the process stops in metaphase. At this point *ovulation* occurs.

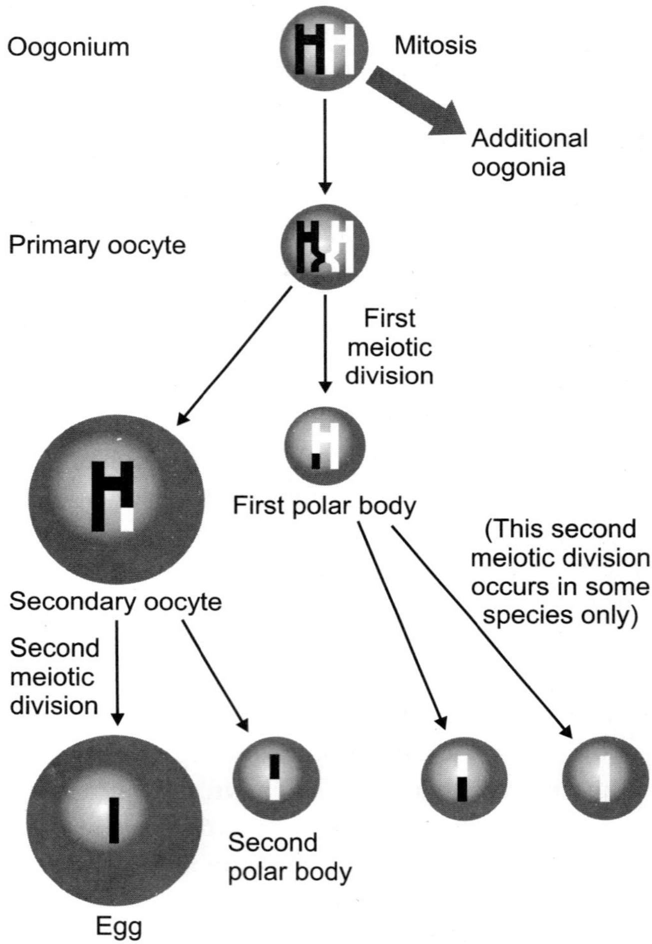

Fig. 14.5 *Process of oogenesis.*

If fertilization occurs, meiosis II continues. Again this is an unequal division with all of the cytoplasm going to the *ovum,* which has 23 single-stranded chromosome. The smaller cell from this division is a second polar body. The first polar body also usually divides in meiosis I to produce two even smaller polar bodies. If fertilization does not occur, the second meiotic division is never completed and the secondary oocyte degenerates.

There are obvious differences between the male and female. In *spermatogenesis,* four functional sperm develop from each primary spermatocyte. In *oogenesis,* only one functional fertilizable cell develops from a primary oocyte. The other three cells are polar bodies and they degenerate.

OVARIAN FOLLICLE DEVELOPMENT

An ovarian follicle consists of a developing oocyte surrounded by one or more layers of cells called *follicular cells*. At the same time that the oocyte is progressing through meiosis, corresponding changes are taking place in the follicular cells. Primordial follicles, which consist of a primary oocyte surrounded by a single layer of flattened cells, develop in the fetus and are the stage that is present in the ovaries at birth and throughout childhood.

Beginning at puberty follicle-stimulating hormone stimulates changes in the primordial follicles. The follicular cells become cuboidal, the primary oocyte enlarges, and it is now a primary follicle. The follicles continue to grow under the influence of follicle-stimulating hormone, and the follicular cells proliferate to form several layers of granulose cells around the primary oocyte. Most of these primary follicles degenerate along with the primary oocytes within them, but usually one continues to develop each month. The granulosa cells start secreting estrogen and a cavity, or antrum, forms within the follicle. When the antrum starts to develop, the follicle becomes a secondary follicle. The granulose cells also secrete a glycoprotein substance that forms a clear membrane, the zona pellucida, around the oocyte. After about 10 days of growth the follicle is a mature vesicular (graafian) follicle, which forms a "blister" on the surface of the ovary and contains a secondary oocyte ready for ovulation.

Ovulation

Ovulation, prompted by luteinizing hormone from the anterior pituitary, occurs when the mature follicle at the surface of the ovary ruptures and releases the secondary oocyte into the peritoneal cavity. The ovulated secondary oocyte, ready for fertilization is still surrounded by the *zona pellucida* and a few layers of cells called the *corona radiata*. If it is not fertilized, the secondary oocyte degenerates in a couple of days. If a sperm passes through the corona radiata and zona pellucida and enters the cytoplasm of the secondary oocyte, the second meiotic division resumes to form a polar body and a mature ovum.

After ovulation and in response to luteinizing hormone, the portion of the follicle that remains in the ovary enlarges and is transformed into a corpus luteum. The *corpus luteum* is a glandular structure that secretes progesterone and some estrogens. Its fate depends on whether fertilization occurs. If fertilization does not take place, the corpus luteum remains functional for about 10 days then it begins to degenerate into a corpus albicans, which is primarily scar tissue, and its hormone output ceases. If fertilization occurs, the corpus luteum persists and continues its hormone functions until the placenta develops sufficiently to secrete the necessary hormones. Again, the corpus luteum ultimately degenerates into corpus albicans, but it remains functional for a longer period of time.

FALLOPIAN TUBES

There are two uterine tubes, also called *fallopian tubes* or *oviducts*. There is one tube associated with each ovary. The end of the tube near the ovary expands to form a funnel-shaped *infundibulum*, which is surrounded by finger-like extensions called *fimbriae*. Because there is no direct connection between the infundibulum and the ovary, the oocyte enters the peritoneal cavity before it enters the fallopian tube. At the time of ovulation, the fimbriae increase their activity and create currents in the peritoneal fluid that help propel the oocyte into the fallopian tube. Once inside the fallopian tube, the oocyte is moved along by the rhythmic beating of cilia on the epithelial lining and by peristaltic action of the smooth muscle in the wall of the tube. The journey through the Fallopian tube takes about 7 days. Because the oocyte is fertile for only 24 to 48 hours, fertilization usually occurs in the Fallopian tube.

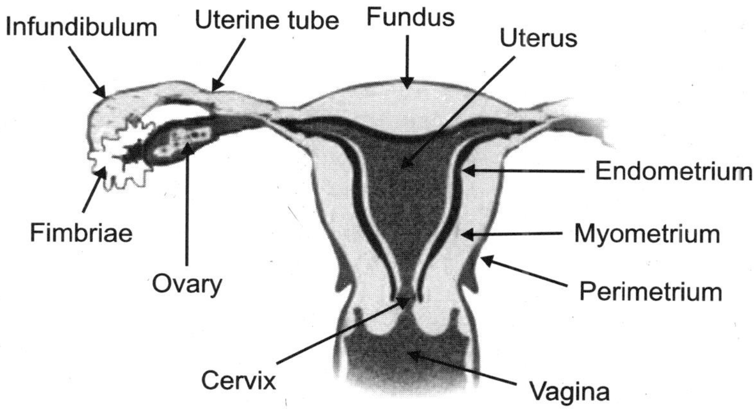

Fig.14.6 *Female reproductive parts.*

UTERUS

The uterus is a muscular organ that receives the fertilized oocyte and provides an appropriate environment for the developing fetus. Before the first pregnancy, the uterus is about the size and shape of a pear, with the narrow portion directed inferiorly. After childbirth, the uterus is usually larger, then regresses after menopause. The uterus is lined with the *endometrium*. The stratum functionale of the endometrium sloughs off during menstruation. The deeper stratum basale provides the foundation for rebuilding the stratum functionale.

VAGINA

The vagina is a fibromuscular tube, about 10 cm long, that extends from the cervix of the uterus to the outside. It is located between the rectum and the urinary bladder. Because the vagina is tilted posteriorly as it ascends and the cervix is tilted anteriorly, the *cervix* projects into the vagina at nearly a right angle. The vagina serves as a passageway for menstrual flow, receives the erect penis during intercourse, and is the birth canal during childbirth.

EXTERNAL GENITALIA

The external genitalia are the accessory structures of the female reproductive system that are external to the vagina. They are also referred to as the vulva or pudendum. The external genitalia include the *labia majora, mons pubis, labia minora, clitoris,* and *glands* within the vestibule. The clitoris is an erectile organ, similar to the male penis, that responds to sexual stimulation. Posterior to the clitoris, the urethra, vagina, paraurethral glands and greater vestibular glands open into the vestibule.

The *female sexual response* includes arousal and orgasm, but there is no ejaculation. A woman may become pregnant without having an orgasm.

Follicle-stimulating hormone, luteinizing hormone, estrogen, and progesterone have major roles in regulating the functions of the female reproductive system.

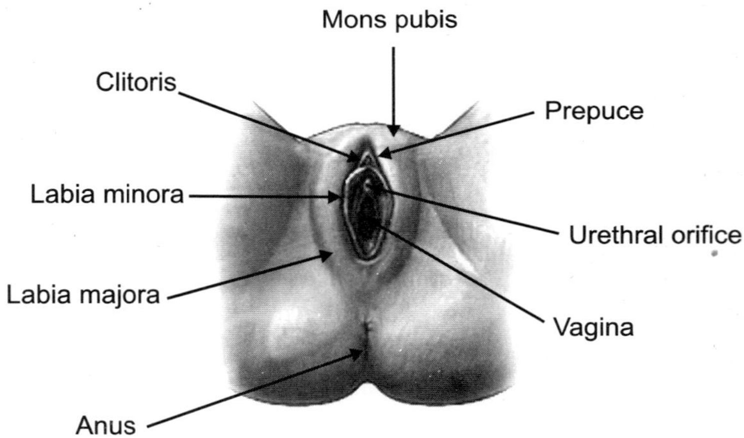

Fig.14.7 *External genitalia.*

At puberty, when the ovaries and uterus are mature enough to respond to hormonal stimulation, certain stimuli cause the hypothalamus to start secreting gonadotropin-releasing hormone. This hormone enters the blood and goes to the anterior pituitary gland where it stimulates the secretion of follicle-stimulating hormone and luteinizing hormone. These hormones, in turn, affect the ovaries and uterus and the monthly cycles begin. A woman's reproductive cycles last from menarche to menopause.

The monthly ovarian cycle begins with the follicle development during the follicular phase, continues with ovulation during the ovulatory phase, and concludes with the development and regression of the *corpus luteum* during the luteal phase.

The uterine cycle takes place simultaneously with the ovarian cycle. The uterine cycle begins with menstruation during the menstrual phase, continues with repair of the endometrium during the proliferative phase, and ends with the growth of glands and blood vessels during the secretory phase.

Menopause occurs when a woman's reproductive cycles stop. This period is marked by decreased levels of ovarian hormones and increased levels of pituitary follicle-stimulating hormone and luteinizing hormone. The changing hormone levels are responsible for the symptoms associated with menopause.

MAMMARY GLANDS

Functionally, the mammary glands produce milk; structurally, they are modified sweat glands. Mammary glands, which are located in the breast overlying the pectoralis major muscles, are present in both sexes, but usually are functional only in the female.

Externally, each breast has a raised nipple, which is surrounded by a circular pigmented area called the *areola*. The nipples are sensitive to touch, due to the fact that they contain smooth muscle that contracts and causes them to become erect in response to stimulation.

Internally, the adult female breast contains 15 to 20 lobes of glandular tissue that radiate around the nipple. The lobes are separated by connective tissue and adipose. The connective tissue helps support the breast. Some bands of connective tissue, called suspensory (Cooper's) ligaments extend through the breast from the skin to the underlying muscles. The amount and distribution of the adipose tissue determines the size and shape of the breast. Each lobe consists of lobules that contain the glandular units. A lactiferous duct collects the milk from the lobules within each lobe and carries it to the nipple. Just before the nipple the lactiferous duct enlarges to form a lactiferous sinus (ampulla), which serves as a reservoir for milk. After the sinus, the duct again narrows and each duct opens independently on the surface of the nipple.

Mammary gland function is regulated by hormones. At puberty, increasing levels of estrogen stimulate the development of glandular tissue in the female breast. Estrogen also causes the breast to increase in size through the accumulation of adipose tissue. Progesterone stimulates the development of the duct system. During pregnancy these hormones enhance further development of the mammary glands. Prolactin from the anterior pituitary stimulates the production of milk within the glandular tissue, and oxytocin causes the ejection of milk from the glands.

COPULATION AND FERTILIZATION

For fertilization to occur, sperm must be deposited in the vagina within a few days before or a day or two after ovulation. Sperm transfer is accomplished by copulation. Sexual excitation dilates the arterioles supplying blood to the penis. Blood accumulates in three cylindrical spongy sinuses that run lengthwise through the penis. The resulting pressure causes the penis to enlarge and erect and thus able to penetrate the vagina.

Movement of the penis back and forth within the vagina causes sexual tension to increase to the point of ejaculation. Contraction of the walls of each vas deferens propels the sperm along. Fluid is added to the sperm by the seminal vesicles, Cowper's glands, and the prostate gland. These fluids provide a source of energy (fructose) and perhaps in other ways provide an optimum chemical environment for the sperm.

The mixture of sperm and accessory fluids is called semen. It passes through the urethra and is expelled into the vagina.

Physiological changes occur in the female as well as the male in response to sexual excitement, although these are not as readily apparent. In contrast to the male, however, such responses are not a prerequisite for copulation and fertilization to occur.

Once deposited within the vagina, the sperm proceed on their journey into and through the uterus and on up into the fallopian tubes. It is here that fertilization may occur if an "egg" is present (strictly speaking, it is still a secondary oocyte until after completion of meiosis II).

Although sperm can swim several millimeters each second, their trip to and through the fallopian tubes may be assisted by muscular contraction of the walls of the uterus and the tubes. There is also evidence that they respond to a chemical attractant produced by the egg or the tissues surrounding it. In any case, sperm may reach the egg within 15 minutes of ejaculation. The trip is also fraught with heavy mortality. An average human ejaculate contains over one hundred million sperm, but only a few dozen complete the journey. And of these, only one will succeed in fertilizing the egg.

Fertilization begins with the binding of a sperm head to the outer coating of the egg (called the zona pellucida). Exocytosis of the acrosome at the tip of the sperm head releases enzymes that digest a path through the zona and enable the sperm head to bind to the plasma membrane of the egg. Fusion of their respective membranes allows the entire contents of the sperm to be drawn into the cytosol of the egg. (Even though the sperm's mitochondria enter the egg, they are almost always destroyed and do not contribute their genes to the embryo. So human mitochondrial DNA is almost always inherited from mothers only.)

Within moments, enzymes released from the egg cytosol act on the zona making it impermeable to the other sperm that arrive. Soon the nucleus of the successful sperm enlarges into the male pronucleus. At the same time, the egg (secondary oocyte) completes meiosis II forming a second polar body and the female pronucleus.

The male and female pronuclei move toward each other while duplicating their DNA in S phase. Their nuclear envelopes disintegrate. A spindle is formed (following replication of the sperm's centriole), and a full set of dyads assembles on it. The fertilized egg or zygote is now ready for its first mitosis. When this is done, 2 cells — each with a diploid set of chromosomes — are formed.

MENSTRUAL CYCLE

Menstruation — having periods — is part of the female reproductive cycle that starts when girls become sexually mature at the time of puberty. During a menstrual period, a woman bleeds from her uterus (womb) via the vagina. This lasts anything from three to seven days. Each period commences approximately every 28 days if the woman does not become pregnant during a given cycle.

Menstruation is a very complicated process involving many different hormones, the woman's sex organs and the brain. A woman's internal sex organs consist of two ovaries, the Fallopian tubes, the uterus (womb) and the vagina. The ovaries contain the eggs with which the woman is born and, during each period, a single egg will usually ripen and mature due to the action of hormones circulating in the bloodstream.

When the egg is mature it bursts from the ovary and drifts through the Fallopian tube down into the uterus. The lining of the uterus — the endometrium — has been thickened by the action of hormones and made ready to receive the fertilised egg.

If the egg is fertilized and the woman becomes pregnant, it will fasten itself onto the endometrium. If the egg is not fertilized, however, resultant hormonal changes cause the endometrium to slip away and menstruation begins.

Menstrual discharge is composed of the endometrium itself, together with a little fresh blood caused by the breaking of very fine blood vessels within the endometrium as it detaches itself from the inside of the uterus.

The amount of blood lost due to the normal monthly period is usually less than 80 ml.

During menstruation, girls begin to menstruate when they are about 10 to 14 years-old. The average age is approximately 12. Women will continue to menstruate until the age of 45 to 55, when menopause begins. A woman will have approximately 500 periods in her lifetime.

Ovulation usually takes place roughly 14 days after the first day of the start of a period; however, the exact timing can vary greatly from woman to woman. Some women know when they are ovulating because they can feel a slight pain in their lower abdomen. Other women may bleed slightly in the middle of their cycle.

Vaginal discharge also changes at ovulation. It increases in amount and becomes more watery due to hormonal changes. This is one of the ways that women who wish to practice natural family planning (NFP) using the mucus test can find out whether it is safe to have sex or not.

Women who do not experience such symptoms during ovulation can find out when they are ovulating by taking their temperature. This will rise by 0.5 degrees Celsius when ovulation occurs. To measure temperature effectively, it must be taken at the same time every morning before getting out of bed.

Temperature readings taken from different parts of the body such as the mouth, under the arm, in the ear or in the rectum will all give a slightly different measurement. For this reason, it is important to choose one location and stick to it. When checking for temperature, rises can occur for a variety of reasons and, therefore, should not be used as the only method of detecting ovulation.

PREGNANCY

Development begins while the fertilized egg is still within the fallopian tube. Repeated mitotic divisions produces a solid ball of cells called a *morula*. Further mitosis and some migration of cells converts this into a hollow ball of cells called the *blastocyst*. Approximately one week after fertilization, the blastocyst embeds itself in the thickened wall of the uterus, a process called *implantation*, and pregnancy is established. The blastocyst produces two major divisions of cells:

(i) Three or four blastocyst cells develop into the inner cell mass, which will form

  (a) 3 extraembryonic membranes: amnion, yolk sac, and

  (b) (a vestigial) allantois and in about 2 months, become the fetus and, ultimately, the baby.

(ii) The remaining 100 or so cells form the trophoblast, which will develop into the chorion that will go on to makeup most of the placenta. All the extraembryonic membranes play vital roles during development but will be discarded at the time of birth.

The placenta grows tightly fused to the wall of the uterus. Its blood vessels, supplied by the fetal heart, are literally bathed in the mother's blood. Although there is normally no mixing of the two blood supplies, the placenta does facilitate the transfer of a variety of materials between the fetus and the mother.

(i) Receiving oxygen and discharging carbon dioxide.

(ii) Discharging urea and other wastes.

(iii) Receiving antibodies (chiefly of the IgG class). These remain for weeks after birth, protecting the baby from the diseases to which the mother is immune.

But the placenta is not simply a transfer device. Using raw materials from the mother's blood, it synthesizes large quantities of proteins and also some hormones. Link to discussion of the placenta as an endocrine gland.

The metabolic activity of the placenta is almost as great as that of the fetus itself. The umbilical cord connects the fetus to the placenta. It receives deoxygenated blood from the iliac arteries of the fetus and returns oxygenated blood to the liver and on to the inferior vena cava. Because its lungs are not functioning, circulation in the fetus differs dramatically from that of the baby after birth. While within the uterus, blood pumped by the right ventricle bypasses the lungs by flowing through the foramen ovale and the ductus arteriosus.

Although the blood in the placenta is in close contact with the mother's blood in the uterus, intermingling of their blood does not normally occur. However, some of the blood cells of the fetus usually do get into the mother's circulation — where they have been know to survive for decades. This raises the possibility of doing prenatal diagnosis of genetic disorders by sampling the mother's blood rather than having to rely on the more invasive procedures of amniocentesis and chorionic villus sampling (CVS).

Far rarer is the leakage of mother's blood cells into the fetus. However, it does occur. A few pregnant women with leukemia or lymphoma have transferred the malignancy to their fetus. Some babies have also acquired melanoma from the transplacental passage of these highly-malignant cells from their mother.

During the first two months of pregnancy, the basic structure of the baby is being formed. This involves cell division, cell migration, and the differentiation of cells into the many types found in the baby. During this period, the developing baby — called an *embryo* — is very sensitive to anything that interferes with the steps involved. Virus infection of the mother, e.g., by *rubella* ("German measles") virus or exposure to certain chemicals may cause malformations in the developing embryo. Such agents are called *teratogens* ("monster-forming"). After about two months, all the systems of the baby have been formed, at least in a rudimentary way. From then on, development of the *fetus,* as it is now called, is primarily a matter of growth and minor structural modifications. The fetus is less susceptible to teratogens than is the embryo. Pregnancy involves a complex interplay of hormones.

ASSISTED REPRODUCTIVE TECHNOLOGY (ART)

Louise Brown recently celebrated her 25th birthday. She was the first of what today number around one million "test tube babies"; that is, she developed from an egg that was fertilized outside her mother's body — the process called *in vitro fertilization (IVF).*

IN VITRO FERTILIZATION (IVF)

IVF involves:

(i) Harvesting mature eggs from the mother. This is not an easy process. The mother must undergo hormonal treatments to produce multiple eggs, which then must be removed (under anesthesia) from her ovaries.

(ii) Harvesting sperm from the father. Harvesting is usually no problem, but often the sperm are defective in their ability to fertilize (so setting the stage for ICSI).

(iii) Mixing sperm and eggs in a culture vessel (in vitro).

(iv) Culturing the fertilized eggs for several days until they have developed to at least the 8-cell stage.

(v) Placing two (usually) of these into the mother's uterus (which her hormone treatments have prepared for implantation).

(vi) Keeping one's fingers crossed — only about one-third of the attempts result in a successful pregnancy).

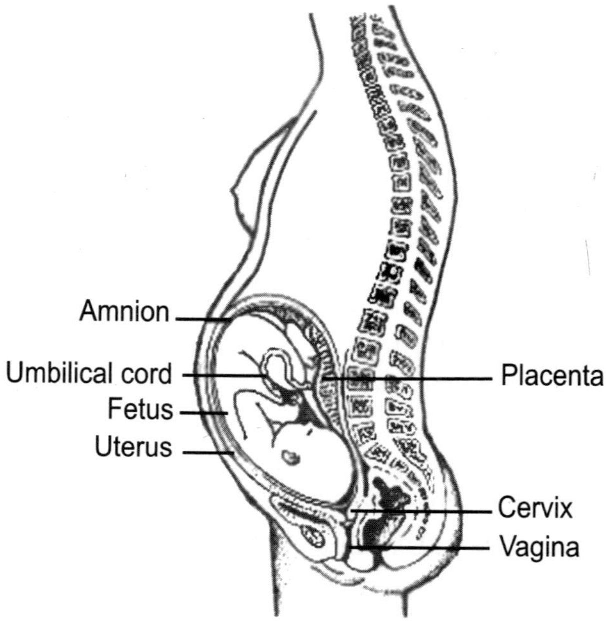

Fig. 14.9 *In Vitro Fertilization (IVF).*

Intracytoplasmic Sperm Injection (ICSI)

Successful IVF assumes the availability of healthy sperm. But many cases of infertility arise from defects in the father's sperm. Often these can be overcome by directly injecting a single sperm into the egg.

Ooplasmic Transfer

Infertility in some cases may stem from defects in the cytoplasm of the mother's egg. To circumvent these, cytoplasm can be removed from the egg of a young, healthy woman (*Donor egg*) and injected — along with a single sperm — into the prospective mother's egg. One reason for concern is that ooplasmic transfer results in an egg carrying both the mother's mitochondria and mitochondria from the donor. This condition — called *heteroplasmy* — creates a child having two different mitochondrial DNA genomes in all of its cells.

In normal fertilization, all the mitochondria in the father's sperm are destroyed in the egg, and perhaps this is important.

Although a few healthy children have been born following ooplasmic transfer, but the current.

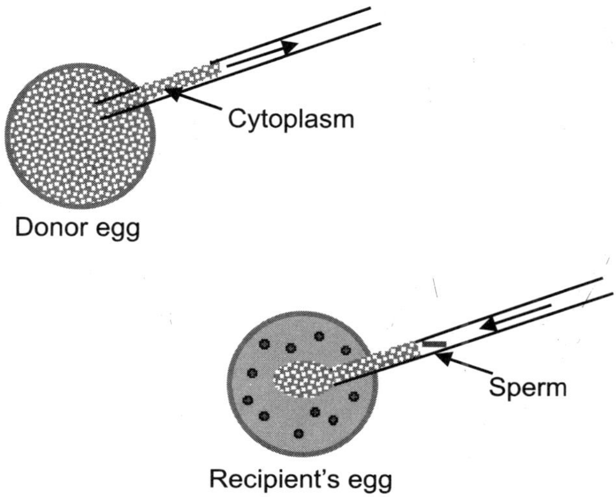

Fig. 14.10 *Ooplasmic transfer.*

The Upside of ART

(i) It has allowed hundreds of thousands of previously-infertile couples to have children.

(i) It permits screening (on one cell removed from the 8-celled morula) for the presence of genetic disorders — thus avoiding starting a pregnancy if a disorder is found. Link to a discussion.

(i) One can use frozen sperm allowing fatherhood for a man who is no longer able to provide fresh sperm.

(i) Because a number of morulas are created, the extras can be frozen, stored, and used later:

(a) If the initial attempt fails (the prospective mother must still receive hormones to prepare her uterus for implantation and the success rate is lower with thawed morulas).

(b) Where regulations permit, the extras can be used as a source of embryonic stem (ES) cells.

THE DOWNSIDE OF ART

Although improving, the success rate is still sufficiently low (~30%) that the process often has to be repeated. Because several morulas are usually transferred, multiple births are common (about 40%), and as is the case with most multiple births, the babies weigh less. To reduce the number of twins, triplets, etc., more ART centers are turning to "single-embryo transfer" (SET).

Some ART centers find that they can increase the success rate — and thus rely more on SET — by culturing the morulas for 5-6 days, instead of the usual 2–3 days, before transferring them (by now they have become blastocysts) to the mother. The risk of birth defects is about doubled (from ~4% in "normal" pregnancies to ~8% in ART pregnancies).

ART procedures in experimental animals often result in a failure of correct gene imprinting. Whether this will pose a problem for humans remains to be seen.

BIRTH AND LACTATION

Exactly what brings about the onset of labor is still not completely understood. Probably a variety of integrated hormonal controls are at work. The first result of labor is the opening of the cervix. With continued powerful contractions, the amnion ruptures and the amniotic fluid (the waters) flows out through the vagina. The baby follows, and its umbilical cord can be cut.

The infant's lungs expand, and it begins breathing. This requires a major switchover in the circulatory system. Blood flow through the umbilical cord, ductus arteriosus, and foramen ovale ceases, and the adult pattern of blood flow through the heart, aorta, and pulmonary arteries begins. In some infants, the switchover is incomplete, and blood flow through the pulmonary arteries is inadequate. Failure to synthesize enough nitric oxide (NO) is one cause.

Shortly after the baby, the placenta and the remains of the umbilical cord (the after birth) are expelled. At the time of birth, and for a few days after, the mother's breasts contain a fluid called *colostrum*. It is rich in calories and protein, including antibodies that provide passive immunity for the newborn infant. Three or four days after delivery, the breasts begin to secrete milk.

(i) Its synthesis is stimulated by the pituitary hormone prolactin (PRL).

(ii) Its release is stimulated by a rise in the level of oxytocin when the baby begins nursing.

(iii) Milk contains an inhibitory peptide. If the breasts are not fully emptied, the peptide accumulates and inhibits milk production. This autocrine action thus matches supply with demand.

STUDY QUESTIONS

1. Discuss the various parts of male reproductive system in male.
2. Discuss the various parts of female reproductive system in female.
3. Write short notes on the following:
   (a) Mammary Glands
   (b) Menstrual Cycle
   (c) Pregnancy
   (d) Birth and Lactation
   (e) Assisted Reproductive Technology (ART).

■■■

INDEX

A

B

C

D

I

J

L

M

N

O

P

R

NOTES

NOTES

NOTES

NOTES